HANNAH ARENDT

The Jew as Pariah:

JEWISH IDENTITY AND POLITICS IN THE MODERN AGE

HANNAH ARENDT

The Jew as Pariah:

JEWISH IDENTITY AND POLITICS IN THE MODERN AGE

EDITED AND WITH AN INTRODUCTION BY
Ron H. Feldman

GROVE PRESS, INC./NEW YORK

Arendt, Hannah. Eichmann in Jerusalem
Eichmann, Adolf, 1906-1962

First Edition 1978
First Printing 1978
ISBN: 0-394-50160-8
Grove Press ISBN: 0-8021-0156-9
Library of Congress Catalog Card Number: 77-18342

First Evergreen Edition 1978
First Printing 1978
ISBN: 0-394-17042-3
Grove Press ISBN: 0-8021-4164-1
Library of Congress Catalog Card Number: 77-18342

Manufactured in the United States of America

Distributed by Random House, Inc., New York

GROVE PRESS, INC., 196 West Houston Street, New York, N.Y. 10014

Jews- History - 1789- 1945
Jews- identity

For גרעין לויתן

May we build a world that
is both Jewish and free
through the power of
our collective action.

Acknowledgments

I first came upon the essays appearing in this volume while doing research for the undergraduate senior thesis I wrote in 1976-77 for the Modern Society and Social Thought major of Stevenson College at the University of California, Santa Cruz. The introduction to this book is a condensation of that thesis. I would like to express my sincere thanks and appreciation to all the people—students, faculty, and staff—with whom I had the opportunity to work and learn in the Modern Society and Social Thought program. This book is, if anything, an example of the results that a personalized, interdisciplinary education in the liberal arts can lead to.

Many people helped me with this project, providing substantive and stylistic criticism as well as personal encouragement. I want to express special thanks to my two thesis advisers, Peter Euben and David Biale. Not only was I fortunate to receive their comments and criticism of my work as it progressed, but their respective expertise in political theory and Jewish history provided me with a valuable contrast. The tension between these two areas that they created in my thinking replicated to some degree the tension I think Hannah Arendt must have felt. This helped me formulate in detail my picture of Arendt as a Jewish pariah. I particularly want to thank Peter for his editorial comments on the introduction.

Larry Fenster suggested that I look into the work of Hannah Arendt, and for this I cannot thank him enough. Moreover, he provided invaluable critical assistance in writing the final draft of the introduction. Chava Haber deserves a special measure of thanks and gratitude; she was the only person besides my advisers who suffered through reading my thesis at all its various stages. As an intelligent person without a specialist's background in either Jewish history or politics, she helped keep me from becoming incomprehensible to the average reader. I will always treasure the memory of all those hours we spent in the Stevenson Coffee House. I am grateful to Leah Bolotin for her critical review of the final draft of my thesis as well as her constant support. My thanks go to Gary Ruchwarger, who went over the very last draft of the introduction with a fine-toothed editorial comb and helped me rework some particularly rough parts.

I want to also thank Steve Ascheim and Ze'ev Mankowitz, who were my teachers at the Institute for Youth Leaders from Abroad in Jerusalem which I attended in 1972–73 as a member of *Hashomer Hazair*. They first introduced me to the serious study of modern Jewish history, instilling in me an appreciation of the subject and an interest in exploring it further.

In addition, I am grateful to all those who read my work at one point or another and provided me with helpful comments, reassurance, or just someone with whom to speak about it: Theda Haber, Avi Schulman, Bert Meyers, Yoav Peled, John Schaar, Betty Ginsburg, Elliot Goldstein, and Charles Pelton.

Alan Rinzler of Grove Press deserves special thanks, for he not only helped turn my idea for this book into a reality, but gave me invaluable encouragement and advice.

And, of course, I want to express my gratitude to my parents and sisters, Saul, Claire, Robin, and Rinah, without whose loving support this would not have been possible.

RON H. FELDMAN
Berkeley, January 1978

Contents

Preface

This volume includes most of the writings published by Hannah Arendt on the subjects of Jewish identity, culture, history, and politics which have not previously been collected into book form. A number of essays are not included because they were preprints or precursors of sections in *The Origins of Totalitarianism*, whose substance is thus already publicly available. In two cases—"The Moral of History" and "Herzl and Lazare"—sections of essays which were excluded from the versions found in *The Origins of Totalitarianism* are included here.

The essays are organized into three sections. "Part I: The Pariah as Rebel" includes essays primarily concerned with Jewish identity, culture, and history; "Part II: Zionism and the Jewish State" includes essays on Jewish politics; "Part III: The Eichmann Controversy" contains writings which preceded and were part of the debate over *Eichmann in Jerusalem* that address the issues of responsibility for the catastrophe of European Jewry and dissent in the Jewish community. The article by Walter Z. Laqueur and the letter by Gershom Scholem are included because they were the triggers for Hannah Arendt's written responses to the controversy and thus provide the polemical context within which her replies appeared and can best be understood.

All the essays are interconnected, however, and the inclusion of the date of each essay's original appearance is meant to ease the reader's attempt to see how Arendt's ideas developed over time. More importantly, the date should help the reader place the writings in the historical context out of which they emerged and to which they were a response.

RON H. FELDMAN

INTRODUCTION

The Jew as Pariah:
The Case of Hannah Arendt

(1906–1975)

I

> All vaunted Jewish qualities—the "Jewish heart," hu-
> manity, humor, disinterested intelligence—are pariah
> qualities. All Jewish shortcomings—tactlessness, political
> stupidity, inferiority complexes and money-grubbing—
> are characteristic of upstarts. There have always been
> Jews who did not think it worth while to change their
> humane attitude and their natural insight into reality
> for the narrowness of caste spirit or the essential
> unreality of financial transactions.[1]

Hannah Arendt's life was played out during the "dark times" of
the twentieth century. She was one of the most remarkable—as
well as one of the last—offspring of a German-Jewish milieu
which produced more than its share of great literary, scientific,
and artistic figures. An outstanding political and cultural critic,
her purpose as a thinker was to help us understand the meaning
and direction of events in a world of deadly chaos.

Probably best know to the general public as the author of
Eichmann in Jerusalem, over which a great storm erupted in
the Jewish community and for which she was vehemently
condemned in the Jewish press, Arendt's reputation as one of
her generation's most gifted political thinkers rests on two
other works: *The Origins of Totalitarianism* and *The Human
Condition*.

Born in Hanover, the only child of a Jewish engineer and
his wife, Hannah Arendt studied philosophy under Karl Jaspers

15

at Heidelberg University, where she received a Ph. D. in 1928 at the age of twenty-two for her thesis *Der Liebesbegriff bei Augustin* (The Concept of Love in St. Augustine). From a foundation in the classics and German philosophy, Arendt spent the next twenty-odd years studying the Jewish experience in the modern age and doing political work in the Jewish community. This began in the early 1930s when she wrote her biography of Rahel Varnhagen, the early nineteenth-century Jewish socialite who kept a famous salon.

With Hitler's rise to power in 1933, Arendt emigrated to France from her native Germany. She worked as an active Zionist in Paris until 1940, serving as chairperson of the French branch of Youth Aliyah and as a special delegate of the Jewish Agency. Youth Aliyah arranged for the emigration of German-Jewish youth to Palestine and reeducated them for their new life there. In 1935 Arendt personally brought a group of children from France to Palestine. After being interned in France in 1940 because she was a German national, she emigrated to the United States in 1941 and became a U.S. citizen in 1950. During the 1940s she was successively the research director of the Conference on Jewish Relations, chief editor of Schocken Books, and executive director for Jewish Cultural Reconstruction. She published a large number of articles, primarily on Jewish topics, and worked on *The Origins of Totalitarianism*. It was during this period that most of the essays in this collection were written. She later was to teach at a number of universities, including Princeton (where she was the first woman appointed to a full professorship), the University of Chicago, and the New School for Social Research.

In the 1950s, Arendt turned her attention to developing her critique of modern society in general. Although it was present in *The Origins of Totalitariansim*, she elaborated it through her essays collected in *Between Past and Future* and, more systematically, in *The Human Condition*. Arendt derives her political theory from a particular interpretation of the experience of the pre-Socratic Greeks, especially the Athenian *polis*. This fascination with ancient Greece is typical of German scholarship and, as Arendt writes in the letter to Gershom Scholem in this collection, "[i]f I can be said to 'have come from anywhere,' it is from the tradition of German philosophy." [2]

In the 1960s, Arendt shifted her attention to her adopted

home, the United States, writing *On Revolution* and the essays collected in *Crises of the Republic*, where she contrasted the American republic with the European nation-state. Her concern with the Jewish world never disappeared, however, and in 1963 she wrote *Eichmann in Jerusalem.* The last section of this volume contains some of the criticism of that book and her written responses. Also included are an earlier essay and letter which show that both the views she expressed in *Eichmann in Jerusalem* and the strong criticism she received had a deep and long history. In her final work, Hannah Arendt returned to philosophy: upon her death she had completed two of the projected three volumes of *The Life of the Mind,* which is at least in part a response to the "banality of evil" she discovered in the person of Adolf Eichmann.

When Hannah Arendt died, she was out of favor with the Jewish community as a consequence of *Eichmann in Jerusalem:* few of the eulogies which traditionally follow upon the death of such a prominent figure appeared in the Jewish press. Partly because she was subjected to a modern form of excommunication from the Jewish community and partly due to the power of her other writings, the essays collected in this volume have been for the most part neglected and forgotten.[3]

This has been most unfortunate, for it has led to a less than complete understanding of both her political theory, for which she was renowned, and her view of modern Jewish history, for which she was castigated. In fact, there is an organic link between her conception of Jewish history and her political theory: her view of the modern Jewish condition serves as an introduction to her political theory, while her political theory illuminates her interpretation of Jewish history.

This collection not only serves to fill the void in the public's knowledge of her work but, more importantly, when taken together these essays are of intrinsic importance inasmuch as they present a coherent and powerful, albeit nonconformist, understanding of what it means to be a Jew in the modern world. Although many of the essays were written over thirty years ago, the issues they deal with continue to be of contemporary importance: the destruction of European Jewry by the Nazis, the relationship of world Jewry to the State of Israel, the relationship of Israel to the Arabs both within the borders of the Jewish state and without, and the peculiar historical position of Jews within modern Western society.

Fundamentally these essays—particularly "We Refugees," "The Jew as Pariah: A Hidden Tradition," and the letter to Gershom Scholem—show that Hannah Arendt chose the role of a "conscious pariah." In Arendt's view, the status of pariah—the social outcast—characterizes the position of the Jews in Western Europe following the Enlightenment and emancipation because they were never truly accepted by European society. "During the 150 years when Jews truly lived amidst, and not just in the neighborhood of, Western European peoples, they always had to pay with political misery for social glory and with social insult for political success."[4] This outsider status gave rise to two particular types: the *conscious pariahs* who were aware of it, and the *parvenus*, who tried to succeed in the world of the Gentiles but could never escape their Jewish roots. For Arendt, the conscious pariahs were

> those who really did most for the spiritual dignity of their people, who were great enough to transcend the bounds of nationality and to weave the strands of their Jewish genius into the general texture of European life ... those bold spirits who tried to make of the emancipation of the Jews that which it really should have been—an admission of Jews *as Jews* to the ranks of humanity, rather than a permit to ape the gentiles or an opportunity to play the parvenu.[5]

By affirming both their Jewish particularity and their right to a place in general European life, the conscious pariahs became marginal not only in relation to European society—as all Jews were—but to the Jewish community as well. They were neither parochially Jewish, like their Eastern European cousins, nor were they part of the wealthy Jewish upper class of bankers and merchants that controlled Jewish-Gentile relations. According to Arendt, the conscious pariah is a hidden tradition: "hidden" because there are few links among the great but isolated individuals who have affirmed their pariah status—such as Heinrich Heine, Rahel Varnhagen, Sholom Aleichem, Bernard Lazare, Franz Kafka, and Walter Benjamin—nor ties between them and the rest of the Jewish community; a "tradition" because "for over a hundred years the same basic conditions have obtained and evoked the same basic reaction."[6]

The parvenus—the upstarts who try to make it in non-Jewish society—are the products of the same historical circumstances and are thus the pariahs' counterparts in Arendt's typology. While the pariahs use their minds and hearts, voluntarily spurning society's insidious gifts, the parvenus use their elbows to raise themselves above their fellow Jews into the "respectable" world of the Gentiles. The parvenus are at best accepted only as "exceptions" to the stereotype of the uncouth, unworldly ghetto Jew—and those Jews who succeed with this ploy feel themselves superior to their fellow Jews. Those Jews who spurn social acceptance on the basis of this self-deceit have been few, but in exchange for their isolation from both Jewish and Gentile society, these conscious pariahs gain the honesty that makes life worth living, a clear view of reality, and a place in both European (and, today, American) and Jewish history.

Not only did Hannah Arendt formulate and celebrate the Jewish pariah as a human type, she epitomized it in her life and thought. As a conscious pariah who was committed to, yet critical of, both her Jewish and European inheritances, her intellectual project as a whole was founded in the problematic of Jewishness in the modern world. The transformation of Judaism into Jewishness in an increasingly secular world meant that, like Kafka, she had lost the Judaic heritage of her fathers without gaining a firmly rooted place in the European polity, which itself was in the process of collapse. As a pariah, her work is characterized by the dialectical tension between her Jewishness and modern Jewish history, on the one side, and her European and generalized human experience in the modern age, on the other. The result was a unique outlook on both Jewish and European concerns in which the specifically Jewish and broadly European experiences constantly inform one another. Arendt's most lauded work, *The Origins of Totalitarianism*, is clearly the product of a conscious pariah, without equal as an intricate and beautiful pattern into which both Jewish and European concerns and history are intentionally woven together.

Not standing exclusively inside or outside either her Jewish or European heritage, Hannah Arendt uses both as platforms from which to gain a critical insight into the other. On the one hand, she consciously stands outside the Jewish tradition, subjecting the experience of the Jews in the modern world to the criticism of a German philosopher rooted in the European classics. Distinguishing between Jewishness—an existential given that one cannot escape—and Judaism—a system of beliefs which one can adopt or reject—she adamantly accepts the one and rejects the other. In doing so, she became a rebel among her own people. On the other hand, Arendt uses her experience as a Jew and her perspective as a conscious pariah standing outside the mainstream of Western society to analyze and gain an understanding of that society. By claiming that "[i]t is no mere accident that the catastrophic defeats of the peoples of Europe began with the catastrophe of the Jewish people," [7] Arendt places the modern Jewish experience at the center of her critique of modern society.

This Jewish-European dialectic in her work has been a perpetual source of misunderstanding on the part of critics concerned with both her Jewish and non-Jewish work, for she falls within no established historical or philosophical perspective. Much like Kafka, with whom Arendt has a feeling of particular closeness and to whom she expresses a particular debt, the Jewish element is crucial though not exclusive: her Jewishness is not her sole concern nor the sole determinant of her work, but our understanding of her work is both diminished and seriously distorted if we overlook it. Arendt's own understanding of her peculiar perspective is best expressed in her letter to Scholem:

> What confuses you is that my arguments and my approach are different from what you are used to; in other words, the trouble is that I am independent. By this I mean, on the one hand, that I do not belong to any organisation and always speak only for myself, and on the other hand, that I have great confidence in Lessing's *selbstdenken* [self-thinking] for which, I think, no ideology, no public opinion, and no "convictions" can ever be a substitute. Whatever objections you may have to the results, you won't understand them unless you realize that they are really my own and nobody else's. [8]

II

The enthusiastic Jewish intellectual dreaming of the paradise on earth, so certain of freedom from all national ties and prejudices, was in fact farther removed

from political reality than his fathers, who had prayed
for the coming of Messiah and the return of the people
to Palestine.[9]

The twentieth century has seen the most momentous
changes in Jewish history since the destruction of the Second
Temple in 70 c.e. The annihilation of European Jewry by the
Nazis during World War II, and the founding of the Jewish
State of Israel shortly thereafter, have radically changed the
position of Jews in the world. The result has been a transformation of relations amongst Jews themselves and between them
and the other peoples of the world. Though inextricably
linked, the Holocaust and the Jewish state raise two different
sets of questions. The Holocaust is the end of an era of Jewish
existence and therefore raises questions about the past—how
and why it happened. The Jewish state is the beginning of a
new era and therefore raises questions about what it means to
be a part of the Jewish people today and in the future. Of
course, the answers to the second set of questions have been
and must be influenced by the answers to the first, whether
explicitly articulated in thought or implicitly contained in
action. The task of trying to understand how and why the
Holocaust happened and what has—or should be—changed as a
result is the central task of Jewish thought in the post-
Holocaust era.

The essays in this volume, particularly when read together
with Arendt's other works in which Jewish history is discussed—
*The Origins of Totalitarianism, Rahel Varnhagen, Men in
Dark Times,* and *Eichmann in Jerusalem*—present Hannah
Arendt's response to this challenge. Not only does she attempt
to understand the sources of modern antisemitism by tracing
the historical relationships of Jews and Gentiles, but she also
criticizes the modes of Jewish self-understanding and world-
understanding that resulted in the Jewish responses of unbelief
and passivity in the face of destruction.

Hannah Arendt's critical assessment of Jewish history is
based on the fundamental political conviction that the world is
what we make of it. There is no Hegelian "cunning of reason,"
but "rather does unreason begin to function automatically
when reason has abdicated to it." [10] The Jews, by the very fact
of their existence, are "one group of people among other
groups, all of which are involved in the business of this world.

And . . . [the Jews do] not simply cease to be coresponsible because . . . [they] became the victim of the world's injustice and cruelty." [11] Unlike both the "scapegoat" theory, which claims that the Jews were accidental victims, and the "eternal antisemitism" theory, which claims that the Jews are inevitable victims, Arendt tries to show that the catastrophic end to the history of the Jews in Europe was neither accidental nor inevitable. Rather, it was the result of the specific history of Jewish-Gentile relationships. If the Jews were so politically blind that they did not understand the implications of their own actions and those of their opponents, it was the result of what Arendt considers the key feature of Jewish history in the modern period: the Jews' *worldlessness*.

> Jewish history offers the extraordinary spectacle of a people, unique in this respect, which began its history with a well-defined concept of history and an almost conscious resolution to achieve a well-circumscribed plan on earth and then, without giving up this concept, avoided all political action for two thousand years. The result was that the political history of the Jewish people became even more dependent upon unforeseen, accidental factors than the history of other nations, so that the Jews stumbled from one role to the other and accepted responsiblity for none. [12]

The continued existence of the Jewish people throughout the period of the Diaspora was until very recently much more the result of Jewish dissociation from the dominant Christian world than Gentile dissociation from the Jews. It is only since the nineteenth century that antisemitism has had a significant effect on Jewish preservation. Given the conditions of the Diaspora, this dissociation was the only possible method of self-preservation and, Arendt claims, survival has been the single aim of Jewish political thought and action since the Babylonian exile. This traditional solution to the problem of survival was to help prepare the basis for the later dissolution of the Jewish people; for, by making dissociation the basis for their survival, the Jews came to conceive of their existence as almost totally separate and independent from the rest of the world. Consequently, the Jews became ignorant of conditions in the real world and incapable of recognizing new opportunities and new threats to their survival as they arose.

By Arendt's account, until the end of the Middle Ages the Jews "had been able to conduct their communal affairs by means of a politics that existed in the realm of imagination alone—the memory of a far-off past and the hope of a far-off future." [13] This conceptual framework was destroyed by an event that ushered in the beginning of the modern age for the Jews: the failure of the mystical messianic movement centered around Sabbatai Zevi in 1666. The great historian of Sabbatai Zevi is Gershom Scholem, and it is in "Jewish History, Revised," her review of Scholem's *Major Trends in Jewish Mysticism*, as well as "The Jewish State: Fifty Years After" that Hannah Arendt presents a unique political twist to the understanding of that event.

Sabbatai Zevi's appearance on the scene was the culmination of a two-century period during which Jewish-Gentile relations were at an all-time low and during which the mysticism of the Kabbalah had become popularized and extremely widespread. Because of their lack of involvement in and control over the political world in which they lived, the Jews were strongly attracted to mystical thought since "these speculations appeal to all who are actually excluded from action, prevented from altering a fate that appears to them unbearable and, feeling themselves helpless victims of incomprehensible forces, are naturally inclined to find some secret means for gaining power for participating in the 'drama of the World.'" [14]

The messianic fervor which gripped the entire Jewish world had no basis in particular events occurring in the non-Jewish world, but was the result of the internal dynamics created by accepting mysticism as a substitute for political action; the Kabbalah saw the events leading to the messianic perfection of the world as a matter exclusively concerning God and His people Israel. When acted upon, the yearning for political reality that was confined within mystical categories could only shatter those categories because they offered no basis for evaluating political realities. Thus, when Zevi turned apostate in the face of the reality of the sultan's power and the popular messianic hope for a physical return to Zion was dashed, the traditional Jewish religious framework for understanding the world was dealt a servere blow.

But, according to Arendt, this confrontation with reality did not engender a more "realistic" understanding among the

Jews; understanding can exist only when there is a framework within which to place events. In her view, the Sabbatai Zevi catastrophe destroyed the traditional framework without replacing it with another. The result was an unprecedented worldlessness:

> In losing their faith in a divine beginning and ultimate culmination of history, the Jews lost their guide through the wilderness of bare facts; for when man is robbed of all means of interpreting events he is left with no sense whatsoever of reality. The present that confronted the Jews after the Sabbatai Zevi debacle was the turmoil of a world whose course no longer made sense and in which, as a result, the Jews could no longer find a place.[15]

In Arendt's view, the Sabbatian movement was "a great political movement" of "real popular action" which let loose onto the public scene what she sees as Jewish mysticism's "exclusive concern with reality and action." [16] The result, however, was a catastrophe "greater for the Jewish people than all other persecutions had been, if we are to measure it by the only available yardstick, its far-reaching influence upon the future of the people. From now on, the Jewish body politic was dead and the people retired from the public scene of history." [17] The legacy of the period of Jewish estrangement from the non-Jewish world, played out in the subsequent history of Hasidism, the Reform movement, attempted assimilation, and revolutionary utopianism, was that the Jews were "even less 'realistic'—that is, less capable than ever before of facing and understanding the real situation." [18]

The "real situation" was that by the seventeenth century the Jews were becoming involved in the world as a whole and moving into positions of potential political power. According to Arendt's analysis, presented in *The Origins of Totalitarianism*, the Jews, in the persons of the court Jews and the international bankers which followed them, were instrumental in the ascendence of the absolute monarchies and the subsequent development of the nation-state. Unlike the declining nobility and the privatistic bourgeoisie, "the Jews were the only part of the population willing to finance the state's beginnings and to tie their destinies to its further development." [19]

While being the state's financiers had great potential for political power, as the antisemites were quick to understand, the worldless mentality of the Jews was such that "they never allied themselves with any specific government, but rather with governments, with authority as such." [20] The wealthy Jews involved in "finance politics" were more concerned with continuing legal discrimination against the poor Jewish masses to preserve their privileged position of prestige and power within the Jewish community than in attaining power over the Gentiles. As the practical rulers of the Jewish community, they were conscientious about their role as its protectors, but ignorant of their real potential among non-Jews. Their political concerns and perceptions never extended further than the pursuit of the only political goal the Jews ever had: survival. "The Jews, without knowledge of or interest in power, never thought of exercising more than mild pressure for minor purposes of self-defense." [21]

The Jews didn't realize that the modern state—a supposedly political entity ruling over class society—soon came into conflict with various classes which comprised that society. Their special services to and special protection from the political authorities prevented either the Jews' submersion in the class system or their emergence as a separate class. They were thus the only distinctive social group that owed its continued existence to the government, unconditionally supported the state as such, and, like the state, stood apart from society and its class distinctions. The result, Arendt observes, was that "each class of society which came into a conflict with the state as such became antisemitic because the only social group which seemed to represent the state were the Jews." [22]

Precisely because they were neither part of class society nor the state's politically active governing clique, the Jews were oblivious to the increasing tension between state and society at the same time that they were driven toward the center of the conflict because they stood between the two as part of neither. Politically naïve enough to believe that their true lack of interest in power would be seen and accepted for what it was, they were taken completely by surprise when twentieth-century political antisemitism rose to power on the basis of charges of a Jewish world conspiracy. This political myopia reflects

the most serious paradox embodied in the curious
political history of the Jews. Of all European peoples,
the Jews had been the only one without a state of their
own and had been, precisely for this reason, so eager and
so suitable for alliances with governments and states as
such, no matter what these governments or states might
represent. On the other hand, the Jews had no political
tradition or experience, and were as little aware of the
tension between society and state as they were of the
obvious risks and power-possibilities of their new role.[23]

Oblivious to the fact that they were instrumental in the
development of the nation-state, the Jews were equally unconcerned with the maintenance of the nation-state system against
the rise of the bourgeoisie's imperialist designs. Indeed, the
Jews unwittingly helped the process along. Having "reached a
saturation point in wealth and economic fortune . . . the sons of
the well-to-do businessmen and, to a lesser extent, bankers,
deserted their fathers' careers for the liberal professions or
purely intellectual pursuits" [24] rather than fighting the growing
influence of big business and industry that was causing a decay
of their political position.

The great Jewish influx into the arts and sciences resulted in
the development of a truly international society whose basis
was the "radiant power of fame." [25] This phenomenon is
extensively discussed in Arendt's essay about Stefan Zweig
included in Part I, "Portrait of a Period." For Arendt, this was
yet another permutation of that quality of the Jewish condition that had made the Jews useful in the first place, their inter-
European, nonnational character. The Jews entered into the
cultural world and became the "outstanding reviewers, critics,
collectors, and organizers of what was famous . . . the living tie
binding famous individuals into a society of the renowned, an
international society by definition, for spiritual achievement
transcends national boundaries." [26]

Although assimilated Jews rarely recognized the fact, since
within this international society their Jewish identity could
effectively be lost, it was precisely those attributes—"kindness,
freedom from prejudice, sensitiveness to injustice," [27] "the
'Jewish heart,' humanity, humor, disinterested intelligence," [28]
and "fraternity" [29]—which were the privileges of the Jews as a
pariah people that produced this particular kind of greatness.

These gifts derived from "the great privilege of being unburdened by care for the world." [30] It is a privilege dearly bought, however, for the price is "real worldlessness. And worldlessness, alas, is always a form of barbarism." [31]

This barbarism was reflected in that Jewish unconcern with the political affairs of the world which developed to such an extent that the assimilated Jews "lost that measure of political responsibility which their origin implied and which the Jewish notables had still felt, albeit in the form of privilege and rulership." [32] They forgot the fact that in every Jew "there still remained something of the old-time pariah, who has no country, for whom human rights do not exist, and whom society would gladly exclude from its privileges."[33] Their activities brought them such social prominence that "Jews became the symbols of Society as such and the objects of hatred for all those whom society did not accept," [34] while at the same time they lost interest in the "finance politics" that had brought them a modicum of protection from the state.

Arendt's critique concludes that Jewish worldlessness, which had its source in the Jews' attempt to preserve themselves by a radical and voluntary separation from the Christian world five hundred years earlier, culminated in the Jews' being more exposed to attack than ever before. More aware of theatrical appearance than political reality, the Jews had a blind faith in the state that had protected them since the emancipation; they forgot that this protection had rested on their performance of unique and necessary functions. The lack of involvement in the political world which had led religious Jews to single out divine providence as the key factor determining the Jews' political fate led secularized Jews to believe that Jewish history "takes place outside all usual historical laws." [35] What had appeared as God's unpredictable will—to which Jews responded with moralizing and penitential prayers—was now viewed as accidental and drew the similarly unpolitical response of Jewish apologetics. Thus, when the Dreyfus Affair demonstrated a very real threat to the Jews' existence and its slogan of 'Death to the Jews" became the rallying cry around which Nazism later grew by leaps and bounds, the Jews, who had become "an object of universal hatred because of [their] useless wealth, and of contempt because of [their] lack of power," [36] were the last to grasp the political significance of events.

In Hannah Arendt's gloomy picture of Jewish political

history there is, however, one positive response to the unreality and worldlessness of the pariah status. This is Zionism, "the only political answer Jews have ever found to antisemitism and the only ideology in which they have ever taken seriously a hostility that would place them in the center of world events." [37]

III

From the "disgrace" of being a Jew there is but one escape—to fight for the honor of the Jewish people as a whole.[38]

The Zionist movement was founded by Theodor Herzl in August 1897, when the first Zionist Congress met and created the World Zionist Organization. Herzl had been a typically assimilated Jew until his Vienna newspaper sent him to cover the Dreyfus case. The impact of this event transformed him into an ardent Jewish nationalist. Herzl saw "the Jewish problem" of the antisemites as the political threat that it was and proposed a radical solution—the creation of a Jewish state. As the essays in the second part of this collection show, Hannah Arendt's view of the Herzlian brand of political Zionism which shaped the movement's perspective and policies is laudatory of its strengths, yet sharply critical of its shortcomings and potential dangers.

According to Hannah Arendt's understanding, Herzl viewed antisemitism as a natural conflict which arose from the fact that the Jews were a national entity separate and different from the nations amongst whom they lived. Because it was natural and inevitable, "Anti-Semitism was an overwhelming force and the Jews would have either to make use of it or be swallowed up by it."[39] Necessarily flowing from the Jews' Diaspora existence, antisemitism was the almost eternal " 'propelling force' responsible for all Jewish suffering since the destruction of the Temple and it would continue to make the Jews suffer until they learned how to use it for their own advantage." [40] Properly handled, it could lead the Jews to control over their destiny: Herzl believed that the antisemites were both rational and honest and that the Jewish problem was the most serious problem facing Europe. The "honest anti-semites" would therefore help him implement his grand scheme to rid them of their Jews, gain Jewish independence, and solve the Jewish problem once and for all. Arendt commends Herzl, for his

> mere will to action was something so startlingly new, so utterly revolutionary in Jewish life, that it spread with the speed of wildfire. Herzl's lasting greatness lay in his very desire to do something about the Jewish question, his desire to act and to solve the problem in political terms. [41]

In Arendt's interpretation, Herzl's political Zionism was not the ideology of a mass revolutionary movement but was, rather, the creed of secularized Western European Jewish intellectuals. Zionism's great asset was that it answered the need that had existed among the Jews since the Sabbatian catastrophe had shattered the traditional Jewish framework of understanding and started the Jews on their perilous journey towards worldlessness: it offered a path back to reality. While its doctrine of eternal antisemitism is similar to other nineteenth-century ideologies which attempted to explain reality in terms of irresistible laws and history in terms of "keys," Zionism and the Zionist movement was unique, according to Arendt, because "the case of the Jews was and still remains different. What they needed was not only a guide to reality, but reality itself; not simply a key to history, but the experience itself of history."[42]

The great achievement of Herzl's Zionist theory is that it escapes the view which sees history as a totally fortuitous series of events understandable only in terms of providence and accident. Its great limitation is that Jewish history is reduced to mere surface manifestations of one unchanging law over which the Jews have no control and whose source is their mere existence as a nation. Thus, while Herzl and his followers were realistic enough to recognize the political actuality of antisemitism, the ideology of "natural" antisemitism meant that no political analysis of it was necessary. Their view, according to Arendt,

> presupposes the eternity of antisemitism in an eternal world of nations, and moreover, denies the Jewish part of responsibility for existing conditions. Thereby it not only cuts off Jewish history from European history and

even from the rest of mankind; it ignores the role that European Jewry played in the construction and functioning of the national state; and thus it is reduced to the assumption, as arbitrary as it is absurd, that every Gentile living with Jews must become a conscious or subconscious Jew-hater.[43]

Impicit in this notion of a natural and inevitable antisemitism was that political reality consisted of an unchanging and unchangeable structure whose main components were the Jews on one side and the nation-states on the other. For the political Zionists, "politics" therefore meant international relations, affairs of state. Herzl's political action consisted of attempts at high-level diplomacy with the great powers, all of which came to nothing. Zionist political policy became one of unrealistic *Realpolitik*. Rather than organizing a powerful popular movement of world Jewry, relying on their own power to achieve their aims, and allying themselves with the oppressed peoples of the Near East, Arendt believes that the Zionist movement "sold out at the very first moment to the powers-that-be." [44] Furthermore, the ideology of eternal antisemitism led the Zionist into another typical response of the persecuted Diaspora Jew: rather than fighting antisemitism on its own ground, the Zionist solution was to escape.

> The up building of Palestine is indeed a great accomplishment and could be made an important and even decisive argument for Jewish claims in Palestine. . . . But the up building of Palestine has little to do with answering the nti-Semites; at most it has "answered" the secret self-hatred and lack of self-confidence on the part of those Jews who have themselves consciously or unconsciously succumbed to some parts of anti-Semitic propaganda.[45]

Another consequence of Herzl's static view of reality was a blind hatred of all revolutionary movements and his patronizing attitude toward the Jewish masses of Eastern Europe. The only political Zionist who ever proposed that the Zionist movement "organize the Jewish people in order to negotiate on the basis of a great revolutionary movement" [46]—what it should have been, according to Arendt—was Bernard Lazare, the

French-Jewish author and lawyer who was the first to publicize the innocence of the accused Captain Dreyfus.

Remembering that Arendt is first and foremost a political thinker,[47] and that her aim is to present a political interpretation of Jewish history, it is understandable that Bernard Lazare (see the essay "The Jew as Pariah" as well as the essays in Part II) stands out as a figure of singular importance and greatness in Arendt's account of Jewish history and Zionism. According to Arendt, Lazare was the first to translate the Jews' social status as a pariah people into terms of political significance by making it a tool for political analysis and the basis for political action.

> Living in the France of the Dreyfus Affair, Lazare could appreciate at first hand the pariah quality of Jewish existence. But he knew where the solution lay: in contrast to his unemancipated brethren who accept their pariah status automatically and unconsciously, the emancipated Jew must awake to an awareness of his position and, conscious of it, become a rebel against it— the champion of an oppressed people. His fight for freedom is part and parcel of that which all the downtrodden of Europe must needs wage to achieve national and social liberation.[48]

Having become a conscious pariah as a result of the Dreyfus Affair, to whom "history is no longer a closed book . . . and politics is no longer the privilege of Gentiles," [49] Lazare perforce became a Zionist.

Lazare belonged to the official Zionist movement only briefly, however. Having attended the Second Zionist Congress in 1898, where he was immediately elected to the Actions Committee, Lazare resigned from the committee and separated himself from the Zionist Organizatin in 1899 because the committee was acting like "a sort of autocratic government [that] seeks to direct the Jewish masses as though they were ignorant chidren." [50] Lazare wanted to promote a revolution within Jewish life, to criticize the role Jewish finance played in internal affairs and the effects it had on the relation of the Jews to non-Jews. But, Arendt claims, there was no possibility for such radical views within "Herzl's essentially reactionary movement."[51]

Herzl's solution of the Jewish problem was, in the final
analysis, escape or deliverance in a homeland. In the
light of the Dreyfus case the whole of the gentile world
seemed to him hostile; there were only Jews and anti-
semites. . . . To Lazare, on the other hand, the territorial
question was secondary—a mere outcome of the primary
demand that "the Jews should be emancipated as a
people and in the form of a nation." What he sought
was not an escape from antisemitism but a mobilization
of the people against its foes.[52]

In terms of the perspective Arendt displays through the
essays in this collection, the importance of Lazare as a model of
what it means to be a political pariah is hard to overestimate. It
is significant to note that Hannah Arendt edited the only
collection of his essays that has appeared in English to this
date, *Job's Dungheap* (1948), writing a short biography for that
volume. Not only is his work the source from which Arendt
derives many of her insights into both modern Jewish history
and Zionism (it was Lazare who first used the terms "pariah"
and "parvenu"), but his experience as an outspoken Jew cast
out from the Jewish community because of his criticism closely
parallels the experience of Arendt herself. Interestingly, in the
1940s, when Arendt wrote about Lazare's exclusion from Jewish
circles due to his views on how the Dreyfus case should have
been handled, she could not have anticipated what was to
cause her a similar experience of modern excommunication: the
trial of Adolf Eichmann. Although in the first case it was the
Jews who were on trial and in the second it was antisemitism,
both Lazare and Arendt based their criticism of the trials'
conduct on the grounds that justice for the defendant must be
the aim of legal proceedings, not political demagoguery and
showmanship.

According to Arendt, the lesson of Lazare's experience as a
Jewish political thinker and actor is that "[a]s soon as the
pariah enters the arena of politics, and translates his status into
political terms, he becomes perforce a rebel." [53] The social
pariahs of the nineteenth century, such as Heine and
Varnhagen, drew comfort from the world of dreams and
fantasy, secure in the knowledge that as compared to nature,
human concerns are pure vanity. In the twentieth century,
however, Arendt believes that such a retreat is no longer

possible: the pariah must become political. Thus, the first consequence of becoming conscious of one's pariah status is the demand that the Jewish people "come to grips with the world of men and women." [54] The duty of the conscious pariah is to awaken one's fellow Jews to a similar consciousness so as to rebel against it. "[Lazare] saw that what was necessary was to rouse the Jewish pariah to fight against the Jewish *parvenu*. There was no other way to save him from the latter's own fate— inevitable destruction." [55] This call to action was founded on the conviction that

> [h]owever much the Jewish pariah might be, from the historical viewpoint, the product of an unjust dispensation ... politically speaking, every pariah who refused to be a rebel was partly responsible for his own position and therewith for the blot on mankind which it represented. From such shame there was no escape, either in art or in nature. For insofar as man is more than a mere creature of nature, more than a mere product of Divine creativity, insofar will he be called to account for the things which men do to men in the world which they themselves condition.[56]

This responsibility for the human world, whether one is a victim or a victimizer, is at the core of Hannah Arendt's political philosophy, and it is the basis for her politically radical, self-critical analysis of the modern Jewish experience that leads to a Zionist conclusion. But Arendt's Zionism is not in the mainstream Herzlian tradition; it is, rather, in the dissident mold of Bernard Lazare, who wanted to be a revolutionary among his own people, not among others. It is well to keep this point in mind as we turn to Arendt's critical assessment of the founding of the Jewish State of Israel.

IV

> The real goal of the Jews in Palestine is the building up of a Jewish homeland. This goal must never be sacrificed to the pseudo-sovereignty of a Jewish State.[57]

Hannah Arendt's essays on Zionism and the Jewish state, collected in Part II of this volume, were written between 1942 and 1950, the most crucial period in the history of the Zionist movement. Her views were shared by only a very small minority of Zionists, most of whom were organized in the *Ihud*, the latest in a long line of small organizations of Palestinian Jews whose purposes were to promote Jewish-Arab understanding and cooperation. Never very large or effectual, the *Ihud* and its advocacy of a binational solution to the Jewish-Arab conflict was well known because it contained a large number of outstanding intellectual, cultural, and philanthropic leaders such as Rabbi Judah Magnes (president of the Hebrew University), Henrietta Szold (the organizer of Youth Aliyah and founder of Hadassah), and Martin Buber.

In the mid-1940s, however, the *Ihud*'s advocacy of binationalism was out of step with the mainstream of the Zionist movement. While for many years the Zionist majority was in favor of coexistence with the Arabs in a binational Palestine, by the end of World War II, in reaction to the genocide of European Jewry, the Zionist maximum—the establishment of a sovereign Jewish state—had become the Zionist minimum. This shift in the Zionist position is the crux of Arendt's criticism of official Zionist policy throughout this period, for she maintained—in 1945, when the Zionist movement demanded a Jewish State in all of Palestine, again in 1948, when they had accepted the principle of partition, and once again, in 1950, after Israel had been established by force of arms—that the creation of a Jewish state was out of touch with the realities of the situation in the Near East and the world at large.[58]

Arendt's criticism of Zionist politics is founded on a deep concern with the fate of the Jewish people following the Holocaust. The realization that millions of Jews had gone to their deaths without resistance resulted in a revolutionary change in Jewish consciousness. "Gone, probably forever, is that chief concern of the Jewish people for centuries: survival at any price. Instead, we find something essentially new among Jews, the desire for dignity at any price."[59] According to Arendt, this shift had the potential to become the basis for "an essentially sane Jewish political movement,"[60] for it indicated a desire to deal with reality and live freely in the world. The problem was that in their desire to overcome the centuries'-long experience of worldlessness, the Jews grasped onto the unrealistic ideological framework of Herzlian Zionism and its doctrine of eternal antisemitism. The result was the famous "Masada complex" in which this newfound desire for dignity was transformed into a potentially suicidal attitude. The danger to the Jewish homeland, as Arendt saw it, was that "[t]here is nothing in Herzlian Zionism that could act as a check on this; on the contrary, the utopian and ideological elements with which he injected the new Jewish will to political action are only too likely to lead the Jews out of reality once more—and out of the sphere of political action." [61]

It was this dangerous course Arendt had in mind when she wrote that "at this moment and under present circumstances a Jewish state can only be erected at the price of the Jewish homeland." [62] Since the "Jewish homeland" has been synonymous with the "Jewish state" for thirty years, it may be difficult to understand Arendt's distinction. In order to do so, we must piece together Arendt's own particular brand of Zionism.

Arendt observes that "Palestine and the building of a Jewish homeland constitute today the great hope and the great pride of Jews all over the world." [63] This deceptively simple sentence contains the essence of her conception of the Jewish homeland as a place that is a *center* and a place that is *built*. Arendt's Zionism is in many ways similar to the "cultural" Zionism of Bialik and Ahad Haam, but she arrives at it for reasons that in her view are highly political. The establishment of a Jewish cultural center in Palestine is a conscious act of creation on the part of the Jewish people; it is a positive response to the crises that have racked Jewish life since the time of Sabbatai Zevi, for it is an attempt by the Jews to create a political realm, take control over their lives, and reenter history after the Diaspora with its accompanying worldlessness and powerlessness. The building of the Jewish homeland is a profoundly political act, for it means not only the fabrication of a "world" within which a truly human life can be lived but the fabrication of a specifically Jewish world. This cultural specificity is of great importance, "[f]or only within the framework of a people can a man live as a man among men." [64]

Many people have recognized that the *Yishuv* (the pre-state Jewish community in Palestine)—and, later, the State of Israel—was a highly artifical creation. This is usually understood to be a criticism of the Jewish homeland, for the whole point of the homeland in Herzl's ideology is to "normalize" and make "natural" the Jews' "unnatural" Diaspora existence. For Arendt, however, it is "precisely this artificiality that gave the

Jewish achievements in Palestine their human significance." [65] The greatness of the *Yishuv* was that it was the conscious product of the concerted will of the Jewish people and *not* the predestined product of any natural forces to which the Jewish people were subject. "The challenges were all there, but none of the responses was 'natural.' " [66] The economic development of the *Yishuv* bore little resemblance to the traditional colonial enterprise. Rather than the usual "original accumulation" in which native riches are exploited with the help and at the expense of native labor in order to enrich the colonial power, the riches of the *Yishuv* "are exclusively the product of Jewish labor." [67] The revival of the Hebrew language, the erection of the Hebrew University, the new modes of human organization and cooperation found in the *kibbutzim*, and the establishment of great health centers "can certainly not be explained by utilitarian reasons." [68]

Unlike those Zionists who considered the establishment of a state to be not only the goal but the ultimate sign of success of the Jewish people's effort to reestablish themselves in their ancient home, Arendt considers the *Yishuv* to already embody the aims of Zionism as she sees them. For Arendt, the Jewish homeland is a political space, a human world created by conscious human effort where a Jewish culture can come into being; this the *Yishuv* achieved, without political sovereignty and without being a majority in Palestine. Precisely because a Jewish community had been built where people could appear to each other, where there was an audience for works of literature and art, Jewish cultural genius no longer needed to either abandon its Jewish roots in favor of "universal" European culture or else be relegated to the category of folklore. It was this political and cultural space of the "Jewish homeland" that Arendt felt was being sacrificed on the altar of the "Jewish state" by the unrealistic political demands of the Zionist movement.

In Arendt's opinion, the demand for a Jewish state simply ignored the fact that the majority of Palestine's population was Arab, and that Palestine itself was surrounded by millions of Arabs in the neighboring countries. The Zionist demand for a state left the Palestinian Arabs with only two choices: emigration or acceptance of their eventual minority status, both of which were unacceptable to a people striving for their independence. The inalterable fact of the Near East was that the Arabs were the Jews' neighbors. In order to preserve the Jewish homeland in Palestine once the British pulled out, the Jews had the choice of either working out an agreement with the Arabs or seeking the protection of one of the great imperial powers. By choosing the latter, the concept of a Jewish state would become farcical and even self-defeating insofar as that state would be a bastion of imperial interests in an area striving to liberate itself from colonialism. On the other hand, Arendt recognized that Arab policies were equally blind in not recognizing the needs and concrete achievements of the Zionists in Palestine.

The unrealistic approach to the Palestinian situation on the part of both the Jews and Arabs, Arendt observed, was the result of the British Mandate under which the British mediated between and separated the two communities from each other. This allowed Jews and Arabs to develop without any political regard or responsibility for each other and made it seem to each of them that the main political issue was how to deal with and ultimately get rid of the British, ignoring the permanent reality of the other's existence. The real issues at the heart of the conflict were "Jewish determination to keep and possibly extend national sovereignty without consideration for Arab interests, and Arab determination to expel the Jewish 'invaders' from Palestine without consideration for Jewish achievements there." [69] The Jewish and Arab claims were perfectly incompatible and mutually irrefutable, for both were the result of nationalistic policies reached within "the closed framework of one's own people and history." [70]

Arendt believed that cooperation between Jews and Arabs in the Near East could, by developing the area, be the basis for true sovereignty and independence. But the only way for this to occur was if both sides gave up their nationalistic and chauvinistic perspectives and claims. "Good relationships between Jews and Arabs will depend upon a changed attitude toward each other, upon a change in the atmosphere in Palestine and the Near East, not necessarily upon a formula." [71] Prophetically, she warned that "if this 'independent and sovereign' behavior goes on unabated, then all independence and sovereignty will be lost." [72]

The inevitable war that would result from the spurious sovereignty upon which the Zionist movement had set its sights would almost certainly destroy those aspects of the Jewish homeland that in Arendt's view had made it "the great hope and the great pride of Jews all over the world." Prior to the *Yishuv*'s success during the War of Liberation (1948–49) the very survival of Israel was highly questionable. Like all Jewish observers then (and now), Arendt's prime concern was with the consequence for the Jewish people of a second catastrophe so soon after Hitler.

> What would happen to Jews, individually and collectively, if this hope and this pride were to be extinguished in another catastrophe is almost beyond imagining. But it is certain that this would become the central fact of Jewish history and it is possible that it might become the beginning of the self-dissolution of the Jewish people. There is no Jew in the world whose whole outlook on life and the world would not be radically changed by such a tragedy.[73]

Today we know that such a tragedy did not occur; but unlike most observers of that period, Arendt asserted that "even if the Jews were to win the war, its end would find the unique possibilities and the unique achievements of Zionism in Palestine destroyed."[74] Without a peace agreement with the Arabs—and the Arabs were not prepared to accept a sovereign Jewish state in their midst—the internal nature of the *Yishuv* would be radically transformed. The result of an uneasy armistice with its neighbors, Arendt predicted, would be that concerns of military self-defense would come to dominate all other public interest and activities. "The growth of a Jewish culture would cease to be the concern of the whole people; social experiments would have to be discarded as impractical luxuries; political thought would center around military strategy; economic development would be determined by the needs of war."[75] With the constant threat from abroad, the country would have to be perpetually prepared for instantaneous mobilization; in order to sustain such a spirit of sacrifice, nationalism and chauvinism would quickly seep into the political and cultural atmosphere. Under these circumstances, a military dictatorship could easily result.

Arendt also felt that as a consequence of statehood the great achievements of the labor movement—particularly the *kibbutzim*—and of the cultural Zionists—particularly the Hebrew University—"would be the first victims of a long period of military insecurity and nationalistic aggressiveness." [76] They would become increasingly isolated as their "anti-nationalist" and "anti-chauvinist" Zionism did not fit the need for a statist ideology. But these would only be the first victims, "[f]or without the cultural and social *hinterland* of Jerusalem and the collective settlements, Tel Aviv could become a Levantine city overnight. Chauvinism ... could use the religious concept of the chosen people and allow its meaning to degenerate into hopeless vulgarity." [77]

With its wars and *raison d'état*, Arendt asserted that statehood would make the Jewish homeland's relationship with the Diaspora problematic. While the cultural center of world Jewry would become a modern-day Sparta, its large expenditures on national defense would lead Israel to excessive financial dependence upon American Jewry. The consequences of this were potentially disastrous:

> Charity money can be mobilized in great quantities only in emergencies, such as the recent catastrophe in Europe or in the Arab-Jewish war; if the Israeli government cannot win its economic independence from such money it will soon find itself in the unenviable position of being forced to create emergencies, that is, forced into a policy of aggressiveness and expansion.[78]

As Arendt warned, Herzl's Jewish state did not solve "the Jewish problem"; the tragic result has been that antisemitism has been transformed into anti-Zionism. With sovereignty, the pariah people has not ceased to be a pariah—it has created a pariah state. As a small state located in a key area of superpower rivalry, Israel's destiny is almost as subject to uncontrollable and unforeseen accidental circumstances as the Jews' fate in the Diaspora. Arendt contends that the often-expressed Israeli belief that they can stand up against the whole world, if necessary, is just as politically unrealistic as the Diasporic unconcern with politics. She feared that it might lead to an equally tragic end.

V

> For the first time Jewish history is not separate but tied up with that of all other nations. The comity of European peoples went to pieces when, and because, it

allowed its weakest member to be excluded and persecuted.[79]

In a complex and largely implicit manner, Hannah Arendt placed the Jews and "the Jewish condition" at the center of her critique of the modern age. By doing so she took one of Karl Marx's ideas and transformed it into part of her own system of thought. In the process she came up with both her own insights and a critique of Marx. A number of aspects of her political theory were arrived at in this fashion, but this case is special. The discovery was not of just one particular quality of modern society but concerns the central category of Arendt's and Marx's respective critiques of the modern age. As Arendt puts it, "[w]orld alienation—and not self-alienation as Marx thought—has been the hallmark of the modern age." [80]

It was Marx, in his essay "On the Jewish Question," who first put forward the thesis that the Jews, rather than being a backward people who had to be "civilized," were actually at the forefront of contemporary developments and embodied the true spirit of the modern age. According to Marx, the reason why "the Jewish question"—whether the Jews were fit for entrance into civil society—was being considered was not that the Jews had become similar to the Christians, but that society was becoming "Jewish":

> The Jew has emancipated himself in a Jewish manner, not only by acquiring the power of money, but also because *money* has become, through him and also apart from him, a world power, while the practical Jewish spirit has become the practical spirit of the Christian nations. The Jews have emancipated themselves in so far as the Christians have become Jews.[81]

It is among the Jews that Marx first discovers money as the "universal *antisocial* element of the *present time*" which is "the *supreme practical* expression of human self-estrangement" that causes "civil society [to] separate itself completely from the life of the state, [to] sever all the species-bonds of man, [and to] dissolve the human world into a world of atomistic, antagonistic individuals." [82] Marx later elaborates the antisocial element inherent in money as such into the social relationship defined by "commodity fetishism" and simultaneously shifts his focus from the Jews to the bourgeoisie. This is no accident, for the Jews were—at most—protocapitalists. As merchants, financiers, and moneylenders, more than any other group they had lived apart from the land and within the money economy during the medieval and early modern periods. It is thus among the Jews, according to Marx, that the real nature of capitalism—the alienation that results from the commodity fetishism inherent in money relations between people—first develops and reveals its inhumanity.

The Jews' social and economic existence within the moneyed sector of the economy in precapitalist society thus foreshadowed the direction in which modern society was moving. With the emergence of industrial capitalism—in Marx's view, the true basis of the modern social structure—Jewish merchant and finance capital became simply a parasitical sector of the capitalist class which received a portion of the surplus value expropriated from the laborer by the industrial bourgeoisie. Thus, while Marx first discovered what he considered to be the "secret" of capitalism by a consideration of the Jews and contended that historically it first developed among the Jews, he believed that the Jews did not have a unique place in the materialist dialectic of capitalist production which ground all people into either capitalists or workers. For Marx, the Jews had become unimportant in society and quickly ceased to figure in his analysis.

Avoiding Marx's misrepresentation of Judaism and his anti-Jewish rhetoric, more subtle and consistent in her analysis of Jews and "the Jewish question," Arendt never makes the facile assertion that modern society is becoming Jewish. Still, the Jews are at the center of her analysis. For Hannah Arendt, history is not made up of the mass of normal, everyday events. Rather, it is made up of the exceptional person and action that reveals the meaning of an historical period.[83] In the modern age, the experience of the Jews is the exception that illuminates the whole modern period, both in terms of the antisemitism that affected them from without and the worldless "Jewish condition" that affected them from within. Thus, while concurring with Marx's analysis that it is among the Jews that the characteristic phenomena of the modern age first appears, she also believes that, as the modern age develops, the dangerous effects of worldlessness are most clearly displayed in the history of the Jews. The very reason why Marx loses interest in the Jews—their marginal and unimportant status in terms of economic life—is precisely the reason why they are significant for Arendt. It is their very superfluousness, their separation from both state and society, that explains why "[i]t was no mere accident that the catastrophic defeats of the peoples of Europe began with the catastrophe of the Jewish people." [84]

In *The Human Condition*—which hardly refers to the Jews or Judaism—Arendt states that

> property, as distinguished from wealth and appropria-
> tion, indicates the privately owned share of a common
> world and therefore is the most elementary political
> condition for man's worldliness. By the same token,
> expropriation and world alienation coincide, and the
> modern age . . . began by alienating certain strata of the
> population from the world.[85]

In context it is clear that she is referring to the uprooting of peasants, but it is equally clear that among the Jews this lack of a "privately owned share of a common world" has been a condition of existence since the beginning of the Diaspora. The rootlessness of "the wandering Jew" antedates the rootlessness of the modern age, and more than any other factor was responsible for the worldless, unrealistic and unpolitical percep-tions Jews had of the world.

Until the Sabbatai Zevi episode this worldlessness was kept within certain bounds. Although separated from the world around them, Arendt asserts that the Jews maintained an internal community whose cohesiveness and distinctiveness was expressed in the concept of exile, a fundamentally political notion which over the centuries had taken on religious form and become one of the central ideas of Judaism. Echoing Marx's analysis, the Jews lived within the market sector of the economy, a realm characterized by "the essential unreality of financial transactions." [86] But it wasn't the spread of the Jewish "god" of money that defined the modern age, as Marx would have it. Rather, the modern age was characterized by the cause which underlay the Jews' reliance on money wealth: the lack of any physical place to which people were rooted and from which they could orient themselves to the world, grasp reality, and experience history. The unique worldless situation of the Jews increasingly became the generalized condition of humankind. And, as the world within which they existed as a pariah people started to disintegrate, the Jews were at the forefront of the process because they had, as it were, a head start.

The atomization of communities into lonely individuals was a process most clearly visible among the assimilating Jews. On the one hand, assimilation spelled the end of the Jewish community. On the other hand, Jews were accepted into the ranks of high society only as exceptions. Thus, in order to become part of society, they had to escape from the Jewish community and become free-floating individuals. The road to assimilation by conforming to the standards laid down by high society was a precursor of the phenomenon of "conformism inherent in society." [87] What was demanded of the Jews was that they behave in an exceptional and peculiar but nevertheless recognizable—and hence stereotypic—"Jewish" way. The result of the ambiguous situation where they were supposed to both be—and not be—Jewish was that introspection characteristic of the "so-called complex psychology of the average Jew." [88]

In Arendt's analysis, the psychological conflict that derived from their unresolved social dilemma was that "Jews felt simultaneously the pariah's regret at not having become a parvenu and the parvenu's bad conscience at having betrayed his people and exchanged equal rights for personal privileges." [89] The result was that

> [i]nstead of being defined by nationality or religion, Jews were being transformed into a social group whose members shared certain psychological attributes and reactions, the sum total of which was supposed to constitute "Jewishness." In other words, Judaism became a psychological quality, and the Jewish question became an involved personal problem for every individual Jew.[90]

The Jews thus constituted the first large-scale example of what happens when political issues are dealt with on an individual, private level rather than a collective, public level. Thinking they were free from the given reality of their Jewish roots, Jews like Rahel Varnhagen tried to overcome their Jewishness by believing that "[e]verything depends on self-thinking." [91] Arendt, speaking from Rahel's point of view, comments that "[s]elf-thinking brings liberation from objects and their reality, creates a sphere of pure ideas and a world which is accessible to any rational being without benefit of knowledge or experience." [92] The result of this alienation from the real world was the breakup of the Jewish community into isolated, lonely individuals. "The terrible and bloody annihilation of individual Jews was preceded by the bloodless destruction of the Jewish people." [93]

For Arendt, the destruction of the Jewish community was only a predecessor to the destruction of communities throughout Europe. The subsequent result was the rise of ideologically based mass movements and the destruction of the nation-state. Despite its many problems and internal contradictions, Arendt does think that for a time prior to the economically inspired imperialism of the nineteenth century, the nation-state had provided a truly political form of human organization. The legal emancipation of the Jews was but one of its logical results. The destruction of the political organization of people in the nation-state and the class society upon which it rested was the first accompishment of the Nazi movement's rise to power. By Arendt's account, class society was absorbed by mass society. The citizen, already turned into the bourgeois, now became the philistine: "the bourgeois isolated from his own class, the atomized indiviudal who is produced by the breakdown of the bourgeois class itself." [94]

Citizenship, the foundation of politics, was now selectively denied to minorities—particularly Jews—on the basis of race. Stateless Jews, rightless people "thrown back into a peculiar state of nature," [95] were among the first to discover that without the rights of the citizen there was no such thing as "the rights of man." The Jews, both pariahs and parvenus, found that once they became "outlaws" literally anything could be done with them, "that a man who is nothing but a man has lost the very qualities which make it possible for other people to treat him as a fellow-man." [96] Expelled from their homes and deprived of even the legal status of the criminal, nobody knew who they were or cared what happened to them. For the stateless, accident reigned supreme. They had absolutely no place on earth to go but internment and concentration camps. Statelessness was the ultimate manifestation of worldlessness, whose logical end is elimination from this world.

Precisely because of their worldless condition, the Jews became the first inhabitants of the laboratory of the concentration camp "in which the fundamental belief of totalitarianism that everything is possible is being verified." [97] It is here that worldlessness and atomization reach their ultimate form and people are reduced to nothing but their biological nature. Both individuality and community are systematically destroyed. The individuals shipped to the concentration camp are more effectively separated from the world of the living than if they were killed, for their very existence and memory are blotted out. World-alienation, a phenomenon which had made its earliest appearance in the modern age among the Jews, reached its climax with their destruction.

VI

> Rahel had remained a Jew and pariah. Only because she
> clung to both conditions did she find a place in the
> history of European humanity.[98]

We are now in a position to briefly consider the bitter controversy which followed the publication of *Eichmann in Jerusalem*. What aroused her critics' ire more than anything else was her assertion that "[w]herever Jews lived, there were recognized Jewish leaders, and this leadership, almost without exception, cooperated in one way or another, for one reason or another, with the Nazis." [99] Gershom Scholem's reaction in his letter to Arendt contained in Part III of this volume was typical: "What perversity! We are asked, it appears, to confess that the Jews too had their 'share' in these acts of genocide." [100]

This criticism totally misses what Hannah Arendt is trying to show about the implications of total worldlessness, for which the "banality of evil" is a corollary. The horror is both that while Eichmann *"never realized what he was doing,"*[101] "the members of the Jewish Councils as a rule were *not* traitors or Gestapo agents, and *still* they became the tools of the Nazis." [102] It was no accident that the Jews were the first victims, and the utmost importance of considering the particularities of modern Jewish history is perhaps most succinctly summed up by Arendt in one of the most important passages in *Eichmann in Jerusalem*:

> It was when the Nazi regime declared that the German
> people not only were unwilling to have any Jews in
> Germany but wished to make the entire Jewish people

disappear from the face of the earth that the new crime, the crime against humanity—in the sense of a crime "against the human status," or against the very nature of mankind—appeared. . . . The supreme crime it [the Israeli court trying Eichmann] was confronted with, the physical extermination of the Jewish people, was a crime against humanity, perpetrated upon the body of the Jewish people, and . . . only the choice of victims, not the nature of the crime, could be derived from the long history of Jew-hatred and anti-Semitism.[103]

For Hannah Arendt the destruction of the Jews is insolubly embedded in European history as a whole. It is only by recognizing the fact that the Jews *were* singled out by the Nazis that the crime against humanity appears, and it is precisely because of this particularity that the experience of the Jews *as* Jews is important for all humankind. It is no accident that the Jews were the first victims of the death factories which constitute the basis of totalitarianism; but they were just that, the *first* victims. Because it is exceptional, the Jews' fate sheds light on the history and experience of all people in the modern age.

As a conscious pariah, Arendt concerns herself with the Jews because she is both a Jew and a European, and she addresses herself to both the world as a whole and the Jews in particular. To the world she is saying that the Jews' condition is connected to everyone's condition, that what happened to the Jews is not an isolated instance but may happen to anybody because the crime itself is not uniquely Jewish, but was only perpetrated upon them. The lack of a political orientation to the world is what links the fate of the Jews to that of modern society as a whole.

Her experience as a Jewish refugee, as expressed in the first essay in this collection, "We Refugees," provided Hannah Arendt with the fundamental experience from which she derived worldliness as her standard of political judgment. Part of her impulse to search for paradigms of political thought and action in the experience of ancient Greece is that she wants to teach a sense of politics to a world in danger of doing what the Jews unwittingly did to themselves as well as what the Nazis did to the Jews. Arendt's great fear is that the condition of worldlessness which has characterized the Jews more than any other people in the modern age may become the generalized condition of our day.

To the Jews, Arendt is saying that part of the reason for the terrible end to their history in Europe is that they did not have a realistic political understanding of the world in which they lived. While Eichmann *"never realized what he was doing,"* the Jews never realized what was happening. In response to the Eichmann controversy, she reminds us that "[n]o State of Israel would ever have come into being if the Jewish people had not created and maintained its own specific in-between space throughout the long centuries of dispersion, that is, prior to the seizure of its old territory." [104] Her aim is to awaken Jews to the fact that whether or not they have been aware of it, they have been able to survive precisely because they have constituted a political community. To survive, they must break with the past in which accident reigned supreme and take conscious control of their destiny. The Zionist movement, and the *kibbutzim* in particular, are important phenomena not only for the Jews but for humankind as a whole because they demonstrate that *even* the Jews can establish a world through the power of collective action and that the so-called natural processes of society produce inevitable results only when human beings desert the realm of politics.

It is only because she was both a Jew and a European who through the darkest of times repudiated neither of these heritages and experiences but rather combined and built on them both that Hannah Arendt achieved distinction as one of the most profound thinkers of our age. Arendt's solution to her own "Jewish problem" was not to repudiate her Jewishness nor blindly affirm it, but to adopt the stance of a conscious pariah— an outsider among non-Jews, and a rebel among her own people. It was because of this marginal position that she was abls to gain critical insights into both the Jewish and non-Jewish worlds. There are, of course, problems with both her version of modern Jewish history and her critique of modern society.[105] But, as is the case with truly original thinkers, the encounter with these problems is a valuable process for the reader.

The controversy over *Eichmann in Jerusalem* not only caused Hannah Arendt much pain and grief, as is evident in the responses to her critics contained in this volume, but has also obscured for too long the real depth of her contribution to understanding the Jewish experience in the modern age. My hope is that this book will help reveal Arendt's views by re-introducing to the public these heretofore scattered essays.

Very few individuals have successfully balanced the reality of being both a Jew and a European, making of the emancipation what it should have been—the emancipation of Jews as Jews. Hannah Arendt provides a striking example of the potential fruitfulness of this combination. The threads of both heritages are woven together in such a way that to overlook or deny the influence of one or the other is to rip apart the very fabric of her life and thought. It is because she remained both a Jew and a European that she gained a place in history, and it is as both a Jew and a European that her life and work should be understood.

The Jewish experience of danger, trauma, and hope in the dark times of the twentieth century was one which Hannah Arendt shared. Very early in her life she took to heart the experience and final words of Rahel Varnhagen:

> The thing which all my life seemed to me the greatest shame, which was the misery and misfortune of my life— having been born a Jewess—this I should on no account now wish to have missed.[106]

NOTES

THE JEW AS PARIAH:
THE CASE OF HANNAH ARENDT (1906-1975)

1. "We Refugees," The Jew as Pariah, p. 66.
2. " 'Eichmann in Jerusalem': An Exchange of Letters between Gershom Scholem and Hannah Arendt" (hereafter referred to as "Exchange") The Jew as Pariah, p. 246.
3. The Spring 1977 issue of Social Research was devoted exclusively to

Hannah Arendt, but not one of the eminent authors who contributed articles so much as mentioned her Jewish writings.
4. *Antisemitism*, p. 56.
5. "The Jew as Pariah: A Hidden Tradition," *The Jew as Pariah*, pp. 67-68.
6. *Ibid.*, p. 68.
7. "The Moral of History," *The Jew as Pariah*, p. 109.
8. "Exchange," *The Jew as Pariah*, p. 250.
9. *Antisemitism*, p. 74.
10. "The Moral of History," *The Jew as Pariah*, p. 109.
11. *Antisemitism*, p. 6.
12. *Ibid.*, p. 8.
13. "The Jewish State: Fifty Years After," *The Jew as Pariah*, p. 167.
14. "Jewish History, Revised," *The Jew as Pariah*, p. 99.
15. "The Jewish State: Fifty Years After," *The Jew as Pariah*, p. 167.
16. "Jewish History, Revised," *The Jew as Pariah*, p. 104. Those familiar with Hannah Arendt's other work will notice the affinity between this account and her discussion of the breakdown of tradition in the modern age presented in *Between Past and Future*, particularly the essays "Tradition and the Modern Age" and "What is Authority?"
17. *Ibid.*, pp. 104-105.
18. "The Jewish State: Fifty Years After," *The Jew as Pariah*, p. 167.
19. *Antisemitism*, p. 17.
20. *Ibid.*, p. 25.
21. *Ibid.*, p. 24.
22. *Ibid.*, p. 25.
23. *Ibid.*, p. 23.
24. *Ibid.*, p. 52.
25. "Portrait of a Period," *The Jew as Pariah*, p. 119.
26. *Antisemitism*, p.53.
27. *Ibid.*, p. 66.
28. "We Refugees," *The Jew as Pariah*, p. 66.
29. "On Humanity in Dark Times: Thoughts About Lessing," *Men in Dark Times*, p. 13.
30. *Ibid.*, p. 14.
31. *Ibid.*, p. 13.
32. *Antisemitism*, p. 83.
33. *Ibid.*, p. 117.
34. *Ibid.*, p. 53.
35. *Imperialism*, p. 120 n.
36. *Antisemitism*, p. 15.
37. *Ibid.*, p. 120.
38. "Portrait of a Period," *The Jew as Pariah*, p. 121.
39. "The Jewish State: Fifty Years After," *The Jew as Pariah*, p. 166.
40. *Ibid.*
41. *Ibid.*
42. *Ibid.*, p. 168.
43. "Zionism Reconsidered," *The Jew as Pariah*, p. 147.
44. *Ibid.*, p. 152.
45. "The Jewish State: Fifty Years After," *The Jew as Pariah*, pp. 172-173.
46. "Zionism Reconsidered," *The Jew as Pariah*, p. 152.
47. It should be remembered that "politics" and "political thought" have special meanings and uncommon implications for Hannah Arendt.

These are implicit throughout her work, but are particularly spelled out in *Between Past and Future* and *The Human Condition*.

48. "The Jew as Pariah: A Hidden Tradition," *The Jew as Pariah*, p. 76.
49. "We Refugees," *The Jew as Pariah*, p. 66.
50. Bernard Lazare, *Job's Dungheap* (New York, Schocken Books, 1948), p. 10.
51. "The Jewish State: Fifty Years After," *The Jew as Pariah*, p. 171.
52. "Herzl and Lazare," *The Jew as Pariah*, pp. 127-128.
53. "The Jew as Pariah: A Hidden Tradition," *The Jew as Pariah*, p. 77.
54. *Ibid.*
55. *Ibid.*, p. 76.
56. *Ibid.*, pp. 77-78.
57. "To Save the Jewish Homeland," *The Jew as Pariah*, p. 192.
58. Foreshadowing the controversy over *Eichmann in Jerusalem*, the continued advocacy of binationalism by Arendt and the *Ihud* was strongly condemned by the mainstream Zionist establishment:

    "Any program which denies these fundamental principles [the Biltmore Program, which called for the creation of a sovereign Jewish Commonwealth], such as advanced by the *Ihud* or any other group, is unacceptable to the Zionist Organization of America and Hadassah, the Women's Zionist Organization of America." (Esco Foundation for Palestine, Inc., *Palestine: A Study of Jewish, Arab, and British Policies*, 2 vols., New Haven, Conn., Yale University Press, 1947, p. 1087.)

    Arendt responded to this criticism in "About 'Collaboration,'" contained in Part III of this volume.
59. "The Jewish State: Fifty Years After," *The Jew as Pariah*, p. 176.
60. *Ibid.*
61. *Ibid.*, pp. 176-177. For Arendt there is an important distinction between ideology and politics: "an ideology differs from a simple [political] opinion in that it claims to possess either the key to history, or the solution for all the 'riddles of the universe,' or the intimate knowledge of the hidden universal laws which are supposed to rule nature and man." (*Imperialism*, p. 39.) Ideology, with its certainty, is the pattern of thought characteristic of totalitarianism, while "common sense," with its element of doubt and opinion, characterizes a truly free political realm.
62. "To Save the Jewish Homeland," *The Jew as Pariah*, p. 188.
63. *Ibid.*, p. 185.
64. "The Jew as Pariah: A Hidden Tradition," *The Jew as Pariah*, p. 90. The relationship between "fabrication" and "the world" is an important but complex one in Arendt's political theory. The interested reader should look at *The Human Condition*, especially the chapters on "Work" and "Action."
65. "Peace or Armistice in the Near East?," *The Jew as Pariah*, p. 206.
66. *Ibid.*, p. 207. The contrast between nature and its necessity on the one hand, and artifice and its freedom on the other, is treated in depth in *The Human Condition*.
67. *Ibid.*, p. 205.
68. *Ibid.*, p. 206.
69. *Ibid.*, p. 197.

70. *Ibid.*, pp. 200-201. The fundamental importance for politics of representative thinking, the ability to see things from another person's point
of view, is discussed by Arendt in "Truth and Politics" in *Between
Past and Future.*

71. *Ibid.*, p. 198.
72. *Ibid.*, p. 197.
73. "To Save the Jewish Homeland," *The Jew as Pariah*, p. 185.
74. *Ibid.*, p. 187.
75. *Ibid.*
76. "Peace or Armistice in the Near East?," *The Jew as Pariah*, p. 222.
77. *Ibid.*
78. *Ibid.*, p. 221.
79. "We Refugees," *The Jew as Pariah*, p. 66.
80. *The Human Condition*, p. 254. Other examples of Arendt's changing the
focus of Marx's analysis are:

(1) Marx believed that the establishment of the nation-state
system was a result of the rise of the bourgeoisie, with imperialism the
logical outcome of the expansion of capital. While Arendt agrees that
imperialism was the result of the growth of capital and the
bourgeoisie's involvement in politics, she asserts that the bourgeoisie's
entrance into politics occurred only in the mid-nineteenth century
and caused the imperilaism which destroyed the nation-state.

(2) Arendt generally follows Marx's analysis in her discussion of
the separation of people from the land and the development of
modern society as a society of laborers "free" from the old "bonds" to
land and community. For Marx the characteristic product of bourgeois society is the proletariat, and it is this class of wage laborers
upon whom the capitalist mode of production is based that is the
vanguard which is to make history. In contrast, Arendt thinks that the
important result of laboring society is the creation of what Marx
called the *lumpenproletariat*, which she expands to include the
déclassé elements of all the classes that came to form the mob, for it
was the mob that prepared the way for the mass movements and
totalitarianism.

I think, in fact, that Arendt's view of the importance of political
action and her notion of both action and freedom, the *raison d'être* of
politics, are actually much closer to those of Marx than she thought.
But this all depends upon which of the many interpretations of Marx
one believes is accurate.

81. Karl Marx, "On the Jewish Question," Robert C. Tucker, ed., *The Marx-
Engels Reader* (New York: W. W. Norton & Company, 1972), p. 47.
82. *Ibid.*, pp. 47-50 *passim.*
83. Arendt's philosophy of history, including her critique of Marxist historiography, is most fully developed in her essay "The Concept of
History: Ancient and Modern" in *Between Past and Future.*
84. "The Moral of History," *The Jew as Pariah*, p. 109.

Arendt's attitude toward history has a certain affinity to that of
her friend Walter Benjamin as expressed in his "Theses on the
Philosophy of History," which he bequeathed to Arendt's guardian-
ship shortly before his death in 1940. "*Thinking* involves not only the
flow of thoughts, but their arrest as well. Where thinking suddenly
stops in a configuration pregnant with tensions, it gives that configura-

tion a shock, by which it *crystallizes* into a monad." (Walter Benjamin, *Illuminations* (New York, Schocken Books, 1969), pp. 262-3, emphasis added.) By comparison, Arendt's overall intellectual project is perhaps most succinctly put in *The Human Condition* (p. 5) where she claims that her purpose "is nothing more than to *think* what we are doing" (emphasis added). This being the case, it is particularly revealing that in her reply to a critique of *The Origins of Totalitarianism* she states:

> I did not write a history of totalitarianism but an analysis in terms of history. . . . The book, therefore, does not really deal with the "origins" of totaritarianism (sic)—as its title unfortunately claims—but gives a historical account of the elements whcih *crystallized* into totalitarianism. ("A Reply," *The Review of Politics*, XV, 1 (January 1953), p. 78, emphasis added.)

85. *The Human Condition*, p. 253.
86. "We Refugees," *The Jew as Pariah*, p. 66.
87. *The Human Condition*, p. 41
88. *Antisemitism*, p. 66.
89. *Ibid.*
90. *Ibid.*
91. *Rahel Varnhagen*, p. 9.
92. *Ibid.* I believe that it is from this experience of the assimilating Jews, in particular Rahel Varhagen and Franz Kafka, that Arendt gained an insight into the phenomenon that she was later to describe as "the subjectivism of modern philosophy" which removed "the Archimedean point" out of the world and into the mind of the human being. See especially the chapter titled "The *Vita Activa* and the Modern Age" in *The Human Condition*.
93. "The Moral of History," *The Jew as Pariah*, p. 109.
94. *Totalitarianism*, p. 36.
95. *Imperialism*, p. 180.
96. *Ibid.*
97. *Totalitarianism*, p. 135.
98. *Rahel Varnhagen*, p. 227.
99. *Eichmann in Jerusalem*, p. 125.
100. Gershom Scholem, "Exchange," *The Jew as Pariah*, p. 243.
101. *Eichmann in Jerusalem*, p. 287.
102. " 'The Formidable Dr. Robinson': A Reply," *The Jew as Pariah*, p. 261.
103. *Eichmann in Jerusalem*, pp. 268-269.
104. *Ibid.*, p. 263.
105. For example, Arendt rarely discusses Eastern European Jewish history and ignores the attempts by Zionist and non-Zionist socialists to organize the Jews into "a great revolutionary movement." In her political theory she aestheticizes and sanitizes politics to such an extent that one often wonders what the exact content of "political action" really is. In a similar vein, her critique of Marx is not always based on a fair representation of his views. And, of course, the accuracy of the historical facts upon which she bases her interpretations of history has been widely questioned, most notably in the case of *Eichmann in Jerusalem*.
106. *Rahel Varnhagen*, p. 3.

PART I

The Pariah
as Rebel

We Refugees

(JANUARY 1943)

In the first place, we don't like to be called "refugees." We ourselves call each other "newcomers" or "immigrants." Our newspapers are papers for "Americans of German language"; and, as far as I know, there is not and never was any club founded by Hitler-persecuted people whose name indicated that its members were refugees.

A refugee used to be a person driven to seek refuge because of some act committed or some political opinion held. Well, it is true we have had to seek refuge; but we committed no acts and most of us never dreamt of having any radical political opinion. With us the meaning of the term "refugee" has changed. Now "refugees" are those of us who have been so unfortunate as to arrive in a new country without means and have to be helped by Refugee Committees.

Before this war broke out we were even more sensitive about being called refugees. We did our best to prove to other people that we were just ordinary immigrants. We declared that we had departed of our own free will to countries of our choice, and we denied that our situation had anything to do with "so-called Jewish problems." Yes, we were "immigrants" or "newcomers" who had left our country because, one fine day, it no longer suited us to stay, or for purely economic reasons. We wanted to rebuild our lives, that was all. In order to rebuild one's life one has to be strong and an optimist. So we are very optimistic.

Our optimism, indeed, is admirable, even if we say so ourselves. The story of our struggle has finally become known. We lost our home, which means the familiarity of daily life.

We lost our occupation, which means the confidence that we are of some use in this world. We lost our language, which means the naturalness of reactions, the simplicity of gestures, the unaffected expression of feelings. We left our relatives in the Polish ghettos and our best friends have been killed in concentration camps, and that means the rupture of our private lives.

Nevertheless, as soon as we were saved—and most of us had to be saved several times—we started our new lives and tried to follow as closely as possible all the good advice our saviors passed on to us. We were told to forget; and we forgot quicker than anybody ever could imagine. In a friendly way we were reminded that the new country would become a new home; and after four weeks in France or six weeks in America, we pretended to be Frenchmen or Americans. The more optimistic among us would even add that their whole former life had been passed in a kind of unconscious exile and only their new country now taught them what a home really looks like. It is true we sometimes raise objections when we are told to forget about our former work; and our former ideals are usually hard to throw over if our social standard is at stake. With the language, however, we find no difficulties: after a single year optimists are convinced they speak English as well as their mother tongue; and after two years they swear solemnly that they speak English better than any other language—their German is a language they hardly remember.

In order to forget more efficiently we rather avoid any allusion to concentration or internment camps we experienced in nearly all European countries—it might be interpreted as pessimism or lack of confidence in the new homeland. Besides, how often have we been told that nobody likes to listen to all that; hell is no longer a religious belief or a fantasy, but something as real as houses and stones and trees. Apparently nobody wants to know that contemporary history has created a new kind of human beings—the kind that are put in concentration camps by their foes and in internment camps by their friends.

Even among ourselves we don't speak about this past. Instead, we have found our own way of mastering an uncertain future. Since everybody plans and wishes and hopes, so do we. Apart from these general human attitudes, however, we try to clear up the future more scientifically. After so much bad luck we want a course as sure as a gun. Therefore, we leave the earth with all its uncertainties behind and we cast our eyes up to the sky. The stars tell us—rather than the newspapers—when Hitler will be defeated and when we shall become American citizens. We think the stars more reliable advisers than all our friends; we learn from the stars when we should have lunch with our benefactors and on what day we have the best chances of filling out one of these countless questionnaires which accompany our present lives. Sometimes we don't rely even on the stars but rather on the lines of our hand or the signs of our handwriting. Thus we learn less about political events but more about our own dear selves, even though somehow psychoanalysis has gone out of fashion. Those happier times are past when bored ladies and gentlemen of high society conversed about the genial misdemeanors of their early childhood. They don't want ghost-stories any more; it is real experiences that make their flesh creep. There is no longer any need of bewitching the past; it is spellbound enough in reality. Thus, in spite of our outspoken optimism, we use all sorts of magical tricks to conjure up the spirits of the future.

I don't know which memories and which thoughts nightly dwell in our dreams. I dare not ask for information, since I, too, had rather be an optimist. But sometimes I imagine that at least nightly we think of our dead or we remember the poems we once loved. I could even understand how our friends of the West coast, during the curfew, should have had such curious notions as to believe that we are not only "prospective citizens" but present "enemy aliens." In daylight, of course, we become only "technically" enemy aliens—all refugees know this. But when technical reasons prevented you from leaving your home during the dark hours, it certainly was not easy to avoid some dark speculations about the relation between technicality and reality.

No, there is something wrong with our optimism. There are those odd optimists among us who, having made a lot of optimistic speeches, go home and turn on the gas or make use of a skyscraper in quite an unexpected way. They seem to prove that our proclaimed cheerfulness is based on a dangerous readiness for death. Brought up in the conviction that life is the highest good and death the greatest dismay, we became witnesses and victims of worse terrors than death—without having been able to discover a higher ideal than life. Thus, although death lost its horror for us, we became neither willing nor capable to risk our lives for a cause. Instead of fighting—or thinking about how to become able to fight back—refugees have got used to wishing death to friends or relatives; if somebody dies, we cheerfully imagine all the trouble he has been saved. Finally many of us end by wishing that we, too, could be saved some trouble, and act accordingly.

Since 1938—since Hitler's invasion of Austria—we have seen how quickly eloquent optimism could change to speechless pessimism. As time went on, we got worse—even more optimistic and even more inclined to suicide. Austrian Jews under Schuschnigg were such a cheerful people—all impartial observers admired them. It was quite wonderful how deeply convinced they were that nothing could happen to them. But when German troops invaded the country and Gentile neighbors started riots at Jewish homes, Austrian Jews began to commit suicide.

Unlike other suicides, our friends leave no explanation of their deed, no indictment, no charge against a world that had forced a desperate man to talk and to behave cheerfully to his very last day. Letters left by them are conventional, meaningless documents. Thus, funeral orations we make at their open graves are brief, embarrassed and very hopeful. Nobody cares about motives, they seem to be clear to all of us.

I speak of unpopular facts; and it makes things worse that in order to prove my point I do not even dispose of the sole arguments which impress modern people—figures. Even those Jews who furiously deny the existence of the Jewish people give us a fair chance of survival as far as figures are concerned—how else could they prove that only a few Jews are criminals and that many Jews are being killed as good patriots in wartime? Through their effort to save the statistical life of the Jewish people we know that Jews had the lowest suicide rate among all civilized nations. I am quite sure those figures are no longer correct, but I cannot prove it with new figures, though I can certainly with new experiences. This might be sufficient for those skeptical souls who never were quite convinced that the measure of one's skull gives the exact idea of its content, or that statistics of crime show the exact level of national ethics. Anyhow, wherever European Jews are living today, they no longer behave according to statistical laws. Suicides occur not only among the panic-stricken people in Berlin and Vienna, in Bucharest or Paris, but in New York and Los Angeles, in Buenos Aires and Montevideo.

On the other hand, there has been little reported about suicides in the ghettoes and concentration camps themselves. True, we had very few reports at all from Poland, but we have been fairly well informed about German and French concentration camps.

At the camp of Gurs, for instance, where I had the opportunity of spending some time, I heard only once about suicide, and that was the suggestion of a collective action, apparently a kind of protest in order to vex the French. When some of us remarked that we had been shipped there *"pour crever"* in any case, the general mood turned suddenly into a violent courage of life. The general opinion held that one had to be abnormally asocial and unconcerned about general events if one was still able to interpret the whole accident as personal and individual bad luck and, accordingly, ended one's life personally and individually. But the same people, as soon as they returned to their own individual lives, being faced with seemingly individual problems, changed once more to this insane optimism which is next door to despair.

We are the first non-religious Jews persecuted—and we are the first ones who, not only *in extremis*, answer with suicide. Perhaps the philosophers are right who teach that suicide is the last and supreme guarantee of human freedom: not being free to create our lives or the world in which we live, we nevertheless are free to throw life away and to leave the world. Pious Jews, certainly, cannot realize this negative liberty; they perceive murder in suicide, that is, destruction of what man never is able to make, interference with the rights of the Creator. *Adonai nathan veadonai lakach* ("The Lord hath given and the Lord hath taken away"); and they would add: *baruch shem adonai* ("blessed be the name of the Lord"). For them suicide, like murder, means a blasphemous attack on creation as a whole. The man who kills himself asserts that life is not worth living and the world not worth sheltering him.

Yet our suicides are no mad rebels who hurl defiance at life and the world, who try to kill in themselves the whole universe. Theirs is a quiet and modest way of vanishing; they seem to apologize for the violent solution they have found for their personal problems. In their opinion, generally, political events had nothing to do with their individual fate; in good or bad times they would believe solely in their personality. Now they find some mysterious shortcomings in themselves which prevent them from getting along. Having felt entitled from their earliest childhood to a certain social standard, they are failures in their own eyes if this standard cannot be kept any longer. Their optimism is the vain attempt to keep head above water. Behind this front of cheerfulness, they constantly struggle with despair of themselves. Finally, they die of a kind of selfishness.

If we are saved we feel humiliated, and if we are helped we feel degraded. We fight like madmen for private existences with individual destinies, since we are afraid of becoming part of that miserable lot of *schnorrers* whom we, many of us former philanthropists, remember only too well. Just as once we failed to understand that the so-called *schnorrer* was a symbol of Jewish destiny and not a *shlemihl,* so today we don't feel entitled to Jewish solidarity; we cannot realize that we by ourselves are not so much concerned as the whole Jewish people. Sometimes this lack of comprehension has been strongly supported by our protectors. Thus, I remember a director of a great charity concern in Paris who, whenever he received the card of a German-Jewish intellectual with the inevitable "Dr." on it, used to exlaim at the top of his voice, "Herr Doktor, Herr Doktor, Herr Schnorrer, Herr Schnorrer!"

The conclusion we drew from such unpleasant experiences was simple enough. To be a doctor of philosophy no longer satisfied us; and we learnt that in order to build a new life, one has first to improve on the old one. A nice little fairy-tale has been invented to describe our behavior; a forlorn émigré dachshund, in his grief, begins to speak: "Once, when I was a St. Bernard ..."

Our new friends, rather overwhelmed by so many stars and famous men, hardly understand that at the basis of all our descriptions of past splendors lies one human truth: once we were somebodies about whom people cared, we were loved by friends, and even known by landlords as paying our rent regularly. Once we could buy our food and ride in the subway without being told we were undesirable. We have become a little hysterical since newspapermen started detecting us and telling us publicly to stop being disagreeable when shopping for milk and bread. We wonder how it can be done; we already are so damnably careful in every moment of our daily lives to avoid anybody guessing who we are, what kind of passport we have, where our birth certificates were filled out—and that Hitler didn't like us. We try the best we can to fit into a world where you have to be sort of politically minded when you buy your food.

Under such circumstances, St. Bernard grows bigger and bigger. I never can forget that young man who, when expected to accept a certain kind of work, sighed out, "You don't know to whom you speak; I was Section-manager in Karstadt's [a great department store in Berlin]." But there is also the deep despair of that middle-aged man who, going through countless shifts of different committees in order to be saved, finally exclaimed, "And nobody here knows who I am!" Since nobody would treat him as a dignified human being, he began sending cables to great personalities and his big relations. He learnt quickly that in this mad world it is much easier to be accepted as a "great man" than as a human being.

The less we are free to decide who we are or to live as we like, the more we try to put up a front, to hide the facts, and to play roles. We were expelled from Germany because we were Jews. But having hardly crossed the French borderline, we were changed into "boches." We were even told that we had to accept this designation if we really were against Hitler's racial theories. During seven years we played the ridiculous role of trying to be Frenchmen—at least, prospective citizens; but at the beginning of the war we were interned as "boches" all the same. In the meantime, however, most of us had indeed become such loyal Frenchmen that we could not even criticize a French governmental order; thus we declared it was all right to be interned. We were the first *"prisonniers volontaires"* history has ever seen. After the Germans invaded the country, the French Government had only to change the name of the firm; having been jailed because we were Germans, we were not freed because we were Jews.

It is the same story all over the world, repeated again and

again. In Europe the nazis confiscated our property; but in Brazil we have to pay 30% of our wealth, like the most loyal member of the *Bund der Auslandsdeutschen*. In Paris we could not leave our homes after eight o'clock because we were Jews; but in Los Angeles we are restricted because we are "enemy aliens." Our identity is changed so frequently that nobody can find out who we actually are.

Unfortunately, things don't look any better when we meet with Jews. French Jewry was absolutely convinced that all Jews coming from beyond the Rhine were what they called *Polaks*—what German Jewry called *Ostjuden*. But those Jews who really came from eastern Europe could not agree with their French brethren and called us *Jaeckes*. The sons of these *Jaecke*-haters—the second generation born in France and already duly assimilated—shared the opinion of the French Jewish upper classes. Thus, in the very same family, you could be called a *Jaecke* by the father and a *Polak* by the son.

Since the outbreak of the war and the catastrophe that has befallen European Jewry, the mere fact of being a refugee has prevented our mingling with native Jewish society, some exceptions only proving the rule. These unwritten social laws, though never publicly admitted, have the great force of public opinion. And such a silent opinion and practice is more important for our daily lives than all official proclamations of hospitality and good will.

Man is a social animal and life is not easy for him when social ties are cut off. Moral standards are much easier kept in the texture of a society. Very few individuals have the strength to conserve their own integrity if their social, political and legal status is completely confused. Lacking the courage to fight for a change of our social and legal status, we have decided instead, so many of us, to try a change of identity. And this curious behavior makes matters much worse. The confusion in which we live is partly our own work.

Some day somebody will write the true story of this Jewish emigration from Germany; and he will have to start with a description of that Mr. Cohn from Berlin who had always been a 150% German, a German super-patriot. In 1933 that Mr. Cohn found refuge in Prague and very quickly became a convinced Czech patriot—as true and as loyal a Czech patriot as he had been a German one. Time went on and about 1937

the Czech Government, already under some nazi p
began to expel its Jewish refugees, disregarding the fa
they felt so strongly as prospective Czech citizens. Ou
Cohn then went to Vienna; to adjust oneself there a de
Austrian patriotism was required. The German invasion forced
Mr. Cohn out that country. He arrived in Paris at a bad
moment and he never did receive a regular residence-permit.
Having already acquired a great skill in wishful thinking, he
refused to take mere administrative measures seriously, convinced that he would spend his future life in France. Therefore,
he prepared his adjustment to the French nation by identifying
himself with "our" ancestor Vercingetorix. I think I had better
not dilate on the further adventures of Mr. Cohn. As long as
Mr. Cohn can't make up his mind to be what he actually is, a
Jew, nobody can foretell all the mad changes he will still have
to go through.

A man who wants to lose his self discovers, indeed, the
possibilites of human existence, which are infinite, as infinite as
is creation. But the recovering of a new personality is as
difficult—and as hopeless—as a new creation of the world.
Whatever we do, whatever we pretend to be, we reveal nothing
but our insane desire to be changed, not to be Jews. All our
activities are directed to attain this aim: we don't want to be
refugees, since we don't want to be Jews; we pretend to be
English-speaking people, since German-speaking immigrants of
recent years are marked as Jews; we don't call ourselves
stateless, since the majority of stateless people in the world are
Jews; we are willing to become loyal Hottentots, only to hide
the fact that we are Jews. We don't succeed and we can't
succeed; under the cover of our "optimism" you can easily
detect the hopeless sadness of assimilationists.

With us from Germany the word assimilation received a
"deep" philosophical meaning. You can hardly realize how
serious we were about it. Assimilation did not mean the
necessary adjustment to the country where we happened to be
born and to the people whose language we happened to speak.
We adjust in principle to everything and everybody. This
attitude became quite clear to me once by the words of one of
my compatriots who, apparently, knew how to express his
feelings. Having just arrived in France, he founded one of these

societies of adjustment in which German Jews asserted to each other that they were already Frenchmen. In his first speech he said: "We have been good Germans in Germany and therefore we shall be good Frenchmen in France." The public applauded enthusiastically and nobody laughed; we were happy to have learnt how to prove our loyalty.

If patriotism were a matter of routine or practice, we should be the most patriotic people in the world. Let us go back to our Mr. Cohn; he certainly has beaten all records. He is that ideal immigrant who always, and in every country into which a terrible fate has driven him, promptly sees and loves the native mountains. But since patriotism is not yet believed to be a matter of practice, it is hard to convince people of the sincerity of our repeated transformations. This struggle makes our own society so intolerant; we demand full affirmation without our own group because we are not in the position to obtain it from the natives. The natives, confronted with such strange beings as we are, become suspicious; from their point of view, as a rule, only a loyalty to our old countries is understandable. That makes life very bitter for us. We might overcome this suspicion if we would explain that, being Jews, our patriotism in our original countries had rather a peculiar aspect. Though it was indeed sincere and deep-rooted. We wrote big volumes to prove it; paid an entire bureaucracy to explore its antiquity and to explain it statistically. We had scholars write philosophical dissertations on the predestined harmony between Jews and Frenchmen, Jews and Germans, Jews and Hungarians, Jews and ... Our so frequently suspected loyalty of today has a long history. It is the history of a hundred and fifty years of assimilated Jewry who performed an unprecedented feat: though proving all the time their non-Jewishness, they succeeded in remaining Jews all the same.

The desperate confusion of these Ulysses-wanderers who, unlike their great prototype, don't know who they are is easily explained by their perfect mania for refusing to keep their identity. This mania is much older than the last ten years which revealed the profound absurdity of our existence. We are like people with a fixed idea who can't help trying continually to disguise an imaginary stigma. Thus we are enthusiastically fond of every new possibility which, being new, seems able to work miracles. We are fascinated by every new nationality in the same way as a woman of tidy size is delighted with every new dress which promises to give her the desired waistline. But she likes the new dress only as long as she believes in its miraculous qualities, and she will throw it away as soon as she discovers that it does not change her stature—or, for that matter, her status.

One may be surprised that the apparent uselessness of all our odd disguises has not yet been able to discourage us. If it is true that men seldom learn from history, it is also true that they may learn from personal experiences which, as in our case, are repeated time and again. But before you cast the first stone at us, remember that being a Jew does not give any legal status in this world. If we should start telling the truth that we are nothing but Jews, it would mean that we expose ourselves to the fate of human beings who, unprotected by any specific law or political convention, are nothing but human beings. I can hardly imagine an attitude more dangerous, since we actually live in a world in which human beings as such have ceased to exist for quite a while; since society has discovered discrimination as the great social weapon by which one may kill men without any bloodshed; since passports or birth certificates, and sometimes even income tax receipts, are no longer formal papers but matters of social distinction. It is true that most of us depend entirely upon social standards; we lose confidence in ourselves if society does not approve us; we are—and always were—ready to pay any price in order to be accepted by society. But it is equally true that the very few among us who have tried to get along without all these tricks and jokes of adjustment and assimilation have paid a much higher price than they could afford: they jeopardized the few chances even outlaws are given in a topsy-turvy world.

The attitude of these few whom, following Bernard Lazare, one may call "conscious pariahs," can as little be explained by recent events alone as the attitude of our Mr. Cohn who tried by every means to become an upstart. Both are sons of the nineteenth century which, not knowing legal or political outlaws, knew only too well social pariahs and their counterpart, social parvenus. Modern Jewish history, having started with court Jews and continuing with Jewish millionaires and philanthropists, is apt to forget about this other trend of Jewish tradition—the tradition of Heine, Rahel Varnhagen, Sholom

Aleichem, of Bernard Lazare, Franz Kafka or even Charlie Chaplin. It is the tradition of a minority of Jews who have not wanted to become upstarts, who preferred the status of "conscious pariah." All vaunted Jewish qualities—the "Jewish heart," humanity, humor, disinterested intelligence—are pariah qualities. All Jewish shortcomings—tactlessness, political stupidity, inferiority complexes and money-grubbing—are characteristic of upstarts. There have always been Jews who did not think it worth while to change their humane attitude and their natural insight into reality for the narrowness of caste spirit or the essential unreality of financial transactions.

History has forced the status of outlaws upon both, upon pariahs and parvenus alike. The latter have not yet accepted the great wisdom of Balzac's *"On ne parvient pas deux fois"*; thus they don't understand the wild dreams of the former and feel humiliated in sharing their fate. Those few refugees who insist upon telling the truth, even to the point of "indecency," get in exchange for their unpopularity one priceless advantage: history is no longer a closed book to them and politics is no longer the privilege of Gentiles. They know that the outlawing of the Jewish people in Europe has been followed closely by the outlawing of most European nations. Refugees driven from country to country represent the vanguard of their peoples—if they keep their identity. For the first time Jewish history is not separate but tied up with that of all other nations. The comity of European peoples went to pieces when, and because, it allowed its weakest member to be excluded and persecuted.

The Jew as Pariah:
A Hidden Tradition

(APRIL 1944)

When it comes to claiming its own in the field of European arts and letters, the attitude of the Jewish people may best be described as one of reckless magnanimity. With a grand gesture and without a murmur of protest it has calmly allowed the credit for its great writers and artists to go to other peoples, itself receiving in return (in punctiliously regular payments) the doubtful privilege of being acclaimed father of every notorious swindler and mountebank. True enough, there has been a tendency in recent years to compile long lists of European worthies who might conceivably claim Jewish descent, but such lists are more in the nature of mass-graves for the forgotten than of enduring monuments to the remembered and cherished. Useful as they may be for purposes of propaganda (offensive as well as defensive), they have not succeeded in reclaiming for the Jews any single writer of note unless he happen to have written specifically in Hebrew or Yiddish. Those who really did most for the spiritual dignity of their people, who were great enough to transcend the bounds of nationality and to weave the strands of their Jewish genius into the general texture of European life, have been given short shrift and perfunctory recognition. With the growing tendency to conceive of the Jewish people as a series of separate territorial units and to resolve its history into so many regional chronicles and parochial records, its great figures have been left perforce to the tender mercies of assimilationist propagandists—to be exploited only in order to bolster selfish interests or furnish alleged illustrations of dubious ideologies.

Note: A slightly revised version of this essay appeared in *Reconstructionist*, March 20, 1959 and April 3, 1959.

No one fares worse from this process than those bold spirits who tried to make of the emancipation of the Jews that which it really should have been—an admission of Jews *as Jews* to the ranks of humanity, rather than a permit to ape the gentiles or an opportunity to play the *parvenu*. Realizing only too well that they did not enjoy political freedom nor full admission to the life of nations, but that, instead, they had been separated from their own people and lost contact with the simple natural life of the common man, these men yet achieved liberty and popularity by the sheer force of imagination. As individuals they started an emancipation of their own, of their own hearts and brains. Such a conception was, of course, a gross misconstruction of what emancipation had been intended to be; but it was also a vision, and out of the impassioned intensity with which it was evinced and expressed it provided the fostering soil on which Jewish creative genius could grow and contribute its products to the general spiritual life of the Western world.

That the status of the Jews in Europe has been not only that of an oppressed people but also of what Max Weber has called a "pariah people" is a fact most clearly appreciated by those who have had practical experience of just how ambiguous is the freedom which emancipation has ensured, and how treacherous the promise of equality which assimilation has held out. In their own position as social outcasts such men reflect the political status of their entire people. It is therefore not surprising that out of their personal experience Jewish poets, writers and artists should have been able to evolve the concept of the pariah as a human type—a concept of supreme importance for the evaluation of mankind in our day and one which has exerted upon the gentile world an influence in strange contrast to the spiritual and political ineffectiveness which has been the fate of these men among their own brethren. Indeed, the concept of the pariah has become traditional, even though the tradition be but tacit and latent, and its continuance automatic and unconscious. Nor need we wonder why: for over a hundred years the same basic conditions have obtained and evoked the same basic reaction.

However slender the basis out of which the concept was created and out of which it was progressively developed, it has nevertheless loomed larger in the thinking of assimilated Jews than might be inferred from standard Jewish histories. It has endured, in fact, from Salomon Maimon in the eighteenth century to Franz Kafka in the early twentieth. But out of the variety of forms which it has assumed we shall here select four, in each of which it expresses an alternative portrayal of the Jewish people. Our first type will be Heinrich Heine's *schlemihl* and "lord of dreams" *(Traumweltherrscher);* our second, Bernard Lazare's "conscious pariah"; our third, Charlie Chaplin's grotesque portrayal of the suspect; [1] and our fourth, Franz Kafka's poetic vision of the fate of the man of goodwill. Between these four types there is a significant connection—a link which in fact unites all genuine concepts and sound ideas when once they achieve historical actuality.

1. HEINRICH HEINE: THE SCHLEMIHL AND LORD OF DREAMS

In his poem, *Princess Sabbath,* the first of his *Hebrew Melodies,* Heinrich Heine depicts for us the national background from which he sprang and which inspired his verses. He portrays his people as a fairy prince turned by witchcraft into a dog. A figure of ridicule throughout the week, every Friday night he suddenly regains his mortal shape, and freed from the preoccupations of his canine existence *(von huendischen Gedanken),* goes forth like a prince to welcome the sabbath bride and to greet her with the traditional hymeneal, *Lecha Dodi.* [2]

This poem, we are informed by Heine, was especially composed for the purpose by the people's poet—the poet who, by a stroke of fortune, escapes the gruelling weekly transformation of his people and who continually leads the sabbath-like existence which is to Heine the only positive mark of Jewish life.

Poets are characterized in greater detail in Part IV of the

1. Chaplin has recently declared that he is of Irish and Gypsy descent, but he has been selected for discussion because, even if not himself a Jew, he has epitomized in an artistic form a character born of the Jewish pariah mentality.

2. Lecha Dodi: "Come, my beloved, to meet the bride; Let us greet the sabbath-tide"—a Hebrew song chanted in the synagogue on Friday night.

poem, where Heine speaks of Yehudah Halevi. They are said to be descended from "Herr Schlemihl ben Zurishaddai"—a name taken from Shelumiel ben Zurishaddai mentioned in the biblical Book of Numbers as the leader of the tribe of Simeon. Heine relates his name to the word schlemihl by the humorous supposition that by standing too close to his brother chieftain Zimri he got himself killed accidentally when the latter was beheaded by the priest Phinehas for dallying with a Midianite woman (cf. Numbers, 25:6-15). But if they may claim Shelumiel as their ancestor,

they must also claim Phinehas—the ruthless Phinehas whose

> ". . . spear is with us,
> And above our heads unpausing
> We can hear its fatal whizzing
> And the noblest hearts it pierces."
> (*Trans. Leland*)

History preserves to us no "deeds heroic" of those "noblest hearts." All we know is that—they were *schlemihls*.

Innocence is the hall-mark of the *schlemihl*. But it is of such innocence that a people's poets—its "lords of dreams"—are born. No heroes they and no stalwarts, they are content to seek their protection in the special tutelage of an ancient Greek deity. For did not Apollo, that "inerrable godhead of delight," proclaim himself once for all the lord of *schlemihls* on the day when—as the legend has it—he pursued the beauteous Daphne only to receive for his pains a crown of laurels? To be sure, times have changed since then, and the transformation of the ancient Olympian has been described by Heine himself in his poem *The God Apollo*. This tells of a nun who falls in love with that great divinity and gives herself up to the search for him who can play the lyre so beautifully and charm hearts so wondrously. In the end, however, after wandering far and wide, she discovers that the Apollo of her dreams exists in the world of reality as Rabbi Faibusch (a Yiddish distortion of Phoebus), cantor in a synagogue at Amsterdam, holder of the humblest office among the humblest of peoples. Nor this alone; the father is a *mohel* (ritual circumciser), and the mother peddles sour pickles and assortments of odd trousers; while the son is a good-for-nothing who makes the rounds of the annual fairs playing the clown and singing the Psalms of David to the accompaniment of a bevy of "Muses" consisting of nine buxom wenches from the Amsterdam casino.

Heine's portrayal of the Jewish people and of himself as their poet-king is, of course, poles apart from the conception entertained by the privileged wealthy Jews of the upper classes. Instead, in its gay, insouciant impudence it is characteristic of the common people. For the pariah, excluded from formal society and with no desire to be embraced within it, turns naturally to that which entertains and delights the common people. Sharing their social ostracism, he also shares their joys and sorrows, their pleasures and their tribulations. He turns, in fact, from the world of men and the fashion thereof to the open and unrestricted bounty of the earth. And this is precisely what Heine did. Stupid and undiscerning critics have called it materialism or atheism, but the truth is that there is only so much of the heathen in it that it seems irreconcilable with certain interpretations of the Christian doctrine of original sin and its consequent sense of perpetual guilt. It is, indeed, no more than that simple *joie de vivre* which one finds everywhere in children and in the common people—that passion which makes them revel in tales and romances, which finds its supreme literary expression in the ballad and which gives to the short love-song its essentially popular character. Stemming as it does from the basic affinity of the pariah to the people, it is something which neither literary criticism nor antisemitism could ever abolish. Though they dub its author "unknown," the Nazis cannot eliminate the *Lorelei* from the repertoire of German song.

It is but natural that the pariah, who receives so little from the world of men that even fame (which the world has been known to bestow on even the most abandoned of her children) is accounted to him a mere sign of *schlemihldom*, should look with an air of innocent amusement, and smile to himself at the spectacle of human beings trying to compete with the divine realities of nature. The bare fact that the sun shines on all alike affords him daily proof that all men are essentially equal. In the presence of such universal things as the sun, music, trees, and children—things which Rahel Varnhagen called "the true realities" just because they are cherished most by those who have no place in the political and social world—the petty dispensations of men which create and maintain inequality must needs appear ridiculous. Confronted with the natural order of things, in which all is equally good, the fabricated order of society, with its manifold classes and ranks, must needs appear a comic, hopeless attempt of creation to throw down the gauntlet to its creator. It is no longer the outcast pariah who appears the *schlemihl*, but those who live in the ordered ranks of society and who have exchanged the generous gifts of nature for the idols of social privilege and prejudice. Especially is this true of the *parvenu* who was not even born to the system, but chose it of his own free will, and who is called upon to pay the cost meticulously and exactly, whereas others can take things in their stride. But no less are they *schlemihls* who enjoy power and high station. It needs but a poet to compare their vaunted grandeur with the real majesty of the sun, shining on king and beggarman alike, in order to demonstrate that all their pomp and circumstance is but sounding brass and a tinkling cymbal. All of these truths are old as the hills. We know them from the songs of oppressed and despised peoples who—so long as man does not aspire to halt the course of the sun—will always seek refuge in nature, hoping that beside nature all the devices of men will reveal themselves as ephemeral trifles.

It is from this shifting of the accent, from this vehement protest on the part of the pariah, from this attitude of denying the reality of the social order and of confronting it, instead, with a higher reality, that Heine's spirit of mockery really stems. It is this too which makes his scorn so pointed. Because he gauges things so consistently by the criterion of what is really and manifestly natural, he is able at once to detect the weak spot in his opponent's armour, the vulnerable point in any particular stupidity which he happens to be exposing. And it is this aloofness of the pariah from all the works of man that Heine regards as the essence of freedom. It is this aloofness that accounts for the divine laughter and the absence of bitterness in his verses. He was the first Jew to whom freedom meant more than mere "liberation from the house of bondage" and in whom it was combined, in equal measure, with the traditional Jewish passion for justice. To Heine, freedom had little to do with liberation from a just or unjust yoke. A man is born free, and he can lose his freedom only by selling himself into bondage. In line with this idea, both in his political poems and in his prose writings Heine vents his anger not only on tyrants but equally on those who put up with them.

The concept of *natural* freedom (conceived, be it noted, by an outcast able to live beyond the struggle between bondage and tyranny) turns both slaves and tyrants into equally unnatural and therefore ludicrous figures of fun. The poet's cheerful insouciance could hardly be expected from the more respectable citizen, caught as he was in the toils of practical affairs and himself partly responsible for the order of things. Even Heine, when confronted with the only social reality from which his pariah existence had not detached him—the rich Jews of his family—loses his serenity and becomes bitter and sarcastic.

To be sure, when measured by the standard of political realities, Heine's attitude of amused indifference seems remote and unreal. When one comes down to earth, one has to admit that laughter does not kill and that neither slaves nor tyrants are extinguished by mere amusement. From this standpoint, however, the pariah is always remote and unreal; whether as *schlemihl* or as "lord of dreams" he stands outside the real world and attacks it from without. Indeed, the Jewish tendency towards utopianism—a propensity most clearly in evidence in the very countries of emancipation—stems, in the last analysis, from just this lack of social roots. The only thing which saved Heine from succumbing to it, and which made him transform the political non-existence and unreality of the pariah into the effective basis of a world of art, was his creativity. Because he sought nothing more than to hold up a mirror to the political world, he was able to avoid becoming a doctrinaire and to keep his passion for freedom unhampered by fetters of dogma. Similarly, because he viewed life through a long-range tele-scope, and not through the prism of an ideology, he was able to see further and clearer than others, and takes his place today among the shrewdest political observers of his time. The basic philosophy of this "prodigal son" who, after "herding the Hegelian swine for many years," at last became even bold enough to embrace a personal god, could always have been epitomized in his own lines:

"Beat on the drum and blow the fife
And kiss the *vivandière*, my boy.
Fear nothing—that's the whole of life,
Its deepest truth, its soundest joy.
Beat reveille, and with a blast
Arouse all men to valiant strife.
Waken the world; and then, at last
March on. . . . That is the whole of life."
                              (*Trans. Untermeyer*).

By fearlessness and divine impudence Heine finally achieved that for which his coreligionists had vainly striven with fear and trembling, now furtively and now ostentatiously, now by preening and vaunting, and now by obsequious sycophancy. Heine is the only German Jew who could truthfully describe himself as both a German and a Jew. He is the only outstanding example of a really happy assimilation in the entire history of that process. By seeing Phoebus Apollo in Rabbi Faibusch, by boldly introducing Yiddish expressions in the German language, he in fact put into practice that true blending of cultures of which others merely talked. One has only to remember how zealously assimilated Jews avoid the mention of a Hebrew word before gentiles, how strenuously they pretend not to understand it if they hear one, to appreciate the full measure of Heine's accomplishment when he wrote, as pure German verse, lines like the following, praising a distinctively Jewish dish:

"Schalet, ray of light immortal
Schalet, daughter of Elysium!
So had Schiller's song resounded,
Had he ever tasted Schalet."
                              (*Trans. Leland*)

In these words, Heine places the fare of Princess Sabbath on the table of the gods, beside nectar and ambrosia.

While the privileged wealthy Jews appealed to the sublimities of the Hebrew prophets in order to prove that they were indeed the descendants of an especially exalted people, or else—like Disraeli—sought to validate their people by endowing it with some extraordinary, mystic power, Heine dispensed with all such rarefied devices and turned to the homespun Judaism of everyday life, to that which really lay in the heart and on the lips of the average Jew; and through the medium of the German language he gave it a place in general European culture. Indeed, it was the very introduciton of these homely Jewish notes that helped to make Heine's works so essentially popular and human.

Heine is perhaps the first German prose writer really to embody the heritage of Lessing. In a manner least expected, he confirmed the queer notion so widely entertained by the early Prussian liberals that once the Jew was emancipated he would become more human, more free and less prejudiced than other men. That this notion involved a gross exaggeration is obvious. In its political implications, too, it was so lacking in elementary understanding as to appeal only to those Jews who imagined— as do so many today—that Jews could exist as "pure human beings" outside the range of peoples and nations. Heine was not deceived by this nonsense of "world-citizenship." He knew that separate peoples are needed to focus the genius of poets and artists; and he had no time for academic pipe-dreams. Just because he refused to give up his allegiance to a people of pariahs and schlemihls, just because he remained consistently attached to them, he takes his place among the most uncompromising of Europe's fighters for freedom—of which, alas, Germany has produced so few. Of all the poets of his time Heine was the one with the most character. And just because German bourgeois society had none of its own, and feared the explosive force of his, it concocted the slanderous legend of his characterlessness. Those who spread this legend, and who hoped thereby to dismiss Heine from serious consideration, included many Jewish journalists. They were averse to adopting the line he had suggested; they did not want to become Germans and Jews in one, because they feared that they would thereby lose their positions in the social order of German Jewry. For Heine's attitude, if only as a poet, was that by achieving emancipation the Jewish people had achieved a genuine freedom. He simply ignored the condition which had characterized emancipation everywhere in Europe—namely, that the Jew might only become a man when he ceased to be a Jew. Because he held this position he was able to do what so few of his contemporaries could—to speak the language of a free man and sing the songs of a natural one.

2. BERNARD LAZARE: THE
CONSCIOUS PARIAH

If it was Heine's achievement to recognize in the figure of the *schlemihl* the essential kinship of the pariah to the poet— both alike excluded from society and never quite at home in this world—and to illustrate by this analogy the position of the Jew in the world of European culture, it was the merit of Bernard Lazare to translate the same basic fact into terms of political significance. Living in the France of the Dreyfus Affair, Lazare could appreciate at first hand the pariah quality of Jewish existence. But he knew where the solution lay: in contrast to his unemancipated brethren who accept their pariah status automatically and unconsciously, the emancipated Jew must awake to an awareness of his position and, conscious of it, become a rebel against it—the champion of an oppressed people. His fight for freedom is part and parcel of that which all the down-trodden of Europe must needs wage to achieve national and social liberation.

In this heroic effort to bring the Jewish question openly into the arena of politics Lazare was to discover certain specific, Jewish factors which Heine had overlooked and could afford to ignore. If Heine could content himself with the bare observation that "Israel is ill-served, with false friends guarding her doors from without and Folly and Dread keeping watch within," Lazare took pains to investigate the political implications of this connection between Jewish folly and gentile duplicity. As the root of the mischief he recognized that "spurious doctrine" (*doctrine bâtarde*) of assimilation, which would have the Jews "abandon all their characteristics, individual and moral alike, and give up distinguishing themselves only by an outward mark of the flesh which served but to expose them to the hatred of other faiths." He saw that what was necessary was to rouse the Jewish pariah to a fight against the Jewish *parvenu*. There was no other way to save him from the latter's own fate—inevitable destruction. Not only, he contended, has the pariah nothing but suffering to expect from the domination of the *parvenu*, but it is he who is destined sooner or later to pay the price of the whole wretched system. "I want no longer," he says in a telling passage, "to have against me not only the wealthy of my people, who exploit me and sell me, but also the rich and poor of other peoples who oppress and torture me in the name of my rich." And in these words he puts his finger squarely on that phenomenon of Jewish life which the historian Jost had so aptly characterized as "double slavery"—dependence, on the one hand, upon the hostile elements of his environment and, on the other, on his own "highly-placed brethren" who are somehow in league with them. Lazare was the first Jew to perceive the connection between these two elements, both equally disastrous to the pariah. His experience of French politics had taught him that whenever the enemy seeks control, he makes a point of using some oppressed element of the population as his lackeys and henchmen, rewarding them with special privileges, as a kind of sop. It was thus that he construed the mechanism which made the rich Jews seek protection behind the notorious general Jewish poverty, to which they referred whenever their own position was jeopardized. This, he divined, was the real basis of their precarious relationship with their poorer brethren—on whom they would be able, at any time it suited them, to turn their backs.

As soon as the pariah enters the arena of politics, and translates his status into political terms, he becomes perforce a rebel. Lazare's idea was, therefore, that the Jew should come out openly as the representative of the pariah, "since it is the duty of every human being to resist oppression." He demanded, that is, that the pariah relinquish once for all the prerogative of the *schlemihl*, cut loose from the world of fancy and illusion, renounce the comfortable protection of nature, and come to grips with the world of men and women. In other words, he wanted him to feel that he was himself responsible for what society had done to him. He wanted him to stop seeking release in an attitude of superior indifference or in lofty and rarefied cogitation about the nature of man *per se*. However much the Jewish pariah might be, from the historical viewpoint, the product of an unjust dispensation ("look what you have made of the people, ye Christians and ye princes of the Jews"), politically speaking, every pariah who refused to be a rebel was partly responsible for his own position and therewith for the blot on mankind which it represented. From such shame there was no escape, either in art or in nature. For insofar as a man is more than a mere creature of nature, more than a mere product of Divine creativity, insofar will he be called to account for the things which men do to men in the world which they themselves condition.

Superficially, it might appear as though Lazare failed because of the organized opposition of the rich, privileged Jews, the nabobs and philanthropists whose leadership he had ventured to challenge and whose lust for power he had dared to denounce. Were this the case, it would be but the beginning of a tradition which might have outlived his own premature death and determined, if not the fate, at least the effective volition of the Jewish people. But it was not the case; and Lazare himself knew—to his own sorrow—the real cause of his failure. The decisive factor was not the *parvenu;* neither was it the existence of a ruling caste which—whatever complexion it might choose to assume—was still very much the same as that of any other people. Immeasurably more serious and decisive was the fact that the pariah simply refused to become a rebel. True to type, he preferred to "play the revolutionary in the society of others, but not in his own," or else to assume the role of *schnorrer* feeding on the crumbs from the rich man's table, like an ancient Roman commoner ready to be fobbed off with the merest trifle that the patrician might toss at him. In either case, he mortgaged himself to the *parvenu,* protecting the latter's position in society and in turn protected by him.

However bitterly they may have attacked him, it was not the hostility of the Jewish nabobs that ruined Lazare. It was the fact that when he tried to stop the pariah from being a *schlemihl,* when he sought to give him a political significance, he encountered only the *schnorrer.* And once the pariah becomes a *schnorrer,* he is nothing worth, not because he is poor and begs, but because he begs from those whom he ought to fight, and because he appraises his poverty by the standards of those who have caused it. Once he adopts the role of *schnorrer,* the pariah becomes automatically one of the props which hold up a social order from which he is himself excluded. For just as *he* cannot live without his benefactors, so *they* cannot live without him. Indeed, it is just by this system of organized charity and alms-giving that the *parvenus* of the Jewish people have contrived to secure control over it, to determine its destinies and set its standards. The *parvenu* who fears lest he become a pariah, and the pariah who aspires to become a *parvenu*, are brothers under the skin and appropriately aware of their kinship. Small wonder, in face of this fact, that of all Lazare's efforts—unique as they were—to forge the peculiar situation of his people into a vital and significant political factor, nothing now remains. Even his memory has faded.

3. CHARLIE CHAPLIN: THE SUSPECT

While lack of political sense and persistence in the obsolete system of making charity the basis of national unity have prevented the Jewish people from taking a positive part in the political life of our day, these very qualities, translated into dramatic forms, have inspired one of the most singular products of modern art—the films of Charlie Chaplin. In Chaplin the most unpopular people in the world inspired what was long the most popular of contemporary figures—not because he was a modern Merry Andrew, but because he represented the revival of a quality long thought to have been killed by a century of class conflict, namely, the entrancing charm of the little people.

In his very first film, Chaplin portrayed he chronic plight of the little man who is incessantly harried and hectored by the guardians of law and order—the representatives of society. To be sure, he too is a *schlemihl*, but not of the old visionary type, not a secret fairy prince, a protégé of Phoebus Apollo. Chaplin's world is of the earth earthy, grotesquely caricatured if you will, but nevertheless hard and real. It is a world from which neither nature nor art can provide escape and against whose slings and arrows the only armor is one's own wits or the kindness and humanity of casual acquaintances.

In the eyes of society, the type which Chaplin portrays is always fundamentally suspect. He may be at odds with the world in a thousand and one ways, and his conflicts with it may assume a manifold variety of forms, but always and everywhere he is under suspicion, so that it is no good arguing rights or wrongs. Long before the refugee was to become, in the guise of the "stateless," the living symbol of the pariah, long before men and women were to be forced in their thousands to depend for their bare existence on their own wits or the chance kindnesses of others, Chaplin's own childhood had taught him two things. On the one hand, it had taught him the traditional

Jewish fear of the "cop"—that seeming incarnation of a hostile world; but on the other, it had taught him the time-honored Jewish truth that, other things being equal, the human ingenuity of a David can sometimes outmatch the animal strength of a Goliath.

Standing outside the pale, suspected by all the world, the pariah—as Chaplin portrays him—could not fail to arouse the sympathy of the common people, who recognized in him the image of what society had done to them. Small wonder, then, that Chaplin became the idol of the masses. If they laughed at the way he was forever falling in love at first sight, they realized at the same time that the kind of love he evinced was their kind of love—however rare it may be.

Chaplin's suspect is linked to Heine's *schlemihl* by the common element of innocence. What might have appeared incredible and untenable if presented as a matter of casuistic discussion, as the theme of high-flown talk about the persecution of the guiltless etc., becomes, in Chaplin's treatment, both warm and convincing. Chaplin's heroes are not paragons of virtue, but little men with a thousand and one little failings, forever clashing with the law. The only point that is made is that the punishment does not always fit the crime, and that for the man who is in any case suspect there is no relation between the offense he commits and the price he pays. He is always being "nabbed" for things he never did, yet somehow he can always slip through the toils of the law, where other men would be caught in them. The innocence of the suspect which Chaplin so consistently portrays in his films is, however, no more a mere trait of character, as in Heine's *schlemihl*; rather is it an expression of the dangerous incompatibility of general laws with individual misdeeds. Although in itself tragic, this incompatibility reveals its comic aspects in the case of the suspect, where it becomes patent. There is obviously no connection at all between what Chaplin does or does not do and the punishment which overtakes him. Because he is suspect, he is called upon to bear the brunt of much that he has not done. Yet at the same time, because he is beyond the pale, unhampered by the trammels of society, he is able to get away with a great deal. Out of this ambivalent situation springs an attitude both of fear and of impudence, fear of the law as if it were an inexorable natural force, and familiar, ironic impudence in the face of its minions. One can cheerfully cock a snoot at them, because one has learned to duck them, as men duck a shower by creeping into holes or under a shelter. And the smaller one is the easier it becomes. Basically, the impudence of Chaplin's suspect is of the same kind as charms us so much in Heine's *schlemihl;* but no longer is it carefree and unperturbed, no longer the divine effrontery of the poet who consorts with heavenly things and can therefore afford to thumb noses at earthly society. On the contrary, it is a worried, careworn impudence—the kind so familiar to generations of Jews, the effrontery of the poor "little Yid" who does not recognize the class order of the world because he sees in it neither order nor justice for himself.

It was in this "little Yid," poor in worldly goods but rich in human experience, that the little man of all peoples most clearly discerned his own image. After all, had he not too to grapple with the problem of circumventing a law which, in its sublime indifference, forbade "rich and poor to sleep under bridges or steal bread?" For a long time he could laugh good-humoredly at himself in the role of a *schlemihl*—laugh at his misfortunes and his comic, sly methods of escape. But then came unemployment, and the thing was not funny any more. He knew he had been caught by a fate which no amount of cunning and smartness could evade. Then came the change. Chaplin's popularity began rapidly to wane, not because of any mounting antisemitism, but because his underlying humanity had lost its meaning. Men had stopped seeking release in laughter; the little man had decided to be a big one.

Today it is not Chaplin, but Superman. When, in *The Dictator,* the comedian tried, by the ingenious device of doubling his role, to point up the contrast between the "little man" and the "big shot," and to show the almost brutal character of the Superman ideal, he was barely understood. And when, at the end of that film, he stepped out of character, and sought, in his own name, to reaffirm and vindicate the simple wisdom and philosophy of the "little man," his moving and impassioned plea fell, for the most part, upon unresponsive audiences. This was not the idol of the thirties.

4. *FRANZ KAFKA: THE MAN OF GOODWILL*

Both Heine's *schlemihl* and Lazare's "conscious pariah" were conceived essentially as Jews, while even Chaplin's suspect betrays what are clearly Jewish traits. Quite different, however, is the case of the last and most recent typification of the pariah—that represented in the work of Franz Kafka. He appears on two occasions, once in the poet's earliest story, *Description of a Fight*, and again in one of his latest novels, entitled *The Castle*.

Description of a Fight is concerned, in a general way, with the problem of social interrelations, and advances the thesis that within the confines of society the effects of genuine or even friendly relations are invariably adverse. Society, we are told, is composed of "nobodies"—"I did wrong to nobody, nobody did wrong to me; but nobody will help me, nothing but nobodies"—and has therefore no real existence. Nevertheless, even the pariah, who is excluded from it, cannot account himself lucky, since society keeps up the pretense that it is somebody and he nobody, that it is "real" and he "unreal." [3] His conflict with it has therefore nothing to do with the question whether society treats him properly or not; the point at issue is simply whether it or he has real existence. And the greatest injury which society can and does inflict on him is to make him doubt the reality and validity of his own existence, to reduce him in his own eyes to a status of nonentity.

The reality of his existence thus assailed, the pariah of the nineteenth century had found escape in two ways, but neither could any longer commend itself to Kafka. The first way led to a society of pariahs, of people in the same situation and—so far as their opposition to society was concerned—of the same outlook. But to take this way was to end in utter detachment from reality—in a bohemian divorce from the actual world. The second way, chosen by many of the better Jews whom society had ostracized, led to an overwhelming preoccupation with the world of beauty, be it the world of nature in which all men were equal beneath an eternal sun, or the realm of art where everyone was welcome who could appreciate eternal genius.

3. Yet of all who have dealt with this age-long conflict Kafka is the first to have started from the basic truth that "society is a nobody in a dress-suit." In a certain sense, he was fortunate to have been born in an epoch when it was already patent and manifest that the wearer of the dress-suit was indeed a nobody. Fifteen years later, when Marcel Proust wanted to characterize French society, he was obliged to use a far grimmer metaphor. He depicted it as a masquerade with a death's head grinning behind every mask.

Nature and art had, in fact, long been regarded as departments of life which were proof against social or political assault; and the pariah therefore retreated to them as to world where he might dwell unmolested. Old cities, reared in beauty and hallowed by tradition, began to attract him with their imposing buildings and spacious plazas. Projected, as it were, from the past into the present, aloof from contemporary rages and passions, they seemed in their timelessness to extend a universal welcome. The gates of the old palaces, built by kings for their own courts, seemed now to be flung open to all, and even unbelievers might pace the great cathedrals of Christ. In such a setting the despised pariah Jew, dismissed by contemporary society as a nobody, could at least share in the glories of the past, for which he often showed a more appreciative eye than the esteemed and full-fledged members of society.

But it is just this method of escape, this retreat into nature and art, against which Kafka directs his shafts in *Description of a Fight*. To his twentieth-century sense of reality, Nature had lost its invulnerable superiority over man since man would not "leave it in peace." He denied, too, the living actuality of monuments which were merely inherited from the dead and abandoned to everybody—that same everybody whom contemporary society would call a "nobody." In his view, the beauties of art and nature when used as an escape mechanism by those to whom its right had been refused were merely products of society. It does no good, he says, to keep thinking of them; in time they die and lose their strength. For Kafka only those things are real whose strength is not impaired but confirmed by thinking. Neither the freedom of the *schlemihl* and poet nor the innocence of the suspect nor the escape into nature and art, but thinking is the new weapon—the only one with which, in Kafka's opinion, the pariah is endowed at birth in his vital struggle against society.

It is, indeed, the use of this contemplative faculty as an instrument of self-preservation that characterizes Kafka's conception of the pariah. Kafka's heroes face society with an attitude of outspoken aggression, poles apart from the ironic condescension and superiority of Heine's "lord of dreams" or the innocent cunning of Chaplin's perpetually harassed little man. The traditional traits of the Jewish pariah, the touching innocence and the enlivening *schlemihldom*, have alike no place in the picture. *The Castle*, the one novel in which Kafka discusses the Jewish problem, is the only one in which the hero is plainly a Jew; yet even there what characterizes him as such is not any typically Jewish trait, but the fact that he in involved in situations and perplexities distinctive of Jewish life.

K. (as the hero is called) is a stranger who can never be brought into line because he belongs neither to the common people nor to its rulers. ("You are not of the Castle and you are not of the village, you are nothing at all.") To be sure, it has something to do with the rulers that he ever came to the village in the first place, but he has no legal title to remain there. In the eyes of the minor bureaucratic officials his very existence was due merely to a bureaucratic "error," while his status as a citizen was a paper one, buried "in piles of document for ever rising and crashing" around him. He is charged continually with being superfluous "unwanted and in everyone's way," with having, as a stranger, to depend on other people's bounty and with being tolerated only by reason of a mysterious act of grace.

K. himself is of the opinion that everything depends on his becoming "indistinguishable," and "that as soon as possible." He admits that the rulers will assuredly obstruct the process. What he seeks, namely, complete assimilation, is something which they are not prepared to recognize—even as an aspiration. In a letter from the castle he is told distinctly that he will have to make up his mind "whether he prefers to become a village worker with a distinctive but merely apparent connection with the Castle or an ostensible village worker whose real occupation is determined through the medium of Barnabas (the court messenger)."

No better analogy could have been found to illustrate the entire dilemma of the modern would-be assimilationist Jew. He, too, is faced with the same alternative, whether to belong ostensibly to the people, but really to the rulers—as their creature and tool—or utterly and forever to renounce their protection and seek his fortune with the masses. "Official" Jewry has preferred always to cling to the rulers, and its representatives are always only "ostensible villagers." But it is with the other sort of Jew that Kafka is concerned and whose fate he portrays. This is the Jew who chooses the alternative way—the way of goodwill, who construes the conventional parlance of assimilation literally. What Kafka depicts is the real drama of assimilation, not its distorted counterpart. He speaks for the average small-time Jew who really wants no more than his rights as a human being: home, work, family and citizenship. He is portrayed as if he were alone on earth, the only Jew in the whole wide world—completely, desolately alone. Here, too, Kafka paints a picture true to reality and to the basic human problem which assimilation involves, if taken seriously. For insofar as the Jew seeks to become "indistinguishable" from his gentile neighbors he has to behave as if he were indeed utterly alone; he has to part company, once and for all, with all who are like him. The hero of Kafka's novel does, in fact, what the whole world wants the Jew to do. His lonely isolation merely reflects the constantly reiterated opinion that if only there were nothing but individual Jews, if only the Jews would not persist in banding together, assimilation would become a farily simple process. Kafka makes his hero follow this "ideal" course in order to show clearly how the experiment in fact works out. To make a thorough success of it, it is, of course, necessary also that a man should renounce all distinctive Jewish traits. In Kafka's treatment, however, this renunciation assumes a significance for the whole problem of mankind, and not merely for the Jewish question. K., in his effort to become "indistinguishable," is interested only in universals, in things which are common to all mankind. His desires are directed only towards those things to which all men have a natural right. He is, in a word, the typical man of goodwill. He demands no more than that which constitutes every man's right, and he will be satisfied with no less. His entire ambition is to have "a home, a position, real work to do," to marry and "to become a member of the community." Because, as a stranger, he is not permitted to enjoy these obvious prerequisites of human existence, he cannot afford to be ambitious. He alone, he thinks (at least at the beginning of the story), must fight for the minimum—for simple human rights, as if it were something which embraced th sum total of all possible demands. And just because he seeks nothing more than his minimum human rights, he cannot consent to obtain his demands—as might otherwise have been possible—in the form of "an act of favor from the Castle." He must perforce stand on his rights."

As soon as the villagers discover that the stranger who has chanced to come into their midst really enjoys the protection of the castle, their original mood of contemptuous indifference turns to one of respectful hostility. From then on their one desire is to cast him back upon the castle as soon as possible; they want no truck with the "upper crust." And when K. refuses, on the grounds that he wants to be free, when he explains that he would rather be a simple but genuine villager than an ostensible one really living under the protection of the castle, their attitude changes in turn to one of suspicion mingled with anxiety—an attitude which, for all his efforts, haunts him continually. The villagers feel uneasy not because he is a stranger, but because he refuses to accept favors. They try constantly to persuade him that his attitude is "dumb," that he lacks acquaintance with conditions as they are. They tell him all kinds of tales concerning the relations of the castle to the villagers, and seek thereby to impart to him something of that knowledge of the world which he so obviously lacks. But all they succeed in doing is to show him, to his increasing alarm, that such things as human instinct, human rights and plain normal life—things which he himself had taken for granted as the indisputed property of all normal human beings—had as little existence for the villagers as for the stranger.

What K. experienced in his efforts to become indistinguishable from the villagers is told in a series of grim and ghastly tales, all of them redolent of human perversity and the slow attrition of human instincts. There is the tale of the inkeeper's wife who had had the "honor" as a girl, to be the short-lived mistress of some underling at the castle, and who so far never forgot it as to turn her marriage into the merest sham. Then there is K.'s own young fiancée who had had the same experience but who, though she was able to forget it long enough to fall genuinely in love with him, could still not endure indefinitely a simple life without "high connections" and who absconded in the end with the aid of the "assistants"—two minor officials of the castle. Last but not least, there is the weird, uncanny story of the Barnabases living under a curse, treated as lepers till they feel themselves such, merely because one of their pretty daughters once dared to reject the indecent advances of an important courtier. The plain villagers, controlled to the last detail by the ruling class, and slaves even in their thoughts to the whims of their all-powerful officials, had long since come to realize that to be in the right or to be in the wrong was for them a matter of pure "fate" which they could not alter. It is not, as K. naively assumes, the sender of an obscene letter that is exposed, but the recipient who becomes branded and tainted. This is what the villagers mean when they speak of their "fate." In K.'s view, "it's unjust and monstrous, but you're the only one in the village of that opinion."

It is the story of the Barnabases that finally makes K. see conditions as they really are. At long last he comes to understand that the realization of his designs, the achievement of basic human rights—the right to work, the right to be useful, the right to found a home and become a member of society— are in no way dependent on complete assimilation to one's *milieu*, on being "indistinguishable." The normal existence which he desires has become something exceptional, no longer to be realized by simple, natural methods. Everything natural and normal in life has been wrested out of men's hands by the prevalent regime of the village, to become a present endowed from without—or, as Kafka puts it, from "above." Whether as fate, as blessing or as curse, it is something dark and mysterious, something which a man receives but does not create, and which he can therefore observe but never fathom. Accordingly K.'s aspiration, far from being commonplace and obvious, is, in fact, exceptional and magnificent. So long as the village remains under the control of the castle, its inhabitants can be nothing but the passive victims of their repective "fates"; there is no place in it for any man of goodwill who wishes to determine his own existence. The simplest inquiry into right and wrong is regarded as querulous disputations; the character of the regime, the power of the castle, are things which may not be questioned. So, when K., thoroughly indignant and outraged, bursts out with the words, "So that's what the officials are like," the whole village trembles as if some vital secret, if not indeed the whole pattern of its life, had been suddenly betrayed.

Even when he loses the innocence of the pariah, K. does not give up the fight. But unlike the hero of Kafka's last novel, *America,* he does not start dreaming of a new world and he does not end in a great "Nature Theatre" where "everyone is welcome," where "there is a place for everyone" in accordance with his talents, his bent and his will. On the contrary, K.'s idea seems to be that much could be accomplished, if only one simple man could achieve to live his own life like a normal human being. Accordingly, he remains in the village and tries, in spite of everything, to establish himself under existent conditions. Only for a single brief moment does the old Jewish ideal stir his heart, and he dreams of the lofty freedom of the pariah—the "lord of dreams." But "nothing more senseless," he observes, "nothing more hopeless than this freedom, this waiting, this inviolability." All these things have no purpose and take no account of men's desire to achieve something in the here below, if it be only the sensible direciton of their lives. Hence, in the end, he reconciles himself readily to the "tyranny of the teacher," takes on "the wretched post" of a school janitor and "does his utmost to get an interview with Klamm"—in a word, he takes his share in the misery and distress of the villagers.

On the face of it, all is fruitless, since K. can and will not divorce himself from the distinction between right and wrong and since he refuses to regard his normal human rights as privileges bestowed by the "powers that be." Because of this, the stories which he hears from the villagers fail to rouse in him that sense of haunting fear with which they take pains to invest them and which endows them with that strange poetic quality so common in the folk-tales of enslaved peoples. And since he cannot share this feeling he can never really be one of them. How baseless a feeling it is, how groundless the fear which seems by some magic to possess the entire village, is clear from the fact that nothing whatever materializes of all the dreadful fate which the villagers predict for K. himself. Nothing more serious happens to him, in fact, than that the authorities at the castle, using a thousand and one excuses, keep holding up his application for legal title of residence.

The whole struggle remains undecided, and K. dies a perfectly natural death; he gets exhausted. What he strove to achieve was beyond the strength of any one man. But though his purpose remained unaccomplished, his life was far from being a complete failure. The very fight he had put up to obtain the few basic things which society owes to men, had opened the eyes of the villagers, or at least of some of them. His story, his behavior, had taught them both that human rights are worth fighting for and that the rule of the castle is not divine law and, consequently, can be attacked. He had made them see, as they put it, that "men who suffered our kind of experiences, who are beset by our kind of fear ... who tremble at every knock at the door, cannot see things straight." And they added: "How lucky are we that you came to us!"

In an epilogue to the novel Max Brod relates with what enthusiasm Kafka once repeated to him the story of how Flaubert, returning from a visit to a simple, happy family of many children had exclaimed spontaneously: *ils sont dans le vrai* ("Those folk are right"). A true human life cannot be led by people who feel themselves detached from the basic and simple laws of humanity nor by those who elect to live in a vacuum, even if they be led to do so by persecution. Men's lives must be nominal, not exceptional.

It was the perception of this truth that made Kafka a Zionist. In Zionism he saw a means of abolishing the "abnormal" position of the Jews, an instrument whereby they might become "a people like other peoples." Perhaps the last of Europe's great poets, he could scarcely have wished to become a nationalist. Indeed, his whole genius, his whole expression of the modern spirit, lay precisely in the fact that what he sought was to be a human being, a normal member of human society. It was not his fault that this society had ceased to be human, and that, trapped within its meshes, those of its members who were really men of goodwill were forced to function within it as something exceptional and abnormal—saints or madmen. If Western Jewry of the nineteenth century had taken assimilation seriously, had really tried to resolve the anomaly of the Jewish people and the problem of the Jewish individual by becoming "indistinguishable" from their neighbors, if they had made equality with others their ultimate objective, they would only have found in the end that they were faced with inequality and that society was slowly but surely disintegrating into a vast complex of inhuman cross-currents. They would have found, in short, the same kind of situation as Kafka portrayed in dealing with the relations of the stranger to the established patterns of village life.

So long as the Jews of Western Europe were pariahs only in a social sense they could find salvation, to a large extent, by becoming *parvenus*. Insecure as their position may have been, they could nevertheless achieve a *modus vivendi* by combining what Ahad Haam described as "inner slavery" with "outward freedom." Moreover those who deemed the price too high could still remain mere pariahs, calmly enjoying the freedom and untouchability of outcasts. Excluded from the world of political realities, they could still retreat into their quiet corners there to preserve the illusion of liberty and unchallenged humanity. The life of the pariah, though shorn of political significance, was by no means senseless.

But today it is. Today the bottom has dropped out of the old ideology. The pariah Jew and the *parvenu* Jew are in the same boat, rowing desperately in the same angry sea. Both are branded with the same mark; both alike are outlaws. Today the truth has come home: there is no protection in heaven or earth against bare murder, and a man can be driven at any moment from the streets and broad places once open to all. At long last, it has become clear that the "senseless freedom" of the individual merely paves the way for the senseless suffering of his entire people.

Social isolation is no longer possible. You cannot stand aloof from society, whether as a *schlemihl* or as a lord of dreams. The old escape-mechanisms have broken down, and a man can no longer come to terms with a world in which the Jew cannot be a human being either as a *parvenu* using his elbows or as a *pariah* voluntarily spurning its gifts. Both the realism of the one and the idealism of the other are today utopian.

There is, however, a third course—the one that Kafka suggests, in which a man may forgo all claims to individual freedom and inviolability and modestly content himself with trying to lead a simple, decent life. But—as Kafka himself points out—this is impossible within the framework of contemporary society. For while the individual might still be allowed to make a career, he is no longer strong enough to fulfill the basic demands of human life. The man of goodwill is driven today into isolation like the Jew-stranger in the castle. He gets lost—or dies from exhaustion. For only within the framework of a people can a man live as a man among men, without exhausting himself. And only when a people lives and functions in consort with other peoples can it contribute to the establishment upon earth of a commonly conditioned and commonly controlled humanity.

Creating a Cultural Atmosphere

(NOVEMBER 1947)

Culture, as we understand it today, made its appearance rather recently and grew out of the secularization of religion and the dissolution of traditional values. When we talk about the Christian culture of the Middle Ages, we are using the term loosely and in a sense that would have been almost incomprehensible to medieval man. The process of secularization may or may not have undermined the foundations of religious faith—I am inclined to think that this undermining has been less decisive than we sometimes assume; in any event secularization transformed religious concepts and the results of religious speculation in such a way that they received new meaning and new relevance independent of faith. This tranformation marked the beginning of culture as we know it—that is, from then on religion became an important part of culture, but it no longer dominated all spiritual achievements.

Even more important for the establishment of culture than the mere dissolution of traditional values, was that great fear of oblivion which followed close upon the 18th century's Enlightenment and which pervaded the whole 19th century. The danger of losing historical continuity as such, along with the treasures of the past, was obvious; the fear of being robbed of the specifically human background of a past, of becoming an abstract ghost like the man without a shadow, was the driving power behind that new passion for impartiality and for the collecting of historical curiosities that gave birth to our present historical and philological sciences as well as to the 19th century's monstrosities of taste. Just because the old traditions were no longer alive, culture was stimulated into being, with all its good and all its ridiculous aspects. The stylelessness of the last century in architecture, its insane attempts to imitate all styles of the past, was only one aspect of what was really a new phenomenon called culture.

Culture is by definition secular. It requires a kind of broad-mindedness of which no religion will ever be capable. It can be thoroughly perverted through ideologies and *Weltanschauungen* which share, though on a lower and more vulgar level, religion's contempt for tolerance and claim to "possess" the truth. Although culture is "hospitable," we should not forget that neither religion nor ideologies will, nor ever can, resign themselves to being only parts of a whole. The historian, though hardly ever the theologian, knows that secularization is not the ending of religion.

It so happened that the Jewish people not only did not share in the slow process of secularization that started in Western Europe with the Renaissance, and out of which modern culture was born, but that the Jews, when confronted with and attracted by Enlightenment and culture, had just emerged from a period in which their own secular learning had sunk to an all-time low. The consequences of this lack of spiritual links between Jews and non-Jewish civilization were as natural as they were unfortunate: Jews who wanted "culture" left Judaism at once, and completely, even though most of them remained conscious of their Jewish origin. Secularization and even secular learning became identified exclusively with non-Jewish culture, so that it never occurred to these Jews that they could have started a process of secularization with regard to their own heritage. Their abandonment of Judaism resulted in a situation within Judaism in which the Jewish spiritual heritage became more than ever before the monopoly of rabbis. The German *Wissenschaft des Judentums,* though it was aware of the danger of a complete loss of all the past's spiritual achievements, took refuge from the real problem in a rather dry scholarship concerned only with preservation, the results of which were at best a collection of museum objects.

While this sudden and radical escape by Jewish intellectuals from everything Jewish prevented the growth of a cultural atmosphere in the Jewish community, it was very favorable for the development of individual creativity. What had been done by the members of other nations as part and parcel of a more collective effort and in the span of several generations, was achieved by individual Jews within the narrow and concentrated framework of a single human lifetime and by the sheer force of personal imagination. It was as individuals, strictly, that the Jews started their emancipation from tradition.

It is true that a unique and impassioned intensity possessed only the few and was paid for by the fact that a particularly high percentage of Jews occupied themselves as pseudo-cultural busybodies and succumbed to mass culture and the mere love of fame. But it still brought forth a remarkably great number of authentic Jewish writers, artists, and thinkers who did not break under the extraordinary effort required of them, and whom this sudden empty freedom of spirit did not debase but on the contrary made creative.

Since, however, their individual achievements did not find reception by a prepared and cultured Jewish audience, they could not found a specifically Jewish tradition in secular writing and thinking—though these Jewish writers, thinkers, and artists had more than one trait in common. Whatever tradition the historian may be able to detect remained tacit and latent, its continuance automatic and unconscious, springing as it did from the basically identical conditions that each of these individuals had to confront all over again for himself, and master by himself without help from his predecessors.

There is no doubt that no blueprint and no program will ever make sense in cultural matters. If there is such a thing as a cultural policy it can aim only at the creation of a cultural atmosphere—that is, in Elliot Cohen's words, a "culture for Jews," but not a Jewish culture. The emergence of talent or genius is independent of such an atmosphere, but whether we shall continue to lose Jewish talent to others, or whether we will become able to keep it within our own community to the same extent that the others do, will be decided by the existence or non-existence of this atmosphere. It is this that seems to me to be the problem. One may give a few suggestions on how to approach it.

There is first of all that great religious and metaphysical post-Biblical tradition which we will have to win back from the theologians and scholars—to both of whom we owe, however, a large debt of gratitude for having preserved it at all. But we shall have to discover and deal with this tradition anew in our own terms, for the sake of people to whom it no longer constitutes a holy past or an untouchable heritage.

There is on the other hand the much smaller body of Jewish secular writings—dating from all periods, but particularly from the 19th century in Eastern Europe; this writing grew out of secular folk life and only the absence of a cultural atmosphere has prevented a portion of it from assuming the status of great literature; instead it was condemned to the doubtful category of folklore. The cultural value of every author or artist really begins to make itself felt when he transcends the boundaries of his own nationality, when he no longer remains significant only to his fellow-Jews, fellow-Frenchmen or fellow-Englishmen. The lack of Jewish culture and the prevalence of folklore in secular Jewish life has denied this transcendence to all Jewish talent that did not simply desert the Jewish community. The rescue of the Yiddish writers of Eastern Europe is of great importance; otherwise they will remain lost to culture generally.

Last but not least, we shall have to make room for all those who either came, and come, into conflict with Jewish orthodoxy or turned their backs on Judaism for the reasons mentioned above. These figures will be of special significance for the whole endeavor; they may even become the supreme test of its success or failure. Not only because creative talent has been especially frequent among them in recent times, but also because they, in their individual efforts towards secularization, offer the first models for that new amalgamation of older traditions with new impulses and awareness without which a specifically Jewish cultural atmosphere is hardly conceivable. These talents do not need us, they achieve culture on their own responsibility. We, on the other hand, do need them since they form the only basis, however small, of culture that we have got; a basis we shall have to extend gradually in both directions: the secularization of religious tradition and rescue from folklore of the great artists (mostly Yiddish) of secular folk life.

Whether such a development will be realized nobody can possibly foretell. *Commentary* looks to me like a good beginning and it certainly is a novum in Jewish cultural life. The reason for some optimism, however, is in the last analysis a political one.

The Yishuv in Palestine is the first Jewish achievement brought about by an entirely secular movement. There is no doubt that whatever may happen to Hebrew literature in the future, Hebrew writers and artists will not need to confine themselves to either folk life or religion in order to remain Jews. They are the first Jews who as Jews are free to start from more than a pre-cultural level.

The Jewish people of America, on the other hand, live a reasonably safe and reasonably free life that permits them to do, relatively, what they please. The central and strongest part of diaspora Jewry no longer exists under the conditions of a nation-state but in a country that would annul its own constitution if ever it demanded homogeneity of population and an ethnic foundation for its state. In America one does not have to pretend that Judaism is nothing but a denomination and resort to all those desperate and crippling disguises that were common among the rich and educated Jews of Europe.

The development of a Jewish culture, in other words, or the lack of it, will from now on not depend upon circumstances beyond the control of the Jewish people, but upon their own will.

Jewish History, Revised

(MARCH 1948)

Jewish historians of the last century, consciously or not, used to ignore all those trends of the Jewish past which did not point to their own major thesis of Diaspora history, according to which the Jewish people did not have a political history of their own but were invariably the innocent victims of a hostile and sometimes brutal environment. Once this environment changed, Jewish history logically would cease to be history at all, as the Jewish people would cease to exist as a people. In sharp contrast to all other nations, the Jews were not history-makers but history-sufferers, preserving a kind of eternal identity of goodness whose monotony was disturbed only by the equally monotonous chronicle of persecutions and pogroms. Within this framework of prejudice and persecution, the historian could still somehow manage to record the main developments of the history of ideas. But Jewish mystical thought, leading as it did to political action in the Sabbatian movement, was so serious an obstacle to this interpretation that it could be overcome only through rash disparagement or complete disregard.

Scholem's new presentation and appreciation of Jewish mysticism [1] not only fills a gap, but actually changes the whole picture of Jewish history. One of the most important changes is his entirely new interpretation of the Reform movement and other modern developments that broke away from orthodoxy. These used to be viewed as the consequences of the emancipation granted to sections of the Jewish people and as the

1. Gershom G. Scholem, *Major Trends in Jewish Mysticism*, (New York: Schocken Books, 1946). Revised edition.

necessary reactions of a new adjustment to the requirements of the Gentile world. But Scholem, in the last chapter of his book, conclusively proves that the Reform movement, with its curiously mixed tendencies toward liquidating Judaism and yet preserving it, was not a mechanical assimilation to the ideas and demands of a foreign environment but the outgrowth of the debacle of the last great Jewish political activity, the Sabbatian movement, of the loss of Messianic hope and of the despair about the ultimate destiny of the people.

A similar collapse of religious standards, followed by a similar despair, was among the outstanding experiences of Europe after the French Revolution. But whereas Romantic pessimism despaired of the political capacities of Man as a law-maker and became resigned to considering him as capable only of obeying laws, whose ultimate legitimation was no longer in God but in history and tradition, Jewish nihilism grew out of the despair of the ability of Man ever to discover the hidden law of God and to act accordingly.

Scholem's book, clarifying for the first time the role played by the Jews in the formation of modern Man, contributes a good deal to more general, typically modern phenomena whose historical origins were never quite understood. In this respect, his discoveries are more likely to reconcile Jewish history with the history of Europe than all apologetic attempts which try to prove the impossible, *i.e.*, the identity between Jews and other nations, or which attempt to demonstrate something essentially inhuman, namely the passivity and thus the irresponsibility of the Jewish people as a whole.

"In (the Kabbalists') interpretation of the religious commandments, these are not represented as allegories of more or less profound ideas, or as pedagogical measures" (as in the interpretation of the philosophers) "but rather as the performance of a secret rite . . . this transformation of Halakhah into a sacrament . . . raised the Halakhah to a position of incomparable importance for the mystic, and strengthened its hold over the people. Every mitzvah became an event of cosmic importance. . . . The religious Jew became a protagonist in the drama of the World; he manipulated the strings behind the scenes."

Kabbalah is a name that covers a great variety of doctrines, from early Gnostic speculations through all kinds of magical

practices up to the great and genuine philosophical speculations of the Book of Zohar. The name expresses the power and
the final victory of Rabbinism, which combats all antagonistic
and heterodox tendencies of Jewish thought by lumping them
under the same name, rather than naming them specifically
and in consonance with the actual content of these thoughts.
But the transformation of Halakhah into magical rite with its
inherent influence upon popular imagination referred to in the
above quotation, seems to form the essential basis for all kinds
of Jewish mystical conceptions. The new interpretation of Law
was based on the new doctrine of the "hidden God" who, in
sharp opposition to the God of the revelation, is impersonal,
"*that* which is infinite" (12), a force instead of a person,
revealing itself only to the "chosen few" but concealed rather
than revealed in the revelation of the Bible. With this concept
of God as an impersonal, divine power is connected that main
heterodox doctrine against which Jewish as well as Christian
orthodoxy have fought their most embittered battles, the
doctrine of the *emanation* of the universe as opposed to the
creation of Man and the world. In all emanation theories, the
primal Man is supposed to be a hidden power, the clear
distinction between God and Man as between creator and
creature disappears, and Man, conceived as a material part of
the divine, becomes endowed with a material-mystical power to
retrace the "hidden path" of emanation that led him away
from the divine, to return into the lap of the substance from
which he emanated and which is expressed by various para-
phrases such as the "*En-Sof*" the "indifferent unity" and, most
characteristically, the *Nothing*. The transformation of Halakhah into a secret rite sprang like all other magical practices,
from these speculations which asserted that the search for the
hidden power may lead to the discovery of secret means by
which Man can regain divine power, and transform himself into
a part of God.

All such doctrines concerned with the "hidden" seem to
have an inherent paradoxical effect. Their adherents always
insisted upon strictest secrecy, exclusiveness, and the esoteric
character of their speculations, which could be revealed only to
the "chosen few." Yet in spite of all these assertions, mystical
ideas did not appeal only to the few but exercised, on the

contrary, an enormous popular influence. Mystical ideas appealed to the masses much more than did the teachings of the learned rabbis and philosophers who maintained that their interpretations could be understood by everybody. This is especially true of the mystical trends in Jewish history, which apparently dominated popular thought and answered the most urgent needs of the common people.

It would be a serious error to think of this paradox as of a problem of the past alone, for this religious past actually survives today in all the superstitious beliefs in "secret societies," in the "hands working behind the scenes" of popular politics, and even in the ideologies that insist on the exclusive power of economic or historical "laws" which, too, work hidden from the eyes of ordinary men. The speculations by which Jewish and Christian mystics transformed the Jewish God of Creation into a secret force were the first form of an essentially materialistic concept, and all modern doctrines asserting that Man is but a part of matter, subject to physical laws and without freedom of action, confront us with the old originally Gnostical belief in emanation. Whether the substance of which Man is held to be a part is material or "divine" has little importance. What matters is that Man is no longer an independent entity, an end in himself.

Today, as in the past, these speculations appeal to all who are actually excluded from action, prevented from altering a fate that appears to them unbearable and, feeling themselves helpless victims of incomprehensible forces, are naturally inclined to find some secret means for gaining power for participating in the "drama of the World." Therefore the secrecy of these speculations has a somewhat artificial character: they are held secret like the discovery of the philosopher's stone, which is supposed to transform all metals into pure gold, which is desired by everybody and, precisely for this reason, is hidden by those who pretend they have discovered it.

More important than this ambiguous esotericism was the mystic's justification of action, even if they offer only a substitute for it. In this connection, it does not greatly matter whether kabbalists were ordinary magicians (usually they were not) or whether they practiced only what Abulafia has admitted and what Scholem calls a "magic of inwardness." In both cases the believers could participate in the power which rules the world.

"The Kabbalists . . . are no friends of mystical autobiography. . . . They glory in objective description and are deeply averse to letting their own personalities intrude into the picture. . . . I am inclined to believe that this dislike of a too personal indulgence in self-expression may have been caused by the fact, among others, that the Jews retained a particularly vivid sense of the incongruity of mystical experience with that idea of God which stressed the aspects of Creator, King and Lawgiver."

The denial of creation and the doctrine of emanation, with the consequent concept of human participation in the drama of the world, was the most striking common feature of Jewish and Gnostic mysticism. The lack of autobiography, the dislike of self-expression, is the most striking contrast of Jewish to Christian mysticism. This restraint is all the more surprising because invariably the main mystical organon of cognition is experience, and never reason, or faith in revelation. This experience comes very close to the modern notion of an experiment: it has to be tested several times before its truth is admitted. (Describing an overwhelming mystical experience as the result of combining the letters of the name of God, a mystical author says: "Once more I took up the Name to do with it as before and, behold, it had exactly the same effect on me. Nevertheless I did not believe until I had tried it four or five times.")

The experimental character of the mystical experience contributed largely to its popularity. It seemed for centuries the only path to the real world, discarded by Rabbinical Judaism. Reality as experienced by the mystics may sometimes appear strange to us; compared with the logistic and legal arguments of orthodoxy, it was as real as real could be, because it was discovered and tested by way of experience, and not by way of interpretation and logic. This approach frequently took the form of interest in one's own soul, because psychological experiences could be repeated and tested indefinitely, the material of the experiments always being at hand, and their results therefore appeared to be the most reliable. Descartes's axiom "*Cogito, ergo sum*" still bears a trace of this tradition: the inner experience of thinking becomes proof of the reality of being. Just as the modern scientific and technical approach toward nature derives from alchemy, so the modern concept of reality as something that can be tested by experiment, and is therefore trusted as permanent, has one of its origins in mystical experience. Mysticism in contrast to orthodox Judaism or Christianity, and modern science in contrast to Jewish or Christian philosophy, trust neither revelation nor pure reasoning but only experience, because they are both concerned not with the problem of truth but with the discovery of a working knowledge of reality.

To the vital concern of Christian mysticism with the problem of reality must be added its equally vital though not specifically mystical concern with the redemption of Man. The subject of Jewish mysticism, on the contrary, "is never man, be he even a saint . . ." (78). Even when Jewish mysticism, in its later phases, leaves the pure sphere of research into reality (as represented by Merkabah Kabbalism) and becomes more concerned with practical life, it merely wants Man to become part of the higher reality and to act accordingly. The eternal question of Christian philosophy, formulated by Augustine as *"quaestio mihi factus sum,"* stimulated Christian mystics more than anything else, but never penetrated into Kabbalah. (And this seems to me one of the reasons for the curious fact that Meister Eckehardt, a true disciple of Augustine, was more strongly influenced by the philosopher Maimonides than any Jewish mystic. In this one respect, Jewish philosophy was much closer to Christian mystical thought than was Jewish mysticism.)

The lack of autobiography in Jewish mysticism and the conscious omission of biographical data seem to mean more than "a particularly vivid sense of the incongruity of mystical experience with [the] idea of God." Autobiographical data are worth retelling only if they are felt to be unique, to possess some unique unrepeatable value. Mystical experiences, on the contrary, were felt to have value only if and insofar as they were repeated, only if they had experimental character. The fact that Christian mystics, in spite of this inherent character of mystical experiences related them in autobiographies, seems to me based not on their being mystics, but on their general philosophical concern with the nature of Man. For Jewish mystics, Man's own self was not subject to salvation and therefore became interesting only as an instrument for supreme action, believed to be a better instrument than the Law. Christian mystics, although they shared with the Jewish mystics in the search for reality, were not primarily interested in action as such, because according to their faith, the supreme event, the salvation of World and Man, had already taken place. It appears as though the same experience was undergone, or rather the same experiments made, by Jewish and Christian mystics alike, by the Jews in order to develop instruments for active participation in the destiny of mankind, but by the Christians as ends in themselves. This might also partly explain the fact that Christian mysticism has always been a matter for individuals and has hardly any continuous tradition of its own, whereas one of the most significant features of Jewish mysticism was that it founded a genuine tradition running parallel to the official tradition of orthodox Judaism. Biographical data, because they stressed individual and unique features, not only appeared irrelevant as to the mystical content but were a real danger to this tradition, which taught Man repeatable experiments and the handling of the supreme instrument that he himself is.

"The doctrine of Tikkun (Lurianic Kabbalah) raised every Jew to the rank of a protagonist in the great process of restitution in a manner never heard of before."

"Sabbatianism represents the first serious revolt in Judaism since the Middle Ages; it was the case of mystical ideas leading directly to the disintegration of the orthodox Judaism of the 'believers.'"

"It was the influence of these elements which had not openly cut themselves off from Rabbinical Judaism which, after the French Revolution, became important in fostering the movement towards reform liberalism and 'enlightenment' in many Jewish circles."

Until the outbreak of the Sabbatian movement, Jewish mysticism had refrained from attacks on orthodoxy and kept itself within the Law. Only after many centuries of rich development did strong antinomian tendencies come out into the open. This might be explained by the political function of the Law in the Diaspora as the only tie for the people. But in spite of cautious restraint and careful avoidance of all conflicts, mystical thought had always prepared its followers for action, thereby breaking with the mere interpretation of the Law and with the mere hope for the coming of the Messiah. In this direction, however, the school of Isaac Luria was bolder than all predecessors when it dared to give a new interpretation of the exile existence of the people: "Formerly (the Diaspora) had been regarded either as a punishment for Israel's sins or as a test of Israel's faith. Now it still is all this, but intrinsically it is a mission: its purpose is to uplift the fallen sparks from all their various locations." For the first time, the role of the "protagonist in the drama of the world" was defined in terms which applied to every Jew.

One remarkable aspect of this "Myth of Exile" is that it served two conflicting purposes: through its mystical interpretation of exile as action instead of suffering, it could rouse the people to hasten the coming of the Messiah and lead to "an explosive manifestation of all those forces to which it owed its rise and its success" in the Sabbatian movement. But after the decline of this movement, it served equally well the needs of the disillusioned people who, having lost the Messianic hope, wanted a new, more general justification of exile, of their inactive existence and mere survival. In the latter form, Isaac Luria's theory has been adopted by assimilated Jewry—though its representatives would not have enjoyed Scholem's discovery that they are the heirs of Kabbalism. This survival of mystical thought in the self-interpretation of assimilated and even dejudaized Jewry was no mere accident, as can be seen from the amazing influence of Khassidism, the other heir of Kabbalism, upon the same 'dejudaized' Jewry when they were initiated into Khassidism at the beginning of our century. A genuine enthusiasm for this last phase of Jewish mysticism spread through the younger generation who generally were quite unconcerned with the intellectual life of their Eastern brethren, but felt themselves surprisingly close to this spiritual world and mentality. The "neutralization of the Messianic element" (that is the neutralization of political attitudes), the outspoken antinomian tendencies, and the conservation of the "Myth of Exile," these three main elements of Khassidism corresponded almost uncannily to the needs of assimilated Jewry. Both Reform Judaism and Khassidism had been concerned solely with Jewish survival, renounced all hope of the restoration of Zion, and accepted the Exile as the ultimate and unchangeable fate of the people. It seems as though the mere loss of Messianic hope, followed by the decline of Rabbinical authority, had essentially identical consequences on the self-interpretation of all sections of the people, widely separated though they were by different social and political conditions. In the long struggle between Jewish orthodoxy and Jewish mysticism, the latter seems to have won the last battle. This victory is all the more surprising, because it was won through defeat.

From its very beginnings, Jewish mysticism had tended toward action and realization; but before ending in utter resignation it attained maximum development in the Sabbatian movement, which, in the new picture given by Scholem, appears as the turning point in Jewish history. It is true that the working power of mystical thought had proved its existence more than once during the Middle Ages in outbreaks of sectarian fanaticism; but never before had a huge popular movement and immediate political action been inspired, prepared, and directed by nothing more than the mobilization of mystical speculations. The hidden experiments of Jewish mystics through the centuries, their efforts to attain a higher reality which, in their opinion, was hidden rather than revealed in the tangible world of everyday life or in the traditional revelation of Mount Sinai, were repeated on a tremendous and absolutely unique scale, by and through the whole Jewish people. For the first time, mysticism showed not only its deep-seated hold on the soul of Man, but its enormous force of action through him. The search for a working knowledge of reality had resulted in a working psychology of the masses, and the powerful will for "realization at any price" had to pay, finally, the price of every tradition, of every established authority and even the price of human standards for truth, as shown by the early acceptance of an apostate Messiah.

Of all mystical trends of the past, Jewish mysticism seems unique in its exclusive concern with reality and action; hence, Jewish mysticism alone was able to bring about a great political movement and to translate itself directly into real popular action. The catastrophe of this victory of mystical thought was greater for the Jewish people than all other persecutions had been, if we are to measure it by the only available yardstick, its far-reaching influence upon the future of the people. From now on, the Jewish body politic was dead and the people retired from the public scene of history.

Perhaps one of the most exciting aspects of the story is the fact that mysticism could survive its own defeat, that its theory as represented in the "Myth of Exile" fitted equally well the needs of popular action and the needs of popular resignation. What survived was the old mystical conception of the actor behind the scenes—one of the favorite ideas of Benjamin Disraeli, for instance—and a general yearning for world redemption as apart from the definite hope of return to Zion—represented by the many "apostles of an unbound political apocalypse" after the outbreak of the French Revolution. With this last allusion, the three spiritual trends in modern Jewish history—Khassidism, Reform movement and "political apocalypse," *i.e.* revolutionary utopianism,—which one used to regard as independent if not contradictory tendencies, are found to stem from the same mighty source, from mysticism. The catastrophe of Sabbatai Zvi, after closing one book of Jewish history, becomes the cradle of a new era.

The Moral of History

(JANUARY 1946)

Die naemlich, welche zu gleicher
Zeit Juden sein und Juden
nicht sein wollen . . ."
—H. E. G. Paulus (1831)

Wilhelm von Humboldt, one of the rare genuine German democrats, who played a big part in the emancipation of Prussian Jewry in 1812 and a still bigger part in the intervention in behalf of the Jews at the Congress of Vienna, looked back in 1816 to the days of his public battle for Jewish rights and his many years of personal intercourse with Jews and said: "I love the Jew really only *en masse; en détail* I strictly avoid him." [1] This amazing and paradoxical utterance, standing as it does in extreme contrast to the personal history of Humboldt—he had many personal friends among Jews—is unique in the history of the arguments presented for Jewish emancipation. Since Lessing and Dohm in Prussia, since Mirabeau and the Abbé Grégoire in France, the advocates of the Jews always based their arguments on the "Jews *en détail,*" on the notable exceptions among the Jewish people. Humboldt's humanism, in the best traditions of Jewish emancipation in France, aimed to liberate the people as a whole, without bestowing special privileges upon individuals. As such his viewpoint was appreciated very little by his contemporaries and it had still less influence on the later history of emancipated Jewry.

More in keeping with the sentiments of the time were the

1. *Wilhelm von Humboldt und Karoline von Humboldt in ihren Briefen* (Berlin 1900) Vol. V, p. 236.

views of H. E. G. Paulus, a liberal Protestant theologian and contemporary of Humboldt. Paulus protested against the idea of emancipating the Jews as a group. Instead he urged that individuals be granted the rights of man according to their personal merits.[2] A few decades later, Gabriel Riesser, the Jewish publicist, vented his irony upon the sort of official Jewish propaganda which based its appeal upon stories of "virtuous Jews" who saved Christians from drowning.[3] The basic principle of granting special privileges to individuals and refusing civic rights to the Jewish people as a group had successfully asserted itself.

In the minds of the privileged Jews such measures taken by the state appeared to be the workings of a sort of heavenly tribunal, by whom the virtuous—who had more than a certain income—were rewarded with human rights, and the unworthy—living in mass concentration in the eastern provinces—were punished as pariahs. Since that time it has become a mark of assimilated Jews to be unable to distinguish between friend and enemy, between compliment and insult, and to feel flattered when an antisemite assures them that he does not mean them, that they are exceptions—exceptional Jews.

The events of recent years have proved that the "excepted Jew" is more the Jew than the exception; no Jew feels quite happy any more about being assured that he is an exception. The extraordinary catastrophe has converted once again all those who fancied themselves extraordinarily favored beings into quite ordinary mortals. Were history a closed book, sealed after each epoch, we would not be much interested in the story

2. Paulus, H. E. G.,*Beitraege von jüdischen und christlichen Gelehrten zur Verbesserung der Bekenner jüdischen Glaubens* (Frankfurt 1817). "The separation of the Jews will only be encouraged if the governments continue to treat them as a whole, in a bad or good sense. If however every one of them is given individual treatment, with justice for every one, according to his behavior, this separation will be dissolved through action." The attack is directed particularly against Humboldt, who defended the cause of the Jews at the Congress of Vienna. Humboldt's argument for the liberation of the Jews *"en masse"* and against a slow method of amelioration, is clearly outlined in his "Expert Opinion" of 1809: "A gradual abolition confirms the separation which it intends to destroy. In all points which are not abolished, it draws attention— by the very fact of the new liberty—to all still existing restrictions and thereby acts against itself." (Cited in: Freund, Ismar, *Die Emanzipation der Juden in Preussen* (Berlin: 1912) Vol. II, p. 270.)

3. Gabriel Riesser, *Gesammelte Schriften (Leipzig:* 1867), Vol. IV, *p.* 290.

of the privileged Jews. The vitality of a nation, however, is measured in terms of the living remembrance of its history. We Jews are inclined to have an inverted historical perspective; the more distantly removed events are from the present, the more sharply, clearly and accurately they appear. Such an inversion of historical perspective means that in our political conscience we do not want to take the responsibility for the immediate past and that we, together with our historians, want to take refuge in periods of the past, which leave us secure in terms of political consequences.

Behind us lies a century of opportunist politics, a century in which an unusual concurrence of circumstances allowed our people to live from day to day. During the same period scholars and philologists have succeeded in estranging history from the people in the same manner as opportunist statesmen alienated them from politics. The sublime concept of human progress was robbed of its historic sense and perverted into a simple natural fact, according to which the son is always presented as better and wiser than his father, the grandson as more enlightened than his grandfather. Or, it was degraded to an economic law, according to which accumulated wealth of the forebears determines the well-being of the sons and grandsons, making each of them advance further in the unending career of the family. In the light of such developments, to forget has become a holy duty, inexperience a privilege and ignorance a guarantee of success.

Since the circumstances under which we live are created by man, the deceased force themselves upon us and upon the institutions that govern us and refuse to disappear into the darkness into which we try to plunge them. The more we try to forget the more their influence dominates us. The succession of generations may be a natural guarantee for the continuity of history but it is certainly not a guarantee of progress. Because we are the sons of our fathers and the grandsons of our grandfathers their misdeeds may persecute us into the third and fourth generations. Inactive ourselves, we cannot even enjoy their deeds for, like all human works, they have the fatal tendency to turn into dross, just as a room painted white always turns black if not repainted frequently.

History, in this sense, has its moral, and if our scholars, with their impartial objectivity, are unable to discover this moral in history, it means only that they are incapable of understanding the world we have created; just like the people who are unable to make use of the very institutions they have produced. History, unfortunately, does not know Hegel's *"List der Vernunft"*; rather does unreason begin to function automatically when reason has abdicated to it.

The automatism of events, reigning since the beginning of the nineteenth century in place of human reason, prepared with incomparable precision for the spiritual collapse of Europe before the bloody idol of race. It is no mere accident that the catastrophic defeats of the peoples of Europe began with the catastrophe of the Jewish people, a people in whose destiny all others thought they could remain uninterested because of the tenet that Jewish history obeys *"exceptional laws."* The defeat of the Jewish people started with the catastrophe of the German Jews, in whom European Jews were not interested because they suddenly discovered that German Jews constituted an exception. The collapse of German Jewry began with its splitting up into innumerable factions, each of which believed that special privileges could protect human rights—e.g., the privilege of having been a veteran of World War I, the child of a war veteran, or if such privileges were not recognized any more, a crippled war veteran or the son of a father killed at the front. Jews *"en masse"* seemed to have disappeared from the earth, it was easy to dispose of Jews *"en détail."* The terrible and bloody annihilation of individual Jews was preceded by the bloodless destruction of the Jewish people.

The European background against which Jewish history appears is complicated and involved. Sometimes the Jewish thread is lost in the maze but most of the time it is easily recognizable. The general history of Europe, from the French Revolution to the beginning of World War I, may be described in its most tragic aspect as the slow but steady transformation of the *citoyen* of the French Revolution into the *bourgeois* of the pre-war period. The stages of the history of this period of nearly 150 years are manifold, and often present magnificent and very human aspects. The period of *enrichissez-vous* (get-rich-quick) was also that of the flowering of French painting; the period of German misery was also that of the great age of classic literature; and we cannot imagine the Victorian age without Dickens. At the end of the era, however, we are confronted by a strange de-humanized kind of humanity. The moral of the history of the nineteenth century is the fact that men who were not ready to assume a responsible role in public affairs in the end were turned into mere beasts who could be used for anything before being led to slaughter. Institutions, moreover, left to themselves without control and guidance by men, turned into monsters devouring nations and countries.

The Jewish phase of 19th century history reveals similar manifestations. While reading Heine and Börne, who just because as Jews they insisted on being considered men and thus were incorporated into the universal history of mankind, we forgot all about the tedious speeches of the representatives of the special group of privileged Jews in Prussia at the same time. In the country which made Disraeli its Prime Minister, the Jew Karl Marx wrote *Das Kapital,* a book which in its fanatical zeal for justice, carried on the Jewish tradition much more efficaciously than all the success of the "chosen man of the chosen race." [4] Finally, who does not, in thinking of the great literary work of Marcel Proust and the powerful bill of indictment by Bernard Lazare, forget those French Jews who filled the aristocratic salons of the Faubourg St. Germain and who, unconsciously following the unseemly example of their Prussian predecessors of the beginning of the nineteenth century, endeavored to be "Jews yet at the same time not Jews"? [5]

This ambiguity became decisive for the social behavior of the assimilated and emancipated Jewry in western Europe. They did not want and could not belong to the Jewish people any more, but they wanted and had to remain Jews—exceptions among the Jewish people. They wanted to and could play their part in non-Jewish society, but they did not desire to and could not disappear among the non-Jewish peoples. Thus they

4. Cf. Horace B. Samuel, *Modernities* (London: 1914), p. 50 ff.
5. Paulus, H. E. G., *Die jüdische Nationalabsonderung nach Ursprung, Folgen und Besserungsmitteln* (1831), p. 6-7.

became exceptions in the non-Jewish world. They maintained they were able to be "men like others on the street but Jews at home." [6] But they felt they were different from other men on the street as Jews, and different from other Jews at home in that they were superior to the masses of the Jewish people.

6. It is not without its irony that this excellent formula which may serve as a motto for western European assimilation as a whole, was propounded by a Russian Jew and first published in Hebrew. It comes from Judah Leib Gordon's Hebrew poem, *Hakitzah ammi* (1863).

Portrait of a Period

(OCTOBER 1943)

A Review of *The World of Yesterday:
An Autobiography*. By Stefan Zweig.
(New York: The Viking Press, 1943)·

In this his last book Stefan Zweig describes a part of the
bourgeois world—the world of the *literati*, which had given him
renown and protected him from the ordinary trials of life.
Concerned only with personal dignity and his art, he had kept
himself so completely aloof from politics that in retrospect the
catastrophe of the last ten years seemed to him like a sudden
monstrous and inconceivable earthquake, in the midst of which
he had tried to safeguard his dignity as long as he could. He
considered it unbearably humiliating when the hitherto wealthy and respected citizens of Vienna had to go begging for visas
to countries which only a few weeks before they would have
been unable even to find on the map. That he himself, only
yesterday so famous and welcome a guest in foreign countries,
should also belong to this miserable host of the homeless and
suspect was simply hell on earth to him. But deeply as the
events of 1933 had changed his personal existence, they could
not touch his standards or his attitudes to the world and to life.
He continued to boast of his unpolitical point of view; it never
occurred to him that, politically speaking, it might be an honor
to stand outside the law when all men were no longer equal
before it. On the contrary, he found himself "one rung lower,"
he "had slipped down to a lesser . . . category." All he realized
was that during the 1930s the better classes in Germany and
elsewhere were steadily yielding to Nazi precepts, and discrimi-

112

nating against those whom the Nazis proscribed and banned: this, in his eyes, meant personal disgrace.

Not one of Stefan Zweig's reactions during all this period was the result of political convictions; they were all dictated by his supersensitiveness to social humiliation. Instead of hating the Nazis, he just wanted to annoy them. Instead of despising those of his coterie who had been *gleichgeschaltet*, he thanked Richard Strauss for continuing to accept his libretti. Instead of fighting he kept silent, happy that his books had not been immediately banned. And later, though comforted by the thought that his works were removed from German bookstores together with those of equally famous authors, this could not reconcile him to the fact that his name had been pilloried by the Nazis like that of a "criminal," and that the famous Stefan Zweig had become the Jew Zweig. He failed to perceive that the dignified restraint, which society had so long considered a criterion of true culture, was under such circumstances tantamount to plain cowardice in public life.

Before Stefan Zweig took his own life he wrote down what the world had given him and then done to him—"the fall into the abyss . . . [and] the height from which it occurred"—with the pitiless accuracy which springs from the calm of absolute despair. He records the pleasures of fame and the curse of humiliation. He tells of the paradise of cultural enjoyments, of meeting men of equal renown. He describes his endless interest in the dead geniuses of history; penetrating their private lives and gathering their personal relics was the most enjoyable pursuit of an inactive existence. And then he tells how he suddenly found himself facing a reality in which there was nothing left to enjoy, in which those as famous as himself either avoided him or pitied him, and in which cultured curiosity about the past was continually and unbearably disturbed by the tumult of the present, the murderous thunder of bombardment, the infinite humiliations at the hands of authorities.

Gone, destroyed forever, was that other world in which, *"frühgereift und zart und traurig"* (Hofmannsthal), one had established oneself so comfortably; razed was that "reservation" for the chosen few connoisseurs who had devoted their lives to the idolatry of Art; broken were the trellises that barred out the *profanum vulgus* of the uncultured more effectively than a

Chinese wall. With that world had passed also its counterpart, the poverty-stricken clique of bohemians. For the young son of a bourgeois household, craving escape from parental protection, bohemians who endured the hardships of ill-success and lack of money became identified with men experienced in the adversities of real life. The "unarrived," dreaming only of large editions of their works, became the symbol of unrecognized genius, and the reflection of the dreadful *dénouement* which destiny might have in store for hopeful and gifted young men.

Naturally, the world which Zweig depicts was anything but *the* world of yesterday; the author of this book lived only on its rim. The gilded trellises of this reservation were very thick, depriving the inmates of every view and every insight that could mar their bliss. Not once does Zweig mention the most ominous manifestation of the postwar period, which struck his native Austria more violently than any other European country—unemployment. But the rare value of his document is nowise lessened by the fact that for us today the trellises behind which these people spent their lives, and to which they owed their extraordinary feeling of security, seem singularly like prison or ghetto walls. It is astounding that there were still men among us whose ignorance was so profound, and whose conscience was so clear, that they could continue to look on the prewar period with the eyes of the nineteenth century. They could regard the impotent pacifism of Geneva and the treacherous lull before the storm, between 1924 and 1933, as a return to normalcy!

It is wryly gratifying that at least one of these men had the courage to record it all in detail, without hiding or prettifying anything. For Zweig finally realized what "chronic fools" they all had been—though the connection between their tragedy and their folly he hardly recognized.

II

The same period which Zweig calls "the Golden Age of Security" was described by his contemporary Charles Péguy (shortly before he fell in the first World War) as the era in which political forms that were presumbaly outmoded lived on with inexplicable monotony—in Russia anachronistic despotism; in Austria the corrupt bureaucracy of the Habsburgs; in

Germany the militarist and stupid regime of the Junkers, hated by the liberal middle class and the workers alike; in France the Third Republic, which was to be granted twenty-odd years more despite its chronic crises. The solution of the puzzle lay in the fact that Europe was much too busy expanding its economic radius for any social stratum or nation to take political questions seriously. Everything could go on because nobody cared. For fifty years—before the opposing economic interests burst into national conflicts, sucking the political systems of all Europe into their vortex—political representation had become a kind of theatrical performance, sometimes an operetta, of varying quality. Simultaneously, in Austria and Russia, the theatre became the focus of national life for the upper crust.

During "the Golden Age of Security" a peculiar dislocation of the balance of power occurred. The enormous development of all industrial and economic potentials produced the steady weakening of purely political factors, while at the same time economic forces grew dominant in the international play of power. Power became synonymous with economic potential, which could bring governments to its feet. This was the real reason why governments played ever-narrowing and empty representative roles, which grew more and more obviously theatrical and operetta-like.

The Jewish bourgeoisie, in sharp contrast to their German and Austrian equivalents, were uninterested in power, even of the economic kind. They were content with their accumulated wealth, happy in the security and peace which their wealth seemed to guarantee. An increasing number of sons from well-to-do homes deserted commercial life, since the mere continued collection of wealth was senseless. They crowded into the cultural occupations; and within a few decades both Germany and Austria saw a great part of their cultural enterprises, such as newspapers, publishing and the theatre, in Jewish hands.

Had the Jews of western and central European countries displayed even a modicum of concern for the political realities of their times, they would have had reason enough not to feel secure. In Germany the first antisemitic parties arose during the 1880's. In his own words, Treitschke made antisemitism "fit for good society." The turn of the century brought the Lueger-

Schoenerer agitation to Austria, ending with the election of
Lueger as Mayor of Vienna. In France the Dreyfus affair
dominated both internal and foreign policies for years. Even as
late as 1940 Zweig could admire Lueger as an "able leader" and
a kindly person whose "official antisemitism never stopped him
from being helpful and friendly to his former Jewish friends."
Among the Jews of Vienna no one took antisemitism, in the
amiable Austrian version Lueger represented, the least bit
seriously—with the exception of the "crazy" feuilleton editor of
the *Neue Freie Presse,* Theodor Herzl.

At least, so it would appear at first glance. Closer examination changes the picture. After Treitschke had made antisemitism fashionable, conversion ceased to be a ticket of admission
to non-Jewish circles in Germany as well as in Austria. Just how
antisemitic the better classes were could not be easily ascer-
tained by the Jewish business men of Austria, for they pursued
only commercial interests and cared nothing about invitations
to non-Jewish groups. But their children discovered soon
enough that there was only one way to be accepted into
society—they must win fame.

On the Jewish situation in this period no more informative
document could be found than the opening chapters of
Zweig's book. They provide the most impressive evidence of
how fame and the will to fame motivated the youth of his
generation. Their ideal was the genius that seemed incarnate in
Goethe. Every Jewish youth able to rhyme passably played the
young Goethe, as every one able to draw a line was a future
Rembrandt and every musical lad an irresistible Beethoven.
The more cultured the parental homes of these *Wunderkinder,*
the more coddled along were the imitations. Nor did this stop
with art itself; it dominated every detail of personal life. They
felt as sublime as Goethe, aped his Olympian aloofness from
politics; they collected rags and fardels that had once belonged
to famous people of other periods; and they strove to come
into direct touch with every living period of renown, as if a tiny
reflection of fame would thus fall upon them—or as if one
could prepare for fame by attending a school of fame.

This idolatry of genius was not restricted to the Jews. It was
a Gentile, Gerhart Hauptmann, who carried it so far as to make
himself look, if not like Goethe, at least like one of the many
cheap busts of the master. And if the parallel enthusiasm which

the German petty bourgeoisie showed for Napoleonic splendor did not actually produce Hitler, it did contribute mightily to the hysterical raptures with which this "great man" was greeted by many German and Austrian intellectuals.

Although deification of the "great man," without much consideration for what he actually achieved, was a general disease of the era, it assumed a special form among the Jews: it was particularly passionate with regard to the great men of culture. In any case, the school of fame which the Jewish youth of Vienna attended was the theatre; the image of fame which they held before them was that of the actor.

But this passion for the theater was by no means exclusively Jewish. In no other European city did the theatre ever acquire the same significance that it had in Vienna during the period of political dissolution. Zweig relates how the death of a famous court actress made his family cook, who had never heard or seen her, burst into tears. Simultaneously, as political activity began to resemble theatre or operetta, the theatre itself developed into a kind of national institution, the actor into a national hero. Since the world had undeniably acquired a theatrical air, the theatre could appear as the world of reality. It is hard for us to believe that even Hugo von Hofmannsthal— the only one of his generation who was not only cultured but, as his later work shows, came close to being a genuine poet— even he fell under the spell of this theatre hysteria, and for many years believed that behind the Viennese absorption in the theatre lay something of the Athenian public spirit. He overlooked the fact that Athenians attended the theatre for the sake of the play, its mythological content and the grandeur of its language, through which they hoped to become the masters of their passions and moulders of their national destiny. The Viennese went to the theatre exclusively for the actors; playwrights wrote for this or that performer; critics discussed only the actor or his part; directors accepted or rejected plays purely on the basis of effective roles for their matinee idols. The star system, as the cinema later perfected it, was completely forecast in Vienna. What was in the making there was not a classical renaissance but Hollywood.

Political conditions facilitated this inversion of being and appearance; but Jews put it into motion, supplied the public demand, propagated it. And since the European world, not unjustifiably, considered Austrian backstage culture typical of the whole period, Zweig is not wrong when he asserts that "nine-tenths of what the world celebrated as Viennese culture in the nineteenth century was promoted, nourished, or even created by Viennese Jewry."

A culture built around an actor or virtuoso established standards as novel as they were dubious. "Posterity weaves no wreaths for the mime"; hence the mime requires an incredible amount of present fame and applause. His vanity is an occupational disease. For to the degree that every artist dreams of leaving his mark on future generations, of transporting his period into another, the artistic impulses of virtuosi and actors are frustrated. Since the actor must renounce immortality, his criterion of greatness depends altogether on contemporary success. Contemporary success was also the only criterion that remained for the "general geniuses," detached from their achievements and considered only in the light of their "inherent greatness." In the field of letters this took the form of biographies describing no more than the appearance, the emotions and the demeanor of great men. This approach not only satisfied vulgar curiosity about the kind of secrets a man's valet would know; it was also prompted by the belief that such idiotic abstraction would clarify the essence of greatness.

In their respect for "inherent greatness" Jews and Gentiles stood side by side. That was why Jewish organization of most cultural enterprises, and particularly of the theatrical culture of Vienna, could go on without restraint, and even become in a sense the epitome of European culture.

III

Stefan Zweig's knowledge of history preserved him from adopting without qualms the worldly yardstick of success. Yet, despite his connoisseurship, he ignored the two great postwar poets in the German language, Franz Kafka and Bertolt Brecht, neither of whom was ever successful. More than that, Zweig confounded the historical significance of writers with the size of their editions. He avers: "Hofmannsthal, Arthur Schnitzler, Beer-Hofmann and Peter Altenberg gave Viennese literature European standing such as it had not possessed under Grillparzer and Stifter."

Precisely because Zweig was modest about himself, discreetly glossing over as uninteresting the personal data in his autobiography, the repeated enumerations of famous people he met is especially striking. It seems like proof that even the best of those cultured Jews could not escape the curse of their time—the worship of that great leveler Success. In his guest-book at Salzburg Zweig gathered "eminent contemporaries" as passionately as he had collected the handwriting and relics of dead poets, musicians and scientists. His own success, the renown of his own accomplishments, failed to sate the appetite of a kind of vanity which could hardly have originated in his character. Presumably the character found it repulsive, but the vanity was deeply and indestructibly rooted in attitude. This began with the search for the "born genius" and "the poet in the flesh"; it considered only a life replete with exciting experiences worth living, and judged an individual by whether or not he belonged to the élite of the chosen few.

Incomplete satisfaction in one's own success, the attempt rather to transform fame into a social background, to create a social caste of famous people like the social caste of aristocrats, to organize a society of the renowned—these were the traits that distinguished the Jews of the period and differentiated their manner from the general genius-lunacy of the times. That was also why the world of art, literature, music and the theatre played right into their hands. They alone were really more interested in those things than even in their own personal achievements or their own fame.

While the turn of the century brought economic security to the Jews and recognized their civic rights as a matter of course, it also made their social position less tenable and their social attitude uncertain, ambiguous. Socially they were pariahs, except when they used extravagant methods (of which fame was one) to enforce their social possibilities. In regard to a *famous* Jew, society would forget its unwritten laws. "The radiant power of fame" was a very real social force, in whose aura one could move freely and even have antisemites for friends, such as Richard Strauss and Karl Haushofer. Fame and success offered means for the socially homeless to create a home and background for themselves. Since outstanding success transcended national frontiers, famous people could easily become the representatives of a nebulous international society, where national prejudices appeared no longer valid. In any case, a famous Austrian Jew was more apt to be accepted as an Austrian in France than in Austria. The world citizenship of this generation, this remarkable nationality which they claimed as soon as their Jewish origin was mentioned, somewhat resembles those modern passports which grant the bearer the right of sojourn in every country except the one that has issued it.

And fame brought also another privilege which, according to Zweig, was at least equally important—the suspension of anonymity, the possibility of being recognized by unknown people, of being admired by strangers. There is no doubt that Zweig feared nothing more than to sink back into obscurity where, stripped of his fame, he would become again what he had been at the beginning of his life. He would be no more than one of the many unfortunates confronted with the almost insuperable problem of conquering a strange world.

Fate, in the form of a political catastrophe, eventually did almost thrust him into this very anonymity. He knew—better than many of his colleagues—that a writer's fame flickers out when he becomes "homeless in borrowed languages." Furthermore, his collections were stolen from him, and with them his intimacy with the famous dead. His house in Salzburg was seized, and with it his bond with the famous men among the living. Taken finally, too, was the invaluable passport, which had not only enabled him to represent his native land in other countries; it had also helped him evade the dubiety of his civic existence in that native land itself.

But again, as during the first World War, it is to Zweig's credit that he did not yield to hysteria, nor take too seriously his newly acquired British citizenship. He could hardly have represented England in other countries. And since the international society of the famous disappeared completely with the second World War, this homeless man lost the only world in which he had once had the delusion of a home.

IV

In a last article, "The Great Silence" (ONA, March 9, 1942), written shortly before his death—an article which seems to me to belong with the finest of Stefan Zweig's work—he tried to take a political stand for the first time in his life. But the word Jew still did not occur to him; Zweig strove once more to represent Europe, at least Central Europe, now choked in "the great silence." Had he spoken about the terrible fate of his own people, he would have been closer to all the European peoples who are today, in the battle against their oppressor, struggling against the persecutor of the Jews. The European peoples know, better than did this self-appointed spokesman who had never in his whole lifetime concerned himself with their political destiny, that yesterday is not detached from today "as if a man had been hurled down from a great height as the result of a violent blow." To them yesterday was neither "an age of reason" nor that "century whose progress, whose silence, whose arts, whose magnificent inventions were the pride and the faith of us all."

Now, without the protective armor of fame, Stefan Zweig was confronted with the reality all-too-familiar to the Jewish people. There had been various escapes from social pariahdom, including the ivory tower of fame. But only flight around the globe could offer salvation from political outlawry. Thus the Jewish bourgeois man of letters, who had never concerned himself with the affairs of his own people, became nevertheless a victim of their foes—and felt so disgraced that he could bear life no longer. Since he had wanted all his life to live in peace with the political and social standards of his environment, he could put up no fight against a world that brands the Jew. When finally the whole structure of his life, with its aloofness from civic struggle and politics, broke down, and he experienced disgrace, he was unable to discover what honor can mean to men.

For honor never will be won by the cult of success or fame, by cultivation of one's own self, nor even by personal dignity. From the "disgrace" of being a Jew there is but one escape—to fight for the honor of the Jewish people as a whole.

Part II:

Zionism and the Jewish State

Herzl and Lazare

(JULY 1942)

To Western Jewry, never really assimilated despite the recourse of some to the antisemitic salons, the Dreyfus case was scarcely of decisive consequence. But to the "modern, cultured Jew who had outgrown the ghetto and its haggling it was a thrust to the heart." [1] For him Herzl's naive generalization was true: it had taken "the common enemy" to make him once more member of a people.[2] These "prodigal sons" had learned a lot from their environment and when they returned to the ancestral hearth they found themselves possessed by that intense discontent which has always been the hallmark of true patriotism and of true devotion to one's people. Sadly and with a certain amazement they came to realize that the moment they proposed improvements in the age-old structure, it was at once decided to expel them from it. And all the time they saw the building in danger of collapse. Theodor Herzl arrived just in time to report the first Dreyfus trial for a Vienna paper. He heard the rabble cry "Death to the Jews!" and proceeded to write *The Jewish State*. Bernard Lazare had come from his home town in the south of France some years before, in the

1. Cf. the remarks of Theodor Herzl in his opening address of the first Zionist Congress (*Gesammelte Werke*, Vol. I, p. 176): "That sense of inner cohesion, with which we have so often and so virulently been charged, was in a state of utter dissolution when antisemitism fell upon us. We have, so to speak, come home. ... But those of us who have returned like prodigal sons to the ancestral hearth find much that urgently requires improvement."

2. Cf. Herzl's statement before the British Aliens Commission: "A nation is an historic group of men united by clearly discernible ties, and held together by a common foe." (*Gesammelte Werke*, Vol. I, p. 474).

midst of the antisemitic furore caused by the Panama scandal. Shortly before the Dreyfus case he had published a two-volume work on antisemitism, in which he had laid it down that this was due, among other things, to the unsocial behavior of the Jews.[3] At that time he believed that he had found in socialism the solution. Lazare likewise was an eyewitness of the Dreyfus trial and he determined not to wait for the world revolution. As he came face to face with the rising hatred of the mob he realized at once that from now on he was an outcast [4] and accepted the challenge. Alone among the champions of Dreyfus he took his place as a conscious Jew, fighting for justice in general but for the Jewish people in particular.[5]

Both men were turned into Jews by antisemitism. Neither concealed the fact.[6] Both realized just because they were so "assimilated" that normal life was possible for them only on the condition that emancipation should not remain a dead letter, while they saw that in reality the Jew had become the pariah of the modern world.[7] Both stood outside the religious tradition of Judaism and neither wished to return to it. Both were removed, as intellectuals, from those narrow and parochial

3. Bernard, Lazare, L'Antisémitisme: son histoire el ses causes (Paris: 1894).
4. Cf. Lazare, Le Fumier de Iob (Paris: 1928) p. 64: "Henceforth I am a pariah."
5. Cf. Péguy, Notre Jeunesse p. 68-69, 74: "The politicians, the rabbis, the official communities of Israel . . . were only too willing to sacrifice Dreyfus for the sake of an illusion. The great mass of the Jews . . . has never been led to its great, if sad, destiny except by force—that is, by a band of fanatics grouped around certain heads, or more precisely, around the prophets of Israel. In this great crisis for Israel and the world the prophet was Bernard Lazare."
6. Cf. Herzl's remark in a letter of the year 1895: "My Judaism was to me a matter of indifference. . . . However, just as antisemitism sent the feeble, cowardly and ambitious Jews into the ranks of Christendom, so it sent me back with renewed vigor to my Judaism." (Tagebücher, Vol. I, pp. 120–21) Similar statements occur passim in his diaries. Bernard Lazare's declaration may be found in his Fumier de Iob: "I am a Jew, yet I ignore everything Jewish. . . . I must needs know who I am, why I am hated and what I might be."
7. Cf. the remark of Herzl at the "family council" of the Rothschilds: "You will never be recognized as full citizens, nay, nor even as second-class (Staatsangehörige);" Tagebücher, Vol. I, p. 187. Similarly in the memoranda for his interview with Baron Hirsch there occurs the observation: "You are pariahs. You have to live on tenterhooks lest anyone deprive you of your rights or property." (Gesammelte Werke, Vol. VI, p. 462) Cf. also Lazare's remark about the "unconscious pariah," i.e., the nonemancipated Jew and the "conscious pariah" of western society, in Le Nationalisme Juif (Paris 1898) p. 8.

Jewish cliques which had somehow grown up within the framework of gentile society. Both were poles apart from that spiritual ghetto which had retained everything of the ghetto's life except its inwardness. Yet both were its natural products; it was from this that both had escaped. When they were drawn back Judaism could no longer mean to them a religion, yet to neither could it mean a half-hearted adherence to one of many cliques. For them their Jewish origin had a political and national significance. They could find no place for themselves in Jewry unless the Jewish people was a nation. In their subsequent careers both men came into serious conflict with the forces which then controlled Jewish politics, namely, the philanthropists. In these conflicts, which in the end exhausted them, both were to learn that the Jewish people was threatened not only by the antisemites from without but also by the influence of its own "benefactors" from within.[8]

But here the similarity ends and there begins that great difference which was to lead ultimately to a personal breach between the two men, when they were serving together on the executive committee of the Zionist Organization. Herzl's solution of the Jewish problem was, in the final analysis, escape or deliverance in a homeland. In the light of the Dreyfus case the whole of the gentile world seemed to him hostile; there were only Jews and antisemites.[9] He considered that he would have to deal with this hostile world and even with avowed antisemites. To him it was a matter of indifference just how hostile a gentile might be; indeed, thought he, the more

8. In his interview with Lord Rothschild, Herzl described Jewish charity as "a mechanism for keeping the needy in subjection." (*Tagebücher*, Vol. III, p. 218) He came into open conflict with the philanthropists when he established the Jewish Colonial Bank and the latter subsequently foundered, as the result of being boycotted by Jewish financial circles. The matter is discussed at length in his *Gesammelte Werke*, Vol. I, p. 406 ff., and there are frequent references to it in the diaries. Similarly Lazare came into conflict with the whole of French Jewry through his championship of Dreyfus. Cf. Baruch Hagani, *Bernard Lazare, 1865–1903* (Paris: 1919), p. 28 ff. That he got the worst of this conflict is shown fully by Péguy, *op. cit.*, p. 75 ff. One example quoted by Péguy (p. 84) is significant: "When negotiations were started for founding a large-scale daily, the Jewish backers always made it a condition that Bernard Lazare should not write for it."

9. Cf. his remark in *Der Judenstaat* (*Gesammelte Werke*, Vol. I, p. 36): "The peoples among whom Jews live are one and all shamefully or shamelessly antisemitic."

antisemitic a man was the more he would appreciate the advantages of a Jewish exodus from Europe! [10] To Lazare, on the other hand, the territorial question was secondary—a mere outcome of the primary demand that "the Jews should be emancipated as a people and in the form of a nation." [11] What he sought was not an escape from antisemitism but a mobilization of the people against its foes. This is shown clearly by his part in the Dreyfus case and by his later memorandum on the persecution of the Jews in Rumania.[12] The consequence of this attitude was that he did not look around for more or less antisemitic protectors but for real comrades-in-arms, whom he hoped to find among all the oppressed groups of contemporary Europe.[13] He knew that antisemitism was neither an isolated nor a universal phenomenon and that the shameful complicity of the Powers in the East-European pogroms had been symptomatic of something far deeper, namely, the threatened collapse of all moral values under the pressure of imperialist politics.[14]

10. Cf. the recurrent observation recorded in his *Tagebücher*, Vol. I, p. 93: "It is the antisemites who will be our staunchest friends, and the antisemitic countries which will be our allies." How he interpreted this notion in practice is revealed in a letter to Katznelson, written in connection with the Kishinev pogroms of 1903. In that letter he seeks to "derive some measure of advantage from the threatening calamity."

11. In *Le Fumier de Iob*.

12. *Les Juifs en Roumanie* (Paris 1902).

13. Characteristic of this attitude is the following passage from his *Juifs en Roumanie*, p. 103: "It may well be that if it [the Rumanian bourgeoisie] plunges the Jew into despair and pushes him to the limit, this very fact, despite his passivity and despite the advice of his wealthy faint-hearts, will forge a link between him and the agricultural laborer and aid both to throw off the yoke." In marked contrast is the attitude of Herzl, as revealed when, following his interview with the sultan, he received telegrams of protest from student-meetings comprising persons of all kinds of oppressed nationalities. He was, he confessed, "pained and distressed," but the only political effect this had on him was to make him talk about using those telegrams in his conversations with the sultan! Cf. *Tagebücher*, Vol. III, p. 103.

14. Cf. his remark in *Les Juifs en Roumanie*, p. 91: "Besides, what other nation dares open its mouth? England, who wiped out the Boers? Russia, who oppressed the Finns and Jews? France, who massacred the Annamites . . . and is now getting ready to butcher the Moors? Italy, who ravages in Eritrea today and in Tripoli tomorrow? Or Germany, the savage executioner of the negroes?"

An interesting insight into the connection between antisemitism's brutalization of peoples and the policies of imperialism is revealed by Fernand Labori, would-be counsel for Dreyfus, in his article "Le Mal politique et les partis," in *La Grande Revue* (October-December, 1901) 276: "Similarly, the

In the light of the Dreyfus case and of his own experience in fighting alongside of Jews for one of their brethren [15] Lazare came to realize that the real obstacle in the path of his people's emancipation was not antisemitism. It was "the demoralization of a people made up of the poor and downtrodden, who live on the alms of their wealthy brethren, a people revolted only by persecution from without but not by oppression from within, revolutionaries in the society of others but not in their own." [16] Ill would it serve the cause of freedom, thought he, if a man were to begin by abandoning his own. Fighters for freedom could be internationalists only if by that they meant that they were prepared to recognize the freedom of all nations; anti-national they could never be.[17] Lazare's criticism of his people was at least as bitter as Herzl's but he never despised them and did not share Herzl's idea that politics must be conducted from above.[18] Faced with the alternative of remaining politically ineffective or of including himself among the élite group of saviors, he preferred to retreat into absolute isolation where, if he could do naught else, he could at least remain one of the people.[19] For Lazare could find no supporters in France. The only element of Western Europe which

---

movement of colonial expansion provides . . . a characteristic trait of the present era. It is a commonplace to point out that this policy has cost humanity moral as well as material sacrifices."

15. Writing in *L'Echo Sioniste* (April 20, 1901) Lazare had the following to say about the French Jews, as he had learned to know them during the Dreyfus crisis: "Take our French Jews. I know that crowd and what they are capable of. It isn't enough for them to reject any solidarity with their foreign-born brethren; they have also to go charging them with all the evils which their own cowardice engenders. They are not content with being more jingoist than the native-born Frenchmen; like all emancipated Jews everywhere they have also, of their own volition, broken all ties of solidarity. Indeed, they go so far that for the three dozen or so men in France who are ready to defend one of their martyred brethren you can find some thousands ready to stand guard over Devil's Island, alongside the most rabid patriots of the country."

16. *Le Fumier de Iob*, p. 151.

17. Péguy, *Notre Jeunesse*, p. 130, stresses this contrast between the international and the anti-national as illustrating Lazare's Jewish patriotism.

18. Cf. *Tagebücher*, vol. i, p. 193.

19. On March 24, 1899 Lazare wrote to Herzl that he felt obliged to resign from the executive committee, which, he added, "tries to direct the Jewish masses as if they were an ignorant child. . . . That is a conception radically opposed to all my political and social opinions and I can therefore not assume responsibility for it;" quoted by Hagani, *Bernard Lazare*, p. 39.

might have responded to his message, the Jews who had outgrown the petty trader's haggling, the intellectuals in the liberal professions, were virtually nonexistent in the country. On the other hand, the impoverished masses, whom he had loved so deeply, and the Jewish oppressed, whom he had championed so devotedly, [20] were separated from him by thousands of miles as well as by a difference in language. In a certain sense, therefore, Herzl with the support of German and Austrian Jewry succeeded where Lazare failed. So utter, indeed, was his failure that he was passed over in silence by his Jewish contemporaries [21] to be recovered to us by Catholic writers. Better than we those men knew that Lazare was a great Jewish patriot as well as a great writer.[22]

20. Péguy, *Notre Jeunesse*, p. 87, describes him as follows: "A heart which beat to all the echoes of the world, a man who could skim four, six, eight or a dozen pages of a newspaper to light, like a streak of lightning, on a single line containing the word Jew . . . a heart which bled in all the ghettos of the world . . . wherever the Jew was oppressed, that is, in a sense; everywhere."

21. *Ibid.*, p. 84: "Everything was set in motion to make him die quietly of hunger."

22. If it were not for Péguy's memoir, "Le portrait de Bernard Lazare," prefixed to the posthumous edition of *Le Fumier de Iob*, we would know little about Lazare. Hagani's biography is based to a large extent on Péguy, while it was only with the latter's help that Lazare himself was able to publish his work on the Jews of Rumania. The saddest part of this sad story is the fact, pointed out by Péguy, that the only man who really appreciated Lazare's greatness and love for Jewry, even though he regarded him as an enemy, was Edouard Drumont.

Zionism Reconsidered

(OCTOBER 1944)

The end result of fifty years of Zionist politics was embodied in the recent resolution of the largest and most influential section of the World Zionist Organization. American Zionists from left to right adopted unanimously, at their last annual convention held in Atlantic City in October, 1944, the demand for a "free and democratic Jewish commonwealth ... [which] shall embrace the whole of Palestine, undivided and undiminished." This is a turning-point in Zionist history; for it means that the Revisionist program, so long bitterly repudiated, has proved finally victorious. The Atlantic City Resolution goes even a step further than the Biltmore Program (1942), in which the Jewish minority had granted minority rights to the Arab majority. This time the Arabs were simply not mentioned in the resolution, which obviously leaves them the choice between voluntary emigration or second-class citizenship. It seems to admit that only opportunist reasons had previously prevented the Zionist movement from stating its final aims. These aims now appear to be completely identical with those of the extremists as far as the future political constitution of Palestine is concerned.[1] It is a deadly blow to those Jewish parties in Palestine itself that have tirelessly preached the necessity of an understanding between the Arab and the Jewish peoples. On the other hand, it will considerably strengthen the majority under the leadership of Ben-Gurion, which, through the pressure of many injustices in Palestine and the terrible catastrophes in Europe, have turned more than ever nationalistic.

1. This program was confirmed by the World Zionist Conference held in London in August 1945.

131

Why "general" Zionists should still quarrel officially with Revisionists is hard to understand, unless it be that the former do not quite believe in the fulfillment of their demands but think it wise to demand the maximum as a base for future compromises, while the latter are serious, honest and intransigent in their nationalism. The general Zionists, furthermore, have set their hopes on the help of the Big Powers, while the Revisionists seem pretty much decided to take matters into their own hands. Foolish and unrealistic as this may be, it will bring to the Revisionists many new adherents from among the most honest and most idealistic elements of Jewry.

In any case, the significant development lies in the unanimous adherence of all Zionist parties to the ultimate aim, the very discussion of which was still tabooed during the 1930's. By stating it with such bluntness in what seemed to them an appropriate moment, Zionists have forfeited for a long time to come any chance of *pourparlers* with Arabs; for whatever Zionists may offer, they will not be trusted. This, in turn, leaves the door wide open for an outside power to take over without asking the advice of either of the two parties most concerned. The Zionists have now indeed done their best to create that insoluble "tragic conflict" which can only be ended through cutting the Gordian knot.

It would certainly be very naive to believe that such a cutting would invariably be to the Jewish advantage, nor is there any reason to assume that it would result in a lasting solution. To be more specific, the British Government may tomorrow decide to partition the country and may sincerely believe it has found a working compromise between Jewish and Arab demands. This belief on the British part would be all the more natural since partition might indeed be an acceptable compromise between the pro-Arab anti-Jewish Colonial administration and the rather pro-Jewish English public opinion: thus it would seem to solve an inner British disagreement over the Palestine question. But it is simply preposterous to believe that further partition of so small a territory whose present border lines are already the result of two previous partitions—the first from Syria and the second from Transjordan—could resolve the conflict of two peoples, especially in a period when similar conflicts are not territorially soluble on much larger areas.

Nationalism is bad enough when it trusts in nothing but

the rude force of the nation. A nationalism that necessarily and admittedly depends upon the force of a foreign nation is certainly worse. This is the threatened fate of Jewish nationalism and of the proposed Jewish State, surrounded inevitably by Arab states and Arab peoples. Even a Jewish majority in Palestine—nay, even a transfer of all Palestine Arabs, which is openly demanded by Revisionists—would not substantially change a situation in which Jews must either ask protection from an outside power against their neighbors or effect a working agreement with their neighbors.

If such an agreement is not brought about, there is the imminent danger that, through their need and willingness to accept any power in the Mediterranean basin which might assure their existence, Jewish interests will clash with those of all other Mediterranean peoples; so that, instead of one "tragic conflict" we shall face tomorrow as many insoluble conflicts as there are Mediterranean nations. For these nations, bound to demand a *mare nostrum* shared only by those who have settled territories along its shores, must in the long run oppose any outside—that is, interfering—power creating or holding a sphere of interest. These outside powers, however powerful at the moment, certainly cannot afford to antagonize the Arabs, one of the most numerous peoples of the Mediterranean basin. If, in the present situation, the powers should be willing to help the establishment of a Jewish homestead, they could do so only on the basis of a broad understanding that takes into account the whole region and the needs of all its peoples. On the other hand, the Zionists, if they continue to ignore the Mediterranean peoples and watch out only for the big faraway powers, will appear only as their tools, the agents of foreign and hostile interests. Jews who know their own history should be aware that such a state of affairs will inevitably lead to a new wave of Jew-hatred; the antisemitism of tomorrow will assert that Jews not only profiteered from the presence of the foreign big powers in that region but had actually plotted it and hence are guilty of the consequences.

The big nations that can afford to play the game of power politics have found it easy to forsake King Arthur's Round Table for the poker table; but small powerless nations that venture their own stakes in that game, and try to mingle with the big, usually end by being sold down the river. The Jews, trying their hand "realistically" in the horse-trading politics of oil in the Near East, are uncomfortably like people who, with a passion for horse-trading but disposing of neither horse nor money, decide to make up for the lack of both by imitating the magnificent shouting that usually accompanies these gaudy transactions.

II

The Revisionist landslide in the Zionist Organization was brought on by the sharpening of political conflicts during the past ten years. None of these conflicts, however, is new; the new factor is the situation in which Zionism is forced to give an answer to questions which for at least twenty years had been held deliberately in suspense. Under Weizmann's leadership in foreign affairs, and partly because of the great achievements of Palestine Jewry, the Zionist Organization had developed a genius for not answering, or answering ambiguously, all questions of political consequence. Everybody was free to interpret Zionism as he pleased; stress was laid, especially in the European countries, on the purely "ideological" elements.

In the light of present decisions, this ideology must appear to any neutral and not too well-informed spectator like deliberately complicated talk designed to hide political intentions. But such an interpretation would not do justice to the majority of Zionists. The truth of the matter is that the Zionist ideology, in the Herzlian version, had a definite tendency toward what later was known as Revisionist attitudes, and could escape from them only through a willful blindness to the real political issues that were at stake.

The political issues on which the course of the whole movement depended were few in number and could be plainly recognized. Foremost among them was the question of which kind of a political body Palestine Jewry was to form. The Revionist insistence on a National State, refusing to accept a mere "national homeland," has proven victorious. Almost as an afterthought of the first came the next question, namely, what relationship this body should have with the Jews of Diaspora countries.

Here enters the double-loyalty conflict, never clearly answered, which is an unavoidable problem of every national movement of a people living within the boundaries of other States and unwilling to resign their civil and political rights therein. For over twenty years the President of the World Zionist Organization and of the Jewish Agency for Palestine has been a British subject whose British patriotism and loyalty are certainly beyond doubt. The trouble is only that by the very nature of his passport he is forced into a theory of predestined harmony of Jewish and British interests in Palestine. Such harmony may or may not exist; but the situation reminds one very vividly of the similar theories of European assimilationists. Here, too, the Revisionists—at least their extreme wing in America, the "Hebrew Committee for National Liberation"—have given the answer which has great chances of being accepted by Zionism, because it corresponds so well with the ideology of most Zionists and fulfills expertly their present needs.

The answer is that in Palestine we have a Hebrew nation, in the Diaspora a Jewish people. This chimes in with the old theory that only the remnant will return, the remnant being the élite of the Jewish people upon whom Jewish survival exclusively depends. This furthermore has the tremendous advantage of fitting in beautifully with the need for a reformulation of Zionism for America. Here not even the pretense of a willingness to move to Palestine is upheld; so here the movement has lost its initial character as that of changing the life of Jews in the Diaspora. The differentiation between the "Jewish people" in America and the "Hebrew nation" in Palestine and Europe could indeed solve, in theory at least, the double-loyalty conflict of American Jews.

Of equal importance has been the question, always open, as to what Jews should do against antisemitism: what kind of fight or explanation the new national movement, which had after all been occasioned by the anti-Jewish agitation of the end of the century, could and would offer. The answer to this, since Herzl's time, has been an utter resignation, an open acceptance of antisemitism as a "fact," and therefore a "realistic" willingness not only to do business with the foes of the Jewish people but also to take propaganda advantage of anti-Jewish hostility. Here, too, the difference between Revisionists and general Zionists has been hard to detect. The while Revisionists were violently criticized by other Zionists for entering into negotiations with the Polish antisemitic prewar Government for the evacuation of a million Polish Jews, in order to win Polish support for extreme Zionist demands before the League of Nations and thus exercise pressure on the British Government, the general Zionists themselves were in constant contact with the Hitler-Government in Germany about the transfer business.

The last, and at the moment certainly most important, issue is the Jewish-Arab conflict in Palestine. The intransigent attitude of the Revisionists is well known. Always claiming the whole of Palestine and Transjordan, they were the first to advocate the transfer of Palestine Arabs to Iraq—a proposition which a few years ago was earnestly discussed in general Zionist circles as well. Since the latest resolution of the American Zionist Organization, from which neither the Jewish Agency nor the Palestine Vaad Leumi differs in principle, leaves practically no choice for the Arabs but minority status in Palestine or voluntary emigration, it is obvious that in this question, too, the Revisionist principle, if not yet the Revisionist methods, has won a decisive victory.

The only distinct difference between the Revisionists and the general Zionists today lies in their attitude towards England, and this is not a fundamental political issue. The Revisionists, decidedly anti-British, share this position, at least on sentimental grounds, with a great many Palestine Jews who have the experience of British Colonial administration. Moreover, they enjoy in this respect the support of many American Zionists who are either influenced by the American distrust of British imperialism or hope that America and not Great Britain will be the future great power in the Near East. The last obstacle between them and victory in this field is Weizmann, who is backed by the English Zionist Organization and a small minority in Palestine.

III

In a rather summary way it may be asserted that the Zionist movement was fathered by two typical nineteenth-century European political ideologies—socialism and nationalism. The amalgam of these two seemingly contradictory doctrines was generally effected long before Zionism came into being: it was effected in all those national-revolutionary movements of small European peoples whose situation was equally one of social as of national oppression. But within the Zionist movement such an amalgam has never been realized. Instead, the movement was split from the beginning between the social-revolutionary forces which had sprung from the east European masses and the aspiration for national emancipation as formulated by Herzl and his followers in the central European countries. The paradox of this split was that, whereas the former was actually a people's movement, caused by national oppression, the latter, created by social discrimination, became the political creed of intellectuals.

For a long time the eastern movement had so strong an affinity with socialism in the Tolstoyan form that its followers almost adopted it as their exclusive ideology. The Marxists among them believed Palestine to be the ideal place to "normalize" the social aspects of Jewish life, by establishing there appropriate conditions for Jewish participation in the all-important class struggle from which the ghetto existence had excluded the Jewish masses: this was to give them a "strategical base" for future participation in the world revolution and the coming classless and nationless society (Borochov). Those who adopted the more eastern variation of the Messianic dream went to Palestine for a kind of personal salvation through work within a collective (A. D. Gordon). Spared the ignominies of capitalist exploitation, they could realize at once and by themselves the ideals they preached, and build up the new social order that was only a far-off dream in the social-revolutionary teachings of the West.

The national aim of the socialist Zionists was attained when they settled in Palestine. Beyond that they had no national aspirations. Absurd as it may sound today, they had not the slightest suspicion of any national conflict with the present inhabitants of the promised land; they did not even stop to think of the very existence of Arabs. Nothing could better prove the entirely unpolitical character of the new movement than this innocent obliviousness. True, those Jews were rebels; but they rebelled not so much against the oppressions of their people as against the crippling, stifling atmosphere of Jewish ghetto-life, on the one hand, and the injustices of social life in general, on the other. From both they hoped to have escaped when once established in Palestine, whose very name was still holy as well as familiar to them, emancipated though they were from Jewish orthodoxy They escaped to Palestine as one might wish to escape to the moon, to a region beyond the wickedness of the world. True to their ideals, they established themselves on the moon; and with the extraordinary strength of their faith they were able to create small islands of perfection.

Out of these social ideals grew the *chalutz* and *kibbutz* movement. Its members, a small minority in their native lands, are a hardly larger minority in Palestine Jewry today. But they did succeed in creating a new type of Jew, even a new kind of aristocracy with their newly established values: their genuine contempt for material wealth, exploitation, and bourgeois life; their unique combination of culture and labor; their rigorous realization of social justice within their small circle; and their loving pride in the fertile soil, the work of their hands, together with an utter and surprising lack of any wish for personal possession.

Great as these achievements are, they have remained without any appreciable political influence. The pioneers were completely content within the small circle where they could realize their ideals for themselves; they were little interested in Jewish or Palestine politics, were in fact frequently wearied by it, unaware of the general destiny of their people. Like all true sectarians, they tried hard to convince people of their way of life, to win over to their convictions as many adherents as possible, even to educate the Jewish youth of the Diaspora to follow in their footsteps. But once in Palestine, and even before within the safe shelter of the various youth movements, these idealists became self-contented, concerned only with the personal realization of lofty ideals, as indifferent as their teachers had been to the world at large which had not accepted the salutary way of living in an agricultural collective. In a sense, indeed, they were too decent for polities, the best among them somehow afraid of soiling their hands with it; but they were also completely disinterested in any event in Jewish life outside Palestine which did not land thousands of Jews as new immigrants; and they were bored by any Jew who was not himself a prospective immigrant. Politics, therefore, they gladly left to the politicians—on condition they were helped with money, left alone with their own social organization, and guaranteed a certain influence upon education of the youth.

Not even the events of 1933 roused their political interest; they were naïve enough to see in them, above all, a God-sent opportunity for an undreamt-of wave of immigration to Palestine. When the Zionist Organization, against the natural impulses of the whole Jewish people, decided to do business with Hitler, to trade German goods against the wealth of German Jewry, to flood the Palestine market with German products and thus make a mockery of the boycott against German-made articles, they found little opposition in the Jewish National Homeland, and least of all among its aristocracy, the so-called *kibbutzniks*. When accused of dealing with the enemy of Jewry and of Labor, these Palestinians used to argue that the Soviet Union too had extended its trade agreements with Germany. Thereby once more these Palestinians underlined the fact that they were interested only in the existing and prospective *Yishuv*, the Jewish settlement, and were quite unwilling to become the protagonists of a world-wide national movement.

This consenting to the Nazi-Zionist transfer agreement is only one outstanding instance among many of the political failure of the aristocracy of Palestine Jewry. Much as, despite their small number, they influenced the social values in Palestine, so little did they exercise their force in Zionist politics. Invariably they submitted to the Organization which, none the less, they held in contempt, as they held in contempt all men who were not producing and living from the work of their hands.

So it has come to pass that this new class of Jews, who possess such a rich new experience in social relationships, have not uttered a single fresh word, have not offered a single new slogan, in the wide field of Jewish politics. They took no differing stand on political antisemitism—content merely with repeating the old socialist or the new nationalist banalities, as though the whole affair did not concern them. Without a single fresh approach to the Arab-Jewish conflict (the "binational State" of *Hashomer Hazair* is no solution since it could be realized only as a result of a solution), they limited themselves to fighting either for or against the slogan of Jewish Labor. Revolutionary as were their background and their ideology, they failed to level a single criticism at Jewish bourgeoisie outside of Palestine, or to attack the role of Jewish finance in the political structure of Jewish life. They even adapted themselves to the charity methods of fund-raising, which they were taught by the Organization when sent to other countries on special missions. Amid the turmoil of conflicts in Palestine today, most of them have become loyal supporters of Ben-Gurion who indeed, in contrast to Weizmann, comes from their own ranks; though many of them have, in the old tradition, simply refused to vote; and only a few of them have protested that under the leadership of Ben-Gurion, whose Revisionist leanings were still violently denounced by Palestine Labor in 1935, the Zionist Organization has adopted the Revionist Jewish State program.

Thus the social-revolutionary Jewish national movement, which started half a century ago with ideals so lofty that it overlooked the particular realities of the Near East and the general wickedness of the world, has ended—as do most such movements—with the unequivocal support not only of national but of chauvinist claims—not against the foes of the Jewish people but against its possible friends and present neighbors.

IV

This voluntary and, in its consequences, tragic abdication of political leadership by the vanguard of the Jewish people left the course free to the devotees of the movement who may be truly called political Zionists. Their Zionism belongs to those nineteenth-century political movements that carried ideologies, *Weltanschauungen*, keys to history, in their portmanteaus. Not less than its better known contemporaries, such as socialism or nationalism, Zionism was once fed on the very life-blood of genuine political passions; and it shares with them the sad fate of having outlived their political conditions only to stalk together like living ghosts amid the ruins of our times.

Socialism—which, despite all its materialist superstitions and naïve atheistic dogmatism, was once an inspiring source of the revolutionary labor movement—laid the heavy hand of "dialectical necessity" upon the heads and hearts of its adherents until they were willing to fit into almost any inhumane conditions. They were so willing because, on the one hand, their genuine political impulses for justice and freedom had grown fainter and fainter and, on the other hand, their fanatical belief in some superhuman, eternally progressive development had grown stronger and stronger. As for nationalism, it never was more evil or more fiercely defended than since it became apparent that this once great and revolutionary principle of the national organization of peoples could no longer either guarantee true sovereignty of the people within or establish a just relationship among different peoples beyond the national borders.

The pressure of this general European situation made itself felt in Jewish life through a new hostile philosophy, which centered its whole outlook around the role of the Jews in political and social life. In a sense, antisemitism was the father of both Assimilationism and Zionism—to such a degree, indeed, that we can hardly understand a single word of the great war of arguments between them, that was to last for decades, without keeping in mind the standard contentions of antisemitism.

At that time antisemitism was still the expression of a typical conflict such as must inevitably occur within the framework of a national state whose fundamental identity between people and territory and state cannot but be disturbed by the presence of another nationality which, in whatever forms, wants to preserve its identity. Within the framework of a national state there are only two alternatives for the solution of nationality-conflicts: either complete assimilation—that is, actual disappearance—or emigration. If, then, the assimilationists had simply preached national suicide for Jewry and the Zionists had simply challenged this in proposing means of national survival, we would have witnessed two factions of Jewry fighting each other on the ground of genuine and serious differences. Instead, both preferred to dodge the issue and to develop each an "ideology." Most of the so-called assimilationists never wanted complete assimilation and national suicide: they imagined that by escaping from actual history into an imaginary history of mankind they had found an excellent method of survival. The Zionists likewise fled the field of actual conflicts into a doctrine of eternal antisemitism governing the relations of Jews and Gentiles everywhere and always, and mainly responsible for the survival of the Jewish people.

Thus both sides relieved themselves of the arduous task of fighting antisemitism on its own grounds, which were political, and even of the unpleasant task of analyzing its true causes. The assimilationists began their futile writing of a ponderous library of refutations which nobody ever read—except perhaps the Zionists. For they obviously accepted the validity of the utterly stupid reasoning, since they concluded from that kind of propaganda that all reasoning was entirely futile—a surprising conclusion if one considers the level of the "reasons."

But now the way was free for talking in general terms and developing the respective *isms*. It was a struggle in which political issues were touched on only when the Zionists charged that the solution of the Jewish problem through assimilation meant suicide. This was true enough; but it was something most of the assimilationists neither wished nor dared to refute. They were frightened by Gentile critics all unaware that they too, the very assimilationists, wanted Jewish survival and were actually engaged in Jewish politics. On the other side, when the assimilationists talked about the danger of double loyalty and the impossibility of being German or French patriots and Zionists at the same time, they rudely raised a problem which for obvious reasons the Zionists did not care to talk of frankly.

Sad as it must be for every believer in government of the people, by the people and for the people, the fact is that a political history of Zionism could easily pass over the genuine national revolutionary movement which sprang from the Jewish masses. The political history of Zionism must be concerned mainly with those elements that did not come of the people: it must be concerned with men who believed in government by the people as little as did Theodor Herzl whom they followed—although it is true that they all emphatically wished to do something for the people. They had the advantage of a general European education and outlook, together with some knowledge of how to approach and deal with governments. They called themselves political Zionists, which indicated clearly their special and one-sided interest in foreign politics. They were confronted by the similarly one-sided concern with domestic politics on the part of the east-European adherents of the movement.

It was only after Herzl's death in 1904, and because of the failure of all of Herzl's ventures into high diplomacy, that they became converts to Weizmann's "practical" Zionism, which preached practical achievements in Palestine as the basis for political success. This approach, however, was to meet with as little actual success. In the absence of a political guarantee (Herzl's famous Charter) and in the presence of the hostile Turkish administration, very few Jews could be induced to settle in Palestine prior to the Balfour Declaration in 1917. This Declaration was not issued—nor was it ever pretended to have been issued—because of practical achievements in Palestine. The practical Zionists, therefore, became "General Zionists," this term designating their ideological creed as opposed to the philosophy of assimilation.

For the most part interested in the relationship between the movement and the Great Powers, and in the propaganda results among a few outstanding personalities, the General Zionists were sufficiently unprejudiced, despite their bourgeois origin, to leave to their eastern brethren—those who actually did go to Palestine—a completely free hand with their experiments in social and economic life, insisting only on an equal chance for capitalist enterprise and investment. Both groups could work together rather smoothly just because of their entirely different outlooks. However, the result of this cooperation, in the actual upbuilding of Palestine, was a most paradoxical conglomerate of radical approach and revolutionary social reforms domestically, with outmoded and outright reactionary political lines in the field of foreign politics, that is, the relationship of the Jews to other nations and peoples.

The men who now assumed Zionist leadership were no less the moral aristocracy of western Jewry than were the founders of the *Kibbutz* and *Chalutz* movement of eastern Jewry. They constituted the best part of that new Jewish intelligentsia in central Europe, whose worst representatives were to be found in the offices of Ullstein and Mosse in Berlin or the *Neue Freie Presse* in Vienna. It was not their fault they were not of the people, for in these western and central European countries a "Jewish people" simply did not exist. Nor can they be blamed for not believing in government by the people, since the central European countries of their birth and upbringing had no political traditions of this kind. Those countries had left their Jewries in a social, if not economic, vacuum wherein they knew the Gentiles of their environment as little as they knew their fellow-Jews who lived far away, beyond the borders of their own native lands. It was their moral courage, their feeling for personal honor and cleanliness in life, which more than anything else served to propagate among them the new solution of the Jewish question. With their stressing of personal salvation from a life of hollow pretenses—something more important to them than the upbuilding of Palestine (where, after all, this type of European Jew appeared in numbers only after the catastrophe of 1933)—they resembled more than they could have known their eastern brethern. Zionism was for the former what socialism had been for the latter; and in both cases Palestine functioned as an ideal place, out of the bleak world, where one might realize one's ideals and find a personal solution for political and social conflicts. It was, indeed, this very factor of personalizing political problems which led western Zionism to an enthusiastic acceptance of the *chaluziuth* ideal of the east. With the difference, however, that this ideal did not actually play any considerable part in the west until the arrival of Hitler. True, it was preached in the Zionist youth movement; but that movement shared with the other German pre-Hitler youth movements the fate that its ideals became only a source of tender recollections in adult life.

Western Zionists, then, were a fraction of those sons of wealthy Jewish bourgeois families who could afford to see their children through the university. Simply by so doing, and without giving the matter much thought, the wealthy Jews, mainly of Germany and Austria-Hungary, created an entirely new class in Jewish life—modern intellectuals given to the liberal professions, to art and science, without either spiritual or ideological link to Judaism. They—"*das moderne gebildete, dem ghetto entwachsene, des Schachers entwoehnte Judentum*" (Herzl)—had to find both their daily bread and their self-respect outside of Jewish society—"*ihr Brod und ihr bisschen Ehre ausserhalb des juedischen Schachers*" (Herzl); and they alone were exposed without shelter and defense to the new Jew-hatred at the turn of the century. If they did not wish to sink to the moral and intellectual level of the Ullstein-Mosse clique, nor to establish themselves as "*freischwebende Intellektuelle*" (Karl Mannheim), they had perforce to go back to Jewish life and find a place for themselves in the midst of their own people.

This, however, quickly proved almost as difficult as complete assimilation with self-respect. For in "the house of their fathers" (Herzl) there was no place for them. The Jewish classes, like Jewish masses, clung together socially, linked by the never-ending chain of family and business connections. Those relationships were further solidified through the charity organization to which every member of the community, though he may never in his life have entered a synagogue, gave his appropriate share. Charity, this leftover of the once autonomous Jewish communities, had proved through two hundred years strong enough to prevent the destruction of the interrelationship of the Jewish people throughout the world. As family and business connections sufficed to keep the Jewry of each country a closely knit social body, Jewish charity had come very near to organize world-Jewry into a curious sort of body politic.

However, the new Jewish intellectuals had not been provided for in this undirected but nevertheless efficiently functioning organization. True, if they were lawyers and doctors—the heart's desire of all Jewish parents—they still needed Jewish social connections for their living. But for those who chose the professions of writers and journalists, of artists or scientists, of teachers or state-employes—as happened frequently—there was no need of Jewish social connections, and Jewish life had no need of those intellectuals. Socially, they were outside the pale. But if they did not fit locally into the social body of emancipated Jewry, still less did they fit into the body politic of charitable world-Jewry. For in this great and truly international organization one had to be either on the receiving or on the giving end in order to be accounted for as a Jew. Now, since these intellectuals were too poor to be philanthropists and too rich to become *schnorrers*, charity took as little interest in them as they could take in charity. Thus were the intellectuals excluded from the only practical way in which Western Jewry proved its solidarity with the Jewish people. The intellectuals didn't belong, either socially or politically; there was no place for them in the house of their fathers. To remain Jews at all they had to build a new house.

Zionism, hence, was destined primarily, in western and central Europe, to offer a solution to these men who were more assimilated than any other class of Jewry and certainly more imbued with European education and cultural values than their opponents. Precisely because they were assimilated enough to understand the structure of the modern national state they realized the political actuality of antisemitism even if they failed to analyze it, and they wanted the same body politic for the Jewish people. The hollow word-struggles between Zionism and assimilationism has completely distorted the simple fact that the Zionists, in a sense, were the only ones who sincerely wanted assimilation, namely, "normalization" of the people ("to be a people like all other peoples"), whereas the assimilationists wanted the Jewish people to retain their unique position.

In sharp contrast to their eastern comrades, these western Zionists were no revolutionaries at all; they neither criticized nor rebelled against the social and political conditions of their time; on the contrary, they wanted only to establish the same set of conditions for their own people. Herzl dreamt of a kind of huge transfer-enterprise by which "the people without a country" was to be transported into "the country without a people"; but the people themselves were to him poor, uneducated and irresponsible masses (an "ignorant child," as Bernard Lazare put it in his critique of Herzl), which had to be led and governed from above. Of a real popular movement Herzl spoke but once—when he wanted to frighten the Rothschilds and other philanthropists into supporting him.

VI

During the decade after Herzl's death until the outbreak of the First World War, Zionism was without any major political success. In this period Zionism developed more and more into an expression of personal affirmation, so to speak—into a type of almost religious confession which helped a man go straight and keep his head high; Zionism lost more and more of that little political impetus it still had until Herzl's death. Instead, and mostly by means of an entirely academic and theoretical critique of Jewish opposition within, it unfolded all the "ideological" elements of Herzl's writings. For the time, during the long stagnation years of the movement, these tenets had but little actual practical significance; anyway they avoided every serious issue. But if ever a fundamentally unpolitical attitude had political consequences, this one had.

First, and for the personal problems of Jewish intellectuals most important of all, was the question of antisemitism. This phenomenon—though extensively described, especially in its rather harmless social aspects—was never analyzed on its political grounds and in context with the general political situation of the time. It was explained as the natural reaction of one people against another, as though they were two natural substances destined by some mysterious natural law to antagonize each other to eternity.

This appraisal of antisemitism—as an eternal phenomenon attending inevitably the course of Jewish history through all the Diaspora countries—sometimes took to more rational forms, as when interpreted with the categories of the national state. Then antisemitism could appear as "a feeling of peripheral tension" comparable to "the tension between nations ... at the national boundaries where the constant human contacts of national elements at variance with each other tend constantly to renew the international conflict" (Kurt Blumenfeld). But even this most advanced interpretation, in which at least one aspect of Jew-hatred is correctly attributed to the national organization of peoples, still presupposes the eternity of antisemitism in an eternal world of nations and, moreover, denies the Jewish part of responsibility for existing conditions. Thereby it not only cuts off Jewish history from European history and even from the rest of mankind; it ignores the role that European Jewry played in the construction and functioning of the national state; and thus it is reduced to the assumption, as arbitrary as it is absurd, that every Gentile living with Jews must become a conscious or subconscious Jew-hater.

This Zionist attitude toward antisemitism—which was held to be sound precisely because it was irrational, and therefore explained something unexplainable and avoided explaining what could be explained—led to a very dangerous misappraisal of political conditions in each country. Antisemitic parties and movements were taken at their face value, were considered genuinely representative of the whole nation, and hence not worthwhile fighting against. And since the Jewish people, still in the manner of antique nations with their own ancient traditions, divided the whole of mankind between themselves and the foreigners, the Jews and the *Goyim*—as the Greeks divided the world between Greeks and *barbaroi*—they were only too willing to accept an unpolitical and unhistorical explanation of the hostility against them. In their estimate of antisemitism Zionists could simply fall back upon this Jewish tradition; they found little serious opposition whether they expressed themselves in half-mystical or, following the fashions of the time, in half-scientific terms, as long as they appealed to this basic Jewish attitude. They fortified the dangerous, time-honored, deep-seated distrust of Jews for Gentiles.

Not less dangerous and quite in accord with this general trend was the sole new piece of historical philosophy which the Zionists contributed out of their own new experiences; "A nation is a group of people ... held together by a common enemy" (Herzl)—an absurd doctrine containing only this bit of truth: that many Zionists had, indeed, been convinced they were Jews by the enemies of the Jewish people. Thereupon these Zionists concluded that without antisemitism the Jewish people would not have survived in the countries of the Diaspora; and hence they were opposed to any attempt to liquidate antisemitism on a large scale. On the contrary, they declared that our foes, the antisemites, "will be our most reliable friends, the antisemitic countries our allies" (Herzl). The result could only be, of course, an utter confusion in which nobody could distinguish between friend and foe, in which the foe became the friend and the friend the hidden, and therefore all the more dangerous, enemy.

Even before the Zionist Organization descended into the shameful position of joining the part of Jewry that willingly treated with its enemy, this doctrine had several not unimportant consequences.

One immediate consequence was that it made superfluous a political understanding of the part Jewish plutocracy played within the framework of national states, and its effects on the life of the Jewish people. The new Zionist definition of a nation as a group of people held together by a common enemy strengthened the general Jewish feeling that "we are all in the same boat"—which simply did not correspond to the realities. Hence the merely sporadic Zionist attacks on the Jewish powers-that-be remained harmless, confined to a few bitter remarks about charity, which Herzl had called the "machinery to suppress the outcries." Even such tame criticisms were silenced ater 1929, the year of the formation of the Jewish

Agency, when the Zionist Organization traded the hope of a larger income (which was not to be realized) against the independence of the only large Jewish organization that had ever been beyond the control of Jewish plutocracy and had ever dared to criticize the Jewish notables. In that year the true revolutionary possibilities of Zionism for Jewish life were definitely sacrificed.

In the second place, the new doctrine of nationalism influenced very strongly the Zionists' attitude toward the Soviet attempt to liquidate antisemitism without liquidating the Jews. This, it was asserted, could in the long and even short run lead only to the disappearance of Russian Jewry. It is true that today little is left of their hostility, although it still plays a role, if only a subordinate one, in the minds of that minority who are wholly tied up with Weizmann and, consequently, hostile to any influence in the Near East besides the British. We witness, rather, a new sympathy for Soviet Russia among Zionists throughout the world. So far it has remained mostly sentimental, ready to admire everything Russian; but, out of disillusionment with Great Britain's promises, there has also arisen a widespread, though politically still inarticulate, hope to see the Soviet Union take an active part in the future of the Near East. The belief in an unalterable friendship of the USSR for the Jews would, of course, be no less naïve than the former belief in England. What every political and national movement in our times should give its utmost attention to with respect to Russia—namely, its entirely new and successful approach to nationality conflicts, its new form of organizing different peoples on the basis of national equality—has been neglected by friends and foes alike.

A third political consequence of a fundamentally unpolitical attitude was the place which Palestine itself was assigned in the philosophy of Zionism. Its clearest expression may be found in Weizmann's dictum during the 'thirties that "the upbuilding of Palestine is our answer to antisemitism"—the absurdity of which was to be shown only a few years later, when Rommel's army threatened Palestine Jewry with exactly the same fate as in European countries. Since antisemitism was taken to be a natural corollary of nationalism, it could not be fomented, it was supposed, against that part of world-Jewry established as a nation. In other words, Palestine was conceived as the place, the only place, where Jews could escape from Jew-hatred. There, in Palestine, they would be safe from their enemies: nay, their very enemies would miraculously change into their friends.

At the core of this hope which—were ideologies not stronger for some people than realities—should by now be blown to bits, we find the old mentality of enslaved peoples, the belief that it does not pay to fight back, that one must dodge and escape in order to survive. How deep-rooted is this conviction could be seen during the first years of the war, when only through the pressure of Jews throughout the world was the Zionist Organization driven to ask for a Jewish Army—which, indeed, was the only important issue in a war against Hitler. Weizmann, however, always refused to make this a major political issue, spoke deprecatingly of a "so-called Jewish Army," and, after five years of war, accepted the "Jewish Brigade," which another spokesman of the Jewish Agency hastened to diminish in importance. The whole matter apparently was, for them, a question of prestige for Palestine Jewry. That an early distinct and demonstrable participation of Jews as Jews in this war would have been the decisive way to prevent the antisemitic slogan which, even before victory was won, already represented Jews as its parasites, apparently never entered their heads.

Ideologically more important was the fact that, by their interpretation of Palestine in the future life of the Jewish people, the Zionists shut themselves off from the destiny of the Jews all over the world. Their doctrine of the inevitable decline of Jewish life in the Galuth, the Diaspora the world over, made it easy for the conscience of the Yishuv, the settlement in Palestine, to develop its attitude of aloofness. Palestine Jewry, instead of making itself the political vanguard of the whole Jewish people, developed a spirit of self-centeredness, though its preoccupation with its own affairs was veiled by its readiness to welcome refugees who would help it become a stronger factor in Palestine. While the assimilated Jewries of the Western world had pretended to ignore the strong ties which had always connected Leningrad with Warsaw, and Warsaw with Berlin, and both with Paris and London, and all together with New York, and had presumed unique unrelated conditions for each country, Zionism followed suit by pretending special conditions for Palestine, unrelated to Jewish destinies elsewhere, while at the same time generalizing adverse conditions for Jews everywhere else in the world.

This pessimism for Jewish life in any other political form, and in any other territory of the earth, seems to be unaffected in the Zionist mind by the very size of Palestine, a small country that at best can give homestead to several millions of the Jewish people but never to all the millions of Jews still remaining throughout the world. Hence only two political solutions could be envisioned. Zionists used to argue that "only the remnant will return," the best, the only ones worth saving; let us establish ourselves as the elite of the Jewish people and we shall be the only surviving Jews in the end; all that matters is our survival; let charity take care of the pressing needs of the masses, we shall not interfere; we are interested in the future of a nation, not in the fate of individuals.

But in the face of the terrible catastrophe in Europe, there are few Zionists left who would stick to their former doctrine of the necessary perishing of *Galuth*-Jewry. Therefore, the alternative solution of the problem, once preached only by Revisionists, has won the day. Now they talk the language of all extreme nationalists. To the puzzling question of how Zionism can serve as an answer to antisemitism for the Jews who remain in the Diaspora they cheerfully assert, "Pan-Semitism is the best answer to anti-Semitism"

VII

It was during and after the First World War that the Zionist attitude toward the Great Powers took definite shape. There had already been, however, almost since the seizure of political leadership by the western branch in the 'nineties, significant signs indicating the way the new national movement was to choose for the realization of its aims. It is well known how Herzl himself started negotiations with Governments, appealing invariably to their interest in getting rid of the Jewish question through the emigration of their Jews. It is known, too, how he invariably failed, and for a simple reason: he was the only one who took the anti-Jewish agitation at its face value. Precisely those Governments that indulged most in Jew-baiting were the least prepared to take his proposal seriously; they could scarcely understand a man who insisted on the spontaneity of a movement which they themselves had stirred up.

Even more significant for the future were Herzl's negotiations with the Turkish Government. The Turkish Empire was one of those nationality-states based on oppression which were already doomed and, indeed, disappeared during the First World War. Yet the Turkish Empire was to be interested in Jewish settlements on this premise: with the Jews a new and completely loyal factor would be introduced into the Near East; and a new loyal element would certainly help to keep down the greatest of the menaces that threatened the Imperial Government from all sides, the menace of an Arab uprising. Therefore when Herzl, during these negotiations, received cables from students of various oppressed nationalities protesting against agreements with a Government which had just slaughtered hundreds of thousands of Armenians, he only observed: "This will be useful for me with the Sultan."

It was in this same spirit, following what had already become a tradition, that as late as 1913 the Zionist leaders, in their reawakened hope to sway the Sultan to their side, broke off negotiations with the Arabs. Whereupon one of the Arab leaders shrewdly remarked: "*Gardez-vous bien, Messieurs les Sionistes, un gouvernement passe, mais un peuple reste.*" (For this and later references to Arab-Jewish negotiations, see M. Perlmann's "Chapters of Arab-Jewish Diplomacy, 1918–1922" in *Jewish Social Studies,* April 1944.)

Those who are dismayed at the spectacle of a national movement that, starting out with such an idealistic élan, sold out at the very first moment to the powers-that-be—that felt no solidarity with other oppressed peoples whose cause, though historically otherwise conditioned, was essentially the same— that endeavored even in the morning-dream of freedom and justice to compromise with the most evil forces of our time by taking advantage of imperialistic interests—those who are dismayed should in fairness consider how exceptionally difficult the conditions were for the Jews who, in contrast to other peoples, did not even possess the territory from which to start their fight for freedom. The alternative to the road that Herzl maked out, and Weizmann followed through to the bitter end, would have been to organize the Jewish people in order to negotiate on the basis of a great revolutionary movement. This would have meant an alliance with all progressive forces in Europe; it would certainly have involved great risks. The only man within the Zionist Organization known to have ever considered this way was the great French Zionist Bernard Lazare, the friend of Charles Péguy—and he had to resign from the Organization at the early date of 1899. From then on no responsible Zionist trusted the Jewish people for the necessary political strength of will to achieve freedom instead of being transported to freedom; thus no official Zionist leader dared to side with the revolutionary forces in Europe.

Instead, the Zionists went on seeking the protection of the Great Powers, trying to trade it against possible services. They realized that what they could offer must be in terms of the interests of the Governments. In the consequent subservience to British policy, which is associated with Weizmann's unswerving loyalty to the cause of the British Empire in the Near East, the Zionists were abetted by sheer ignorance of the new imperialist forces at work. Though these forces had been active ever since the 'eighties of the last century, they had begun to show clearly in all their intricacies only at the beginning of the twentieth century. Since theirs was a national movement, the Zionists could think only in national terms, seemingly unaware of the fact that imperialism was a nation-destroying force, and therefore, for a small people, it was near-suicide to attempt to become its allies or its agents. Nor have they even yet realized that protection by these interests supports a people as the rope supports for hanging. When challenged by opponents the Zionists would answer that British national interests and Jewish national interests happen to be identical and therefore this is a case not of protection but of alliance. It is rather hard to see what national, and not imperial, interest England could possibly have in the Near East; though it has never been hard to foretell that, till we achieve the bliss of messianic times, an alliance between a lion and a lamb can have disastrous consequences for the lamb.

Opposition from within the ranks of Zionists themselves never gained enough numerical strength to offset the official political line; moreover, any such opposition always showed itself hesitant in action, uneasy and weak in argument as though it were insecure in thought as well as in conscience. Such leftist groups as *Hashomer Hazair*—which have a radical program for world politics, so radical that, at the beginning of this war, they even opposed it on the ground of its being an "imperialist war"—express themselves only by abstention when it comes to vital questions of Palestine foreign policy. In other words, they sometimes, in spite of the undoubted personal integrity of most of their members, give the all too familiar impression of leftist groups of other countries, that hide under official protests their secret relief at having the majority parties do the dirty work for them.

This uneasiness of conscience, widespread among other leftist groups and explainable by the general bankruptcy of socialism, is among Zionists older than the general conditions and points to other and more special reasons. Since the days of Borochov, whose adherents can still be found in the small sectarian group of Poale-Zion, the leftist Zionists never thought of developing any answer of their own to the national question: they simply added official Zionism to their socialism. This addition hasn't made for an amalgam, since it claims socialism for domestic and nationalist Zionism for foreign affairs. The result is the existing situation between Jews and Arabs.

In fact, the uneasiness of conscience dates from the days of the surprising discovery that within the very domestic field, in the upbuilding of Palestine, there were factors present of foreign policy—by the existence of "a foreign people." Since that time Jewish Labor has fought against Arab Labor under the pretense of class-struggle against the Jewish planters, who certainly did employ Arabs for capitalist reasons. During this fight—which more than anything else, up to 1936, poisoned the Palestine atmosphere—no attention was paid to the economic conditions of the Arabs who, through the introduction of Jewish capital and labor and the industrialization of the country, found themselves changed overnight into potential proletarians, without much chance to find the corresponding work positions. Instead, Zionist Labor repeated the true but wholly inadequate arguments regarding the feudal character of Arab society, the progressive character of capitalism, and the general rise of the Palestine standard of life shared in by the Arabs. How blind people can become if their real or supposed interests are at stake is shown by the preposterous slogan they used: although Jewish Labor fought as much for its economic position as for its national aim, the cry was always for *"Avodah Ivrith"* ("Jewish Labor"); and one had to peer behind the scenes to detect that their chief menace was not simply Arab labor but, more actually, *"avodah zolah"* (cheap labor), represented, it is true, by the unorganized backward Arab worker.

In the resulting pickets of Jewish workers against Arab workers the leftist groups, most important among them *Hashomer Hazair*, did not directly participate; but they did little else: they remained abstentionists. The consequent local troubles, the latent internal war which has been going on in Palestine since the early 'twenties, interrupted by more and more frequent outbreaks, in turn strengthened the attitude of official Zionism. The less able was Palestine Jewry to find allies among the neighbors, the more the Zionists had to look upon Great Britain as the great protecting power.

Outstanding among the reasons why Labor and left-wing groups consented to this policy is again the general outlook of Zionism they had accepted. With an eye only for "the unique character" of Jewish history, insisting on the unparalleled nature of Jewish political conditions which were held to be unrelated to any other factors in European history and politics, the Zionists had ideologically placed the center of the Jewish people's existence outside the pale of European peoples and outside the destiny of the European continent.

Among all the misconceptions harbored by the Zionist movement because it had been influenced so strongly by antisemitism, this false notion of the non-European character of the Jews has had probably the most far-reaching and the worst consequences. Not only did the Zionists break the necessary solidarity of European peoples—necessary not only for the weak but for the strong as well; incredibly, they would even deprive the Jews of the only historical and cultural homestead they possibly can have; for Palestine together with the whole Mediterranean basin has always belonged to the European continent, geographically, historically, culturally, if not at all times politically. Thus the Zionists would deprive the Jewish people of its just share in the roots and development of what we generally call Western culture. Indeed, the attempts were numerous to interpret Jewish history as the history of an Asiatic people that had been driven by misfortune into a foreign comity of nations and culture wherein, regarded as an eternal stranger, it could never feel at home. (The absurdity of this kind of argumentation could be proved by citing the example of the Hungarian people alone: the Hungarians were of Asiatic origin, but had always been accepted as members of the European family since they were christianized.) Yet no serious attempt was ever made to integrate the Jewish people into the pattern of Asiatic politics, for that could only mean an alliance with the national-revolutionary peoples of Asia and participation in their struggle against imperialism. In the official Zionist conception, it seems, the Jewish people is uprooted from its European background and left somehow in the air, while Palestine is a place in the moon where such footless aloofness may be realized.

Only in its Zionist variant has such a crazy isolationism gone to the extreme of escape from Europe altogether. But its underlying national philosophy is far more general; indeed, it has been the ideology of most central European national movements. It is nothing else than the uncritical acceptance of German-inspired nationalism. This holds a nation to be an eternal organic body, the product of inevitable natural growth of inherent qualities; and it explains peoples, not in terms of political organizations, but in terms of biological superhuman personalities. In this conception European history is split up into the stories of unrelated organic bodies, and the grand French idea of the sovereignty of the people is perverted into the nationalist claims to autarchical existence. Zionism, closely tied up with that tradition of nationalist thinking, never bothered much about sovereignty of the people, which is the prerequisite for the formation of a nation, but wanted from the beginning that utopian nationalist independence.

To such an independence, it was believed, the Jewish nation could arrive under the protecting wings of any great power strong enough to shelter its growth. Paradoxical as it may sound, it was precisely because of this nationalist misconception of the inherent independence of a nation that the Zionists ended by making the Jewish national emancipation entirely dependent upon the material interests of another nation.

The actual result was a return of the new movement to the traditional methods of *shtadlonus*, which the Zionists once had so bitterly despised and violently denounced. Now Zionists too knew no better place politically than the lobbies of the powerful, and no sounder basis for agreements than their good services as agents of foreign interests. It was in the interest of foreign powers that the so-called Weizmann-Feisal agreement was "allowed to pass into oblivion until 1936. It also stands to reason that British apprehension and compromise was behind the tacit abandonment. . . ." (Perlmann, cited above.) When in 1922 new Arab-Jewish negotiations took place, the British Ambassador in Rome was kept fully informed, with the result that the British asked a postponement until "the Mandate has been conferred"; the Jewish representative, Asher Saphir, held "little doubt that members of a certain political school took the view that it was not in the interest of the peaceful administration of Near and Middle Eastern territories that the two Semitic races . . . should cooperate again on the platform of the recognition of Jewish rights in Palestine." (Perlmann) From then onward Arab hostility has grown year by year; and Jewish dependence on British protection has become so desperate a need that one may well call it a curious case of voluntary unconditional surrender.

VIII

This, then, is the tradition to fall back upon in times of crisis and emergency like ours—these the political weapons with which to handle the new political situation of tomorrow—these the "ideological categories" to utilize the new experiences of the Jewish people. Up to now no new approaches, no new insights, no reformulation of Zionism or the demands of the Jewish people have been visible. And it is therefore only in the light of this past, with consideration of this present, that we can gauge the chances of the future.

One new factor, however, should be noted, although so far it has not brought about anything like a fundamental change. It is the tremendously increased importance of American Jewry and American Zionism within the World Zionist Organization. Never before has any Jewry of any country produced such a large number of members of the Zionist Organization, together with an even larger number of sympathizers. Indeed, the election planks of both the Democratic and Republican parties last year, the declarations of both President Roosevelt and Governor Dewey at election time, would seem to prove that the great majority of voting Jews in America are regarded as pro-Palestinians and that, so far as there is "a Jewish vote," it is influenced by the program for Palestine to the same degree as the Polish vote is influenced by American foreign policy toward Poland and the Italian vote by events in Italy.

The Zionism of the American Jewish masses, however, differs remarkably from Zionism in the countries of the old continent. The men and women who are members of the Zionist Organization here would have been found in Europe in the so-called Pro-Palestine Committees. In those Committees were organized the people who held Palestine to be a good solution for oppressed and poor Jews, the best of all philanthropic enterprises, but who never considered Palestine to be a solution for their own problems, the very existence of which they were rather inclined to deny. At the same time, most of those who here in America call themselves non-Zionists also have a pronounced tendency towards this pro-Palestine view; at any rate, they take a much more positive and constructive attitude towards the Palestine enterprise, and for the rights of the Jewish people as a people, than did the "assimilants" in Europe.

The reason is to be found in the political structure of the United States, which is not a national state in the European sense of the word. A vital interest in Palestine as the homeland of the Jewish people is only natural, needs no excuses, in a country where so many national splinter groups show loyalty to their mother-countries. Indeed, a Jewish mother-country might thus rather tend to "normalize" the situation of the Jews in America and be a good argument against political anti-semitism.

However, this "normalization," inherent in pro-Palestinism, would instantly be thrown into reverse if Zionism in the official sense of the term were to get hold of American Jews. Then they would have to start a really national movement, at least preach if not actually practice *chaluziuth* (pioneering and self-realization); they would have to insist in principle on *aliyah* (immigration to Zion) for every Zionist. In fact, Weizmann has recently called on American Jews to come and settle in Palestine. The old question of double loyalty would emerge again, in a more violent form than in any other country, because of the multi-national structure of the United States. Just because the American body politic can afford a far greater tolerance for community life of the numerous nationalities which all together form and determine the life of the American nation, this country could never permit one of these "splinter groups" to start a movement to take them away from the American continent. The argument once heard in European Zionist discussions that, after all, the European countries could get along very well without their Jews, whereas the Jewish people needs to reclaim its best sons, can never be valid here. On the contrary, it would set a dangerous precedent; it could easily serve to upset the balance of a community of peoples who need to get along with each other within the limits of the American constitution and on the territory of the American continent. It is for this reason—because of the acute menace of any outright national movement for the constitution of a nationality-state—that the Zionist movement has been so bitterly opposed in Soviet Russia.

Probably on account of this unique position of theirs in the World Zionist Organization, their vague if not explicit consciousness of it, American Zionists have not attempted to change the general ideological outlook. That is held to be good enough for European Jews who, after all, are the principal ones concerned. Instead, American Zionists have simply taken the pragmatic stand of the Palestine maximalists, and hope—together with them, though for more complex reasons—that American interest and power will at least equal the English influence in the Near East. This would, of course, be the best way to solve all their problems. If Palestine Jewry could be charged with a share in the care-taking of American interests in that part of the world, the famous dictum of Justice Brandeis would indeed come true: you would have to be a Zionist in order to be a perfect American patriot. And why should this good fortune not come to pass? Has it not been for more than twenty-five years the foundation of British Zionism that one had to be a good Zionist to be a good British patriot—that by supporting the Balfour Declaration one supported the very Government whose loyal subject one was? We should be prepared to see a similar, though government-inspired, "Zionism" among Russian Jewry, if and when Soviet Russia takes up her old claims to Near Eastern politics. Should this happen, it will quickly enough become clear to what an extent Zionism has inherited the burden of assimilationist politics.

It must be admitted, however, that while the question of present and future power politics in the Near East are very much in the foreground today, the political realities and experiences of the Jewish people are very much in the background, and they have only too little connection with the main movements in the world. But the new experiences of Jewry are as numerous as the fundamental changes in the world are tremendous; and the chief question to be addressed to Zionism is how well it is prepared to take both into consideration and act accordingly.

IX

The most important new experience of the Jewish people is again concerned with antisemitism. It is a matter of record that the Zionist outlook for the future of emancipated Jewry has always been dark, and Zionists occasionally boast of their foresight. Compared with the earthquake that has shaken the world in our time, those predictions read like prophecies of a storm in a teacup. The fierce outburst of popular hatred which Zionism predicted, and which fitted well with its general distrust of the peoples and over confidence in Governments, did not take place. Rather, in a number of countries it was replaced by concerted Government action, which proved infinitely more detrimental than any popular outburst of Jew-hatred had ever been.

The point is that antisemitism, in Europe at least, has been discovered as the best political, and not merely demagogic, weapon of imperialism. Wherever politics are centered around the race concept, the Jews will be in the center of hostility. It would lead us too far here to ask the reasons for this entirely new state of affairs. But one thing is certain. Inasmuch as imperialism—in sharp contrast to nationalism—does not think in terms of limited territories but, as the saying goes, "in continents," Jews will be secure from this new type of antisemitism nowhere in the world, and certainly not in Palestine, one of the center-spots of imperialist interests. The question to be asked of Zionists today would therefore be what political stand they propose to take in view of a hostility that is far less concerned with dispersed Jewish individuals than with the people as a whole, no matter where it happens to live.

Another question to be asked of Zionists concerns national organization. We have been seeing the catastrophic decline of the national-state system in our time. The new feeling, that has grown among European peoples since the first war, is that the national state is neither capable of protecting the existence of the nation nor able to guarantee the sovereignty of the people. The national border lines, once the very symbol of security against invasion as well as against an unwelcome overflow of foreigners, have proved to be no longer of any real avail. And while the old western nations were threatened either by lack of manpower and the resulting lag in industrialization, or by an influx of foreigners they could not assimilate, the eastern countries gave the best possible examples that the national state cannot exist with a mixed population.

For Jews, however, there is only too little reason for rejoicing in the decline of the national state and of nationalism. We cannot foretell the next steps of human history, but the alternatives seem to be clear. The resurgent problem of how to organize politically will be solved by adopting either the form of empires or the form of federations. The latter would give the Jewish people, together with other small peoples, a reasonably fair chance for survival. The former may not be possible without arousing imperialist passions as a substitute for outdated nationalism, once the motor to set men into action. Heaven help us if that comes to pass.

X

It is within this general framework of realities and possibilities that the Zionists propose to solve the Jewish question by means of a national state. Yet the essential characteristic of a national state, sovereignty, is not even hoped for. Suppose the Zionists had succeeded twenty-five years ago in securing Palestine as a Jewish Commonwealth: what would have happened? We should have seen the Arabs turn against the Jews as the Slovaks turned against the Czechs in Czechoslovakia, and the Croats against the Serbs in Yugoslavia. And though not a single Arab were left in Palestine, the lack of real sovereignty amid Arab States, or peoples hostile to the Jewish State, would have had exactly the same result.

In other words, the slogan of a Jewish Commonwealth or a Jewish State actually means that Jews propose to establish themselves from the very beginning as a "sphere of interest" under the delusion of nationhood. Either a bi-national Palestine State or a Jewish Commonwealth might conceivably have been the outcome of a working agreement with Arabs and other Mediterranean peoples. But to think that by putting the cart before the horse one can solve genuine conflicts between peoples is a fantastic assumption. The erection of a Jewish State within an imperial sphere of interest may look like a very nice solution to some Zionists, though to others as something desperate but unavoidable. In the long run, there is hardly any course imaginable that would be more dangerous, more in the style of an adventure. It is, indeed, very bad luck for a small people to be placed without any fault of its own in the territory of a "sphere of interest," though one can hardly see where else it could be placed in the economically and politically shrunken world of today. But only folly could dictate a policy which trusts a distant imperial power for protection, while alienating the good will of neighbors. What then, one is prompted to ask, will be the future policy of Zionism with respect to big powers, and what program have Zionists to offer for a solution of the Arab-Jewish conflict?

In this connection there is a further question. The most optimistic estimates hope for annual postwar emigration from Europe to Palestine of about 100,000 Jews, during at least ten years. Assuming this can be brought about, what is to happen to those who are not in the first groups of immigrants? What status are they to have in Europe? What kind of social, economic, political life will they lead? Zionists apparently hope for restoration of the *status quo ante*. In that case, will the restored Jews be willing to go to Palestine after, say, a period of five years which, even under the darkest circumstances, would mean a period of normalization? For if European Jews are not at once claimed as the prospective citizens of the new Jewish Commonwealth (to say nothing of the question of their admission), there will be the additional trouble of claiming majority rights in a country where Jews are very clearly a minority. Such a claim, on the other hand, if granted, would of course exclude a restoration of the *status quo* in Europe, and thus possibly create a not entirely harmless precedent. Even the most superficial restoration of the *status quo* in Europe would still make it well-nigh impossible to cloud the double-loyalty issue with the same meaningless generalities as in the good old days of the past.

The last question, then, which Zionism has so far succeeded in not answering, solemnly protesting that an answer would be "beneath its dignity," is this old problem of the relationship between the proposed new State and the Diaspora. And this problem is by no means restricted to European Jewries.

It is a matter of record, ideologies notwithstanding, that up to now the *Yishuv* has been not only an asylum for persecuted Jews from some Diaspora countries. It is also a community which has had to be supported by other Diaspora Jewries. Without the power and resources of American Jewry, above all, the catastrophe in Europe would have been a deadly blow to Palestine Jewry, politically as well as economically. If a Jewish Commonwealth will be obtained in the near future—with or without partition—it will be due to the political influence of American Jews. This would not need to affect their status of American citizenship if their "homeland," or "mother country," were a politically autonomous entity in a normal sense, or if their help were likely to be only temporary. But if the Jewish Commonwealth is proclaimed against the will of the Arabs and without the support of the Mediterranean peoples, not only financial help but political support will be necessary for a long time to come. And that may turn out to be very troublesome indeed for Jews in this country, who after all have no power to direct the political destinies of the Near East. It may eventually be far more of a responsibility than today they imagine or tomorrow can make good.

These are some of the questions Zionism will face in the very near future. To answer them sincerely, with political sense and responsibility, Zionism will have to reconsider its whole obsolete set of doctrines. It will not be easy either to save the Jews or to save Palestine in the twentieth century; that it can be done with categories and methods of the nineteenth century seems at the very most highly improbable. If Zionists persevere in retaining their sectarian ideology and continue with their short-sighted "realism," they will have forfeited even the small chances that small peoples still have in this none too beautiful world of ours.

The Jewish State:
Fifty Years After
Where Have Herzl's Politics Led?

(MAY 1946)

Rereading Herzl's The Jewish State today is a peculiar experience. One becomes aware that those things in it that Herzl's own contemporaries would have called utopian now actually determine the ideology and policies of the Zionist movement; while those of Herzl's practical proposals for the building of a Jewish homeland which must have appeared quite realistic fifty years ago have had no influence whatsoever.

The last is all the more surprising because these practical proposals are far from antiquated even for our own age. Herzl proposed a "Jewish Company" that would build a state with "Relief by Labor"—that is, by paying a "good-for-nothing beggar" charity rates for forced full-time work—and by the "truck system" consisting of labor gangs "drafted from place to place like a body of troops" and paid in goods instead of wages. Herzl was also determined to suppress all "opposition" in case of lack of gratitude on the part of people to whom the land would be given. All this sounds only too familiar. And it is altogether to the honor of the Jewish people that nobody—as far as I know—ever discussed these "realistic" proposals seriously, and that Palestinian reality has turned out to be almost the opposite of what Herzl dreamt.

The above features of Herzl's program, though happily forgotten in the present political state of affairs in Palestine, are nevertheless significant. For all their innocence, they show to which category of politician in the framework of European history Herzl belonged. When he wrote The Jewish State Herzl was deeply convinced that he was under some sort of higher inspiration, yet at the same time he was earnestly afraid of making a fool of himself. This extreme self-esteem mixed with self-doubt is not rare phenomenon; it is usually the sign of the "crackpot." And in a sense this Viennese whose style, manner and ideals hardly differed from those of his more obscure fellow-journalists was indeed a crackpot.

But even in Herzl's time—the time of the Dreyfus Affair, when the crackpots were just embarking on their political careers in many movements functioning outside the parliaments and the regular parties—even then they were already in closer touch with the subterranean currents of history and the deep desires of the folk than were all the sane leaders of affairs with their balanced outlooks and utterly uncomprehending mentalties. The crackpots were already beginning to be prominent everywhere—the anti-Semites Stoecker and Ahlwardt in Germany, Schoenerer and Lueger in Austria, and Drumont and Deroulède in France.

Herzl wrote *The Jewish State* under the direct and violent impact of these new political forces. And he was among the first to estimate correctly their chances of ultimate success. Even more important, however, than the correctness of his forecast was the fact that he was not altogether out of sympathy with the new movements. When he said, "I believe that I understand anti-Semitism," he meant that he not only understood historical causes and political constellations, but also that he understood—and to a certain extent, correctly—the man who hated Jews. It is true, his frequent appeals to "honest anti-Semites" to "subscribe small amounts" to the national fund for the establishment of a Jewish state were not very realistic; and he was equally unrealistic when he invited them: "whilst preserving their independence [to] combine with our officials in controlling the transfer of our estates" from the Diaspora to the Jewish homeland; and he frequently asserted, in all innocence, that anti-Semites would be the Jews' best friends and anti-Semitic governments their best allies. But this faith in anti-Semites expressed very eloquently and even touchingly how close his own state of mind was to that of his hostile environment and how intimately he did belong to the "alien" world.

With the demagogic politicians of his own and more recent times, Herzl shared both a contempt for the masses and a very real affinity with them. And like these same politicians, he was more an incarnation than a representative of the strata of

society to which he belonged. He did more than "love" or
simply speak for the new and ever increasing class of Jewish
"intellects that we produce so super-abundantly and that are
persecuted everywhere"; he did more than merely discern in
these intellectuals the real *luftmenschen* of Western Jewry—
that is, Jews who, though economically secure, had no place in
either Jewish or Gentile society and whose personal problems
could be solved only by a reorientation of the Jewish people as
a whole. Herzl actually incarnated these Jewish intellectuals in
himself in the sense that everything he said or did was exactly
what they would have, had they shown an equal amount of
moral courage in revealing their inmost secret thoughts.

Another trait Herzl shared with the leaders of the new anti-
Semitic movements by whose hostility he was so deeply
impressed was the furious will to action at any price—action,
however, that was to be conducted according to certain
supposedly immutable and inevitable laws and inspired and
supported by invincible natural forces. Herzl's conviction that
he was in alliance with history and nature themselves saved him
from the suspicion that he himself might have been insane.
Anti-Semitism was an overwhelming force and the Jews would
have either to make use of it or be swallowed up by it. In his
own words, anti-Semitism was the "propelling force" responsible for all Jewish suffering since the destruction of the Temple
and it would continue to' make the Jews suffer until they
learned how to use it for their own advantage. In expert hands
this "propelling force" would prove the most salutary factor in
Jewish life: it would be used the same way that boiling water is
used to produce steam power.

This mere will to action was something so startlingly new,
so utterly revolutionary in Jewish life, that it spread with the
speed of wildfire. Herzl's lasting greatness lay in his very desire
to do something about the Jewish question, his desire to act
and to solve the problem in political terms.

During the twenty centuries of their Diaspora the Jews have
made only two attempts to change their condition by direct
political action. The first was the Sabbatai Zevi movement, the
mystic-political movement for the salvation of Jewry which
terminated the Jewish Middle Ages and brought about a
catastrophe whose consequences determined Jewish attitudes

and basic convictions for over two centuries thereafter. In preparing as they did to follow Sabbatai Zevi, the self-appointed "Messiah," back to Palestine in the mid–1600s, the Jews assumed that their ultimate hope of a Messianic millennium was about to be realized. Until Sabbatai Zevi's time they had been able to conduct their communal affairs by means of a politics that existed in the realm of imagination alone—the memory of a far-off past and the hope of a far-off future. With the Sabbatai Zevi movement these centuries-old memories and hopes culminated in a single exalted moment. Its catastrophical aftermath brought to be a close—probably forever—the period in which religion alone could provide the Jews with a firm framework within which to satisfy their political, spiritual and everyday needs. The attendant disillusionment was lasting in so far as from then on their religion no longer afforded the Jews an adequate means of evaluating and dealing with contemporary events, political or otherwise. Whether a Jew was pious or not, whether he kept the Law or lived outside its fence, he was henceforth to judge secular events on a secular basis and make secular decisions in secular terms.

Jewish secularization culminated at last in a second attempt to dissolve the Diaspora. This was the rise of the Zionist movement.

The mere fact that a catastrophe had thrown the Jews from the two extremes of the past and the future into the middle ground of the present does not signify that they had now become "realistic." To be confronted by reality does not automatically produce an understanding of reality or make one feel at home in it. On the contrary, the process of secularization made Jews even less "realistic"—that is, less capable than ever before of facing and understanding the real situation. In losing their faith in a divine beginning and ultimate culmination of history, the Jews lost their guide through the wilderness of bare facts; for when man is robbed of all means of interpreting events he is left with no sense whatsoever of reality. The present that confronted the Jews after the Sabbatai Zevi debacle was the turmoil of a world whose course no longer made sense and in which, as a result, the Jews could no longer find a place.

The need for a guide or key to history was felt by all Jews alike. But by the 19th century it was a need that was not at all specific to the Jews alone. In this context Zionism can be included among the many "isms" of that period, each of which claimed to explain reality and predict the future in terms of irresistible laws and forces. Yet the case of the Jews was and still remains different. What they needed was not only a guide to reality, but reality itself; not simply a key to history, but the experience itself of history.

As I have just indicated, this need of reality had existed since the collapse of the Sabbatai Zevi movement and the disappearance of Messianic hope as a lively factor in the consciousness of the Jewish masses. But it became an effective force only at the end of the 19th century, mainly because of two entirely separate factors whose coincidence produced Zionism and formed Herzl's ideology.

The first of these factors had little to do, essentially, with Jewish history. It so happened that in the 80's of the last century anti-Semitism sprang up as a political force simultaneously in Russia, Germany, Austria and France. The pogroms of 1881 in Russia set in motion that huge migratory movement from East to West which remained the most characteristic single feature of modern Jewish history until 1933. Moreover, the emergence of political anti-Semitism at exactly the same moment in both Central and Western Europe and the support, if not leadership, given it by sizable sections of the European intelligentsia refuted beyond doubt the traditional liberal contention that Jew-hatred was only a remnant of the so-called Dark Ages.

But even more important for the political history of the Jewish people was the fact that the Westward migration—despite the objections to the *"Ostjuden"* so loudly voiced by the emancipated Jews of the West—brought together the two main sections of Jewry, laid the foundation for a new feeling of solidarity—at least among the moral elite—and taught both Eastern and Western Jews to see their situation in identical terms. The Russian Jew who came to Germany in flight from persecution discovered that enlightenment had not extinguished violent Jew-hatred, and the German Jew who saw the homelessness of his Eastern brother began to view his own situation in a different light.

The second factor responsible for the rise of Zionism was entirely Jewish—it was the emergence of a class entirely new to

Jewish society, the intellectuals, of whom Herzl became the main spokesman and whom he himself termed the class of "average *(durchschnittliche)* intellects." These intellectuals resembled their brethren in the more traditional Jewish occupations in so far as they, too, were entirely de-Judaized in respect to culture and religion. What distinguished them was that they no longer lived in a cultural vacuum; they had actually become "assimilated": they were not only de-Judaized, they were also Westernized. This, however, did not make for their social adjustment. Although Gentile society did not receive them on equal terms, they had no place in Jewish society either, because they did not fit into its atmosphere of business and family connections.

The psychological result of their situation was to make these Jewish intellectuals the first Jews in history capable of understanding anti-Semitism on its own political terms, and even to make them susceptible to the deeper and more basic political attitudes of which anti-Semitism was but one expression among others.

The two classic pamphlets of Zionist literature, Pinsker's *Auto-emancipation* and Herzl's *The Jewish State,* were written by members of this new Jewish class. For the first time Jews saw themselves as a people through the eyes of the nations: "To the living the Jew is a corpse, to the native a foreigner, to the homesteader a vagrant, to the proprietor a beggar, to the poor an exploiter and millionaire, to the patriot a man without a country, to all a hated rival"—this was the characteristically precise and sober way Pinsker put it. Both Herzl and Pinsker identified the Jewish question in all its aspects and connections with the fact of anti-Semitism, which both conceived of as the natural reaction of all peoples, always and everywhere, to the very existence of Jews. As Pinsker put it, and as both believed, the Jewish question could be solved only by "finding a means of reintegrating this exclusive element in the family of nations so that the basis of the Jewish question would be permanently removed."

What still is Zionism's advantage over assimilationism is that it placed the whole question on a political level from the very beginning and asked for this "readjustment" in political terms. The assimilationists sought readjustment no less desper-

ately, but spent their energies in founding innumerable voca-
tional-training societies for Jews without, however, having the
least power to force Jews to change their occupations. The
intellectual followers of assimilationism carefully avoided political issues and invented the "salt of the earth" theory, making
it quite clear that they would prefer the crudest secularization
of the Jewish religious concept of chosenness to any radical re-
definition of the Jewish position in the world of nations.

In other words, the great advantage of the Zionists'
approach lay in the fact that their will to convert the Jews into
a "nation like all other nations" saved them from falling into
that Jewish brand of chauvinism automatically produced by
secularization, which somehow persuades the average de-
Judaized Jew that, although he no longer believes in a God
who chooses or rejects, he is still a superior being simply
because he happened to be born a Jew—the salt of the earth—
or the motor of history.

The Zionist will to action, to come to grips with reality,
embodied a second advantage—this time over the internationalist and revolutionary approach to the Jewish question.
This approach, no less than assimilationist chauvinism, was the
consequence of the secularization of religious attitudes. But it
was not initiated by average Jews, rather by an élite. Having
lost their hope of a Messianic millennium that would bring
about the final reconciliation of all peoples, these Jews
transferred their hopes to the progressive forces of history
which would solve the Jewish question automatically, along
with all other injustices. Revolutions in the social systems of
other peoples would create a mankind without classes and
nations; the Jews together with their problems would be
dissolved in this new mankind—at the end of days somehow.
What happened in the meantime did not count so much; Jews
would have to suffer as a matter of course along with all other
persecuted classes and peoples.

The Zionists' fight against this spurious selflessness—which
could only arouse suspicion as to the ultimate aims and motives
of a policy that expected one's own people to behave like saints
and to make the chief sacrifices—has been of great importance
because it tried to teach the Jews to solve their problems by
their own efforts, not by those of others.

But this struggle hardly enters the picture of Herzl's

Zionism. He had a blind hatred of all revolutionary movements as such and an equally blind faith in the goodness and stability of the society of his times. The aspect of Zionism here in question received its best expression in the writings of the great French Jewish writer, Bernard Lazare. Lazare wanted to be a revolutionary among his own people, not among others, and could find no place in Herzl's essentially reactionary movement.

Yet in considering Herzl's movement as a whole and in assessing his definite merits within the given historical situation, it is necessary to say that Zionism opposed a comparatively sound nationalism to the hidden chauvinism of assimilationism and a relatively sound realism to the obvious utopianism of Jewish radicals.

However, the more ideological and utopian elements expressed in *The Jewish State* had greater influence in the long run on the formulations and practice of Zionism than did the undeniable assets set forth above. Herzl's will to reality at any price rested on a view that held reality to be an unchanging and unchangeable structure, always identical with itself. In this reality he saw little else but eternally established nation-states arrayed compactly against the Jews on one side, and on the other side the Jews themselves, in dispersion and eternally persecuted. Nothing else mattered: differences in class structure, differences between political parties or movements, between various countries or various periods of history did not exist for Herzl. All that did exist were unchanging bodies of people viewed as biological organisms mysteriously endowed with eternal life; these bodies breathed an unchanging hostility toward the Jews that was ready to take the form of pogroms or persecution at any moment. Any segment of reality that could not be defined by anti-Semitism was not taken into account and any group that could not be definitely classed as anti-Semitic was not taken seriously as a political force.

Jewish political action meant for Herzl finding a place within the unchanging structure of this reality, a place where Jews would be safe from hatred and eventual persecution. A people without a country would have to escape to a country without a people; there the Jews, unhampered by relations with other nations, would be able to develop their own isolated organism.

Herzl thought in terms of nationalism inspired from German sources—as opposed to the French variety, which could never quite repudiate its original relationship to the political ideas of the French Revolution. He did not realize that the country he dreamt of did not exist, that there was no place on earth where a people could live like the organic national body he had in mind and that the real historical development of a nation does not take place inside the closed walls of a biological entity. And even if there had been a country without a people and even if questions of foreign policy had not arisen in Palestine itself, Herzl's brand of political philosophy would still have given rise to serious difficulties in the relations of the new Jewish state with other nations.

Even more unrealistic but just as influential was Herzl's belief that the establishment of a Jewish state would automatically wipe out anti-Semitism. This belief was based on his assumption of the essential honesty and sincerity of the anti-Semites, in whom he saw nothing but nationalists pure and simple. This point of view may have been appropriate before the end of the 19th century, when anti-Semitism did actually derive more or less from the feeling that Jews were strangers within any given homogeneous society. But by Herzl's own time anti-Semitism had become transformed into a political weapon of a new kind and was supported by the new sect of racists whose loyalties and hatreds did not stop at national boundaries.

The fault in Herzl's approach to anti-Semitism lay in the fact that the anti-Semites he had in view were hardly extant anymore—or if they were, they no longer determined anti-Semitic politics. The real anti-Semites had become dishonest and wanted to preserve the availability of the Jews as a scapegoat in case of domestic difficulties; or else, if they were "honest," they wanted to exterminate the Jews wherever they happened to live. There was no escape from either variety of anti-Semite into a promised land "whose upbuilding"—in Weizmann's words—"would be the answer to anti-Semitism."

The building up of Palestine is indeed a great accomplishment and could be made an important and even decisive argument for Jewish claims in Palestine—at least a better and more convincing one than the current pleas that argue our desperate situation in Europe and the justifiability, therefore, of the "lesser injustice" that would be done to the Arabs. But the upbuilding of Palestine has little to do with answering the anti-Semites; at most it has "answered" the secret self-hatred and lack of self-confidence on the part of those Jews who have themselves consciously or unconsciously succumbed to some parts of anti-Semitic propaganda.

The third thesis of Herzl's political philosophy was the Jewish state. Though for Herzl himself this was certainly the most daring and attractive facet of the whole, the demand for a state seemed neither doctrinaire nor utopian at the time his book was first published. In Herzl's view reality could hardly express itself in any other form than that of the nation-state. In his period, indeed, the claim for national self-determination of peoples was almost self-evident justice as far as the oppressed peoples of Europe were concerned, and so there was nothing absurd or wrong in a demand made by Jews for the same kind of emancipation and freedom. And that the whole structure of sovereign national states, great and small, would crumble within another fifty years under imperialist expansion and in the face of a new power situation, was more than Herzl could have foreseen. His demand for a state has been made utopian only by more recent Zionist policy—which did not ask for a state at a time when it might have been granted by everybody, but did ask for one only when the whole concept of national sovereignty had become a mockery.

Justified as Herzl's demand for a Jewish state may have been in his own time, his way of advancing it showed the same unrealistic touch as elsewhere. The opportunism with which he carried on his negotiations to this end stemmed from a political concept that saw the destinies of the Jews as completely without connection with the destinies of other nations, and saw Jewish demands as unrelated to all other events and trends. Although the demand for a state could be understood in his period only in terms of national self-determination, Herzl was very careful not to tie the claims for Jewish liberation to the claims of other peoples. He was even ready to profit by the minority troubles of the Turkish empire and he offered the rulers of that empire Jewish aid in coping with them. In this instance Herzl's was the classical example of a policy hardboiled enough to seem "realistic," but in reality completely utopian because it failed to take into account either one's own or the other party's relative strength.

The constant miscalculations that were to become so characteristic of Zionist policy are not accidental. The universality with which Herzl applied his concept of anti-Semitism to all non-Jewish peoples made it impossible from the very beginning for the Zionists to seek truly loyal allies. His notion of reality as an eternal, unchanging hostile structure—all *goyim* everlastingly against all Jews—made the identification of hardboiledness with realism plausible because it rendered any empirical analysis of actual political factors seemingly superfluous. All one had to do was use the "propelling force of anti-Semitism," which, like "the wave of the future," would bring the Jews into the promised land.

Today reality has become a nightmare. Looked at through the eyes of Herzl, who from the outside sought a place inside reality into which the Jews could fit and where at the same time they could isolate themselves from it—looked at in this way, reality is horrible beyond the scope of the human imagination and hopeless beyond the strength of human despair. Only when we come to feel ourselves part and parcel of a world in which we, like everybody else, are engaged in a struggle against great and sometimes overwhelming odds, and yet with a chance of victory, however small, and with allies, however few—only when we recognize the human background against which recent events have taken place, knowing that what was done was done by men and therefore can and must be prevented by men—only then will we be able to rid the world of its nightmarish quality. That quality taken in itself and viewed from the outside—by people who consider themselves as cut off from the nightmarish world in principle and who are thus ready to accept the course of that world "realistically"— can inhibit all action and exclude us altogether from the human community.

Herzl's picture of the Jewish people as surrounded and forced together by a world of enemies has in our day conquered the Zionist movement and become the common sentiment of the Jewish masses. Our failure to be surprised at this development does not make Herzl's picture any truer—it only makes it more dangerous. If we actually are faced with open or concealed enemies on every side, if the whole world is ultimately against us, then we are lost.

For Herzl's way out has been closed—his hope in an escape from the world and his naive faith in appeasement through escape have been rendered illusory. *Altneuland* is no longer a dream. It has become a very real place where Jews live together with Arabs and it has also become a central junction of world communications. Whatever else it may be, Palestine is not a place where Jews can live in isolation, nor is it a promised land where they would be safe from anti-Semitism. The simple truth is that Jews will have to fight anti-Semitism everywhere or else be exterminated everywhere. Though Zionists no longer regard anti-Semitism as an ally, they do, however, seem to be more convinced than ever that struggle against it is hopeless—if only because we would have to fight the whole world.

The danger of the present situation—in which Herzl's Zionism is accepted as a matter of course as the determinant of Zionist policy—lies in the semblance to common sense that the recent experiences of the Jews in Europe have lent Herzl's philosophy. Beyond doubt, the center of Jewish politics today is constituted by the remnants of European Jewry now in the camps of Germany. Not only is all our political activity concentrated upon them—even more important is the fact that our whole political outlook springs of necessity from their experiences, from our solidarity with them.

Every one of these surviving Jews is the last survivor of a family, every one of them was saved only by a miracle, every one of them has had the basic experience of witnessing and feeling the complete breakdown of international solidarity. Among all those who were persecuted, only Jews were singled out for certain death. What the Nazis or the Germans did was not decisive in this connection; what was decisive was the experiences of the Jews with the majority of all the other nationalities and even with the political prisoners in the concentration camps. The question is not whether the non-Jewish anti-fascists could have done more than they actually did for their Jewish comrades—the essential point is that only the Jews were sent inevitably to the gas chambers; and this was enough to draw a line between them that, perhaps, no amount of good will could have erased. For the Jews who experienced this, all Gentiles became alike. This is what lies at the bottom of their present strong desire to go to Palestine. It is not that they imagine they will be safe there—it is only that they want to live among Jews alone, come what may.

Another experience—also of great importance to the future of Jewish politics—was gained from the realization, not that six million Jews had been killed, but that they had been driven to death helplessly, like cattle. There are stories telling how Jews tried to obviate the indignity of this death by their attitude and bearing as they were marched to the gas chambers—they sang or they made defiant gestures indicating that they did not accept their fate as the last word upon them.

What the survivors now want above all else is the right to die with dignity—in case of attack, with weapons in their hands. Gone, probably forever, is that chief concern of the Jewish people for centuries: survival at any price. Instead, we find something essentially new among Jews, the desire for dignity at any price.

As great an asset as this new development would be to an essentially sane Jewish political movement, it nevertheless constitutes something of a danger within the present framework of Zionist attitudes. Herzl's doctrine, deprived as it now is of its original confidence in the helpful nature of anti-Semitism, can only encourage suicidal gestures for whose ends the natural heroism of people who have become accustomed to death can be easily exploited. Some of the Zionist leaders pretend to believe that the Jews can maintain themselves in Palestine against the whole world and that they themselves can persevere in claiming everything or nothing against everybody and everything. However, behind this spurious optimism lurks a despair of everything and a genuine readiness for suicide that can become extremely dangerous should they grow to be the mood and atmosphere of Palestinian politics.

There is nothing in Herzlian Zionism that could act as a check on this; on the contrary, the utopian and ideological elements with which he injected the new Jewish will to political action are only too likely to lead the Jews out of reality once more—and out of the sphere of political action. I do not know—nor do I even want to know—what would happen to Jews all over the world and to Jewish history in the future should we meet with a catastrophe in Palestine. But the parallels with the Sabbatai Zevi episode have become terribly close.

To Save The Jewish Homeland

There Is Still Time

(MAY 1948)

When, on November 29, 1947, the partition of Palestine and
the establishment of a Jewish state were accepted by the
United Nations, it was assumed that no outside force would be
necessary to implement this decision.

It took the Arabs less than two months to destroy this
illusion and it took the United States less than three months to
reverse its stand on partition, withdraw its support in the
United Nations, and propose a trusteeship for Palestine. Of all
the member states of the United Nations, only Soviet Russia
and her satellites made it unequivocally clear that they still
favored partition and the immediate proclamation of a Jewish
state.

Trusteeship was at once rejected by both the Jewish Agency
and the Arab Higher Committee. The Jews claimed the moral
right to adhere to the original United Nations decision; the
Arabs claimed an equally moral right to adhere to the League
of Nations principle of self-determination, according to which
Palestine would be ruled by its present Arab majority and the
Jews be granted minority rights. The Jewish Agency, on its part,
announced the proclamation of a Jewish state for May 16,
regardless of any United Nations decision. It remains a fact,
meanwhile, that trusteeship, like partition, would have to be
enforced by an outside power.

A last-minute appeal for a truce, made to both parties
under the auspices of the United States, broke down in two
days. Upon this appeal had rested the last chance of avoiding
foreign intervention, at least temporarily. As matters stand at

this moment, not a single possible solution or proposition affecting the Palestinian conflict is in sight that could be realized without enforcement by external authority.

The past few weeks of guerrilla warfare should have shown both Arabs and Jews how costly and destructive the war upon which they have embarked promises to be. In recent days, the Jews have won a few initial successes that prove their relative superiority over present Arab forces in Palestine. The Arabs, however, instead of concluding at least local truce agreements, have decided to evacuate whole cities and towns rather than stay in Jewish-dominated territory. This behavior declares more effectively than all proclamations the Arab refusal of any compromise; it is obvious that they have decided to expend in time and numbers whatever it may take to win a decisive victory. The Jews, on the other hand, living on a small island in an Arab sea, might well be expected to jump at the chance to exploit their present advantage by offering a negotiated peace. Their military situation is such that time and numbers necessarily work against them. If one takes into account the objective vital interests of the Arab and the Jewish peoples, especially in terms of the present situation and future well-being of the Near East—where a full-fledged war will inevitably invite all kinds of international interventions—the present desire of both peoples to fight it out at any price is nothing less than sheer irrationality.

One of the reasons for this unnatural and, as far as the Jewish people are concerned, tragic development is a decisive change in Jewish public opinion that has accompanied the confusing political decisions of the great powers.

The fact is that Zionism has won its most significant victory among the Jewish people at the very moment when its achievements in Palestine are in gravest danger. This may not seem extraordinary to those who have always believed that the building of a Jewish homeland was the most important—perhaps the only real—achievement of Jews in our century, and that ultimately no individual who wanted to stay a Jew could remain aloof from events in Palestine. Nevertheless, Zionism had in actuality always been a partisan and controversial issue; the Jewish Agency, though claiming to speak for the Jewish people as a whole, was still well aware that it represented only a fraction of them. This situation has changed overnight. With the exception of a few anti-Zionist diehards, whom nobody can take very seriously, there is now no organization and almost no individual Jew that doesn't privately or publicly support partition and the establishment of a Jewish state.

Jewish left-wing intellectuals who a relatively short time ago still looked down upon Zionism as an ideology for the feeble-minded, and viewed the building of a Jewish homeland as a hopeless enterprise that they, in their great wisdom, had rejected before it was ever started; Jewish businessmen whose interest in Jewish politics had always been determined by the all-important question of how to keep Jews out of newspaper headlines; Jewish philanthropists who had resented Palestine as a terribly expensive charity, draining off funds from other "more worthy" purposes; the readers of the Yiddish press, who for decades had been sincerely, if naively, convinced that America was the promised land—all these, from the Bronx to Park Avenue down to Greenwich Village and over to Brooklyn are united today in the firm conviction that a Jewish state is needed, that America has betrayed the Jewish people, that the reign of terror by the Irgun and the Stern groups is more or less justified, and that Rabbi Silver, David Ben Gurion, and Moshe Shertok are the real, if somewhat too moderate, statesmen of the Jewish people.

Something very similar to this growing unanimity among American Jews has arisen in Palestine itself. Just as Zionism had been a partisan issue among American Jews, so the Arab question and the state issue had been controversial issues within the Zionist movement and in Palestine. Political opinion was sharply divided there between the chauvinism of the Revisionists, the middle-of-the-road nationalism of the majority party, and the vehemently anti-nationalist, anti-state sentiments of a large part of the kibbutz movement, particularly the Hashomer Hatzair. Very little is now left of these differences of opinion.

The Hashomer Hatzair has formed one party with the Ahdut Avodah, sacrificing its age-old bi-national program to the "accomplished fact" of the United Nations decision—a body, by the way, for which they never had too much respect when it was still called the League of Nations. The small Aliya Hadasha, mostly composed of recent immigrants from Central

Europe, still retains some of its old moderation and its sympathies for England, and it would certainly prefer Weizmann to Ben Gurion—but since Weizmann and most of its members have always been committed to partition, and, like everybody else, to the Biltmore Program, this opposition does not amount to much more than a difference over personalities.

The general mood of the country, moreover, has been such that terrorism and the growth of totalitarian methods are silently tolerated and secretly applauded; and the general, underlying public opinion with which anybody desiring to appeal to the Yishuv has to reckon shows no notable divisions at all.

Even more surprising than the growing unanimity of opinion among Palestinian Jews on one hand and American Jews on the other, is the fact that they are essentially in agreement on the following more or less roughly stated propositions: the moment has now come to get everything or nothing, victory or death; Arab and Jewish claims are irreconcilable and only a military decision can settle the issue; the Arabs—all Arabs—are our enemies and we accept this fact; only outmoded liberals believe in compromises, only philistines believe in justice, and only *shlemiels* prefer truth and negotiation to propaganda and machine guns; Jewish experience in the last decades—or over the last centuries, or over the last two thousand years—has finally awakened us and taught us to look out for ourselves; this alone is reality, everything else is stupid sentimentality; everybody is against us, Great Britain is anti-Semitic, the United States is imperialist—but Russia might be our ally for a certain period because her interests happen to coincide with ours; yet in the final analysis we count upon nobody except ourselves; in sum—we are ready to go down fighting, and we will consider anybody who stands in our way a traitor and anything done to hinder us a stab in the back.

It would be frivolous to deny the intimate connection between this mood on the part of Jews everywhere and the recent European catastrophe, with the subsequent fantastic injustice and callousness toward the surviving remnant that were thereby so ruthlessly transformed into displaced persons. The result has been an amazing and rapid change in what we call national character. After two thousand years of "Galut mentality," the Jewish people have suddenly ceased to believe in survival as an ultimate good in itself and have gone over in a few years to the opposite extreme. Now Jews believe in fighting at any price and feel that "going down" is a sensible method of politics.

Unanimity of opinion is a very ominous phenomenon, and one characteristic of our modern mass age. It destroys social and personal life, which is based on the fact that we are different by nature and by conviction. To hold different opinions and to be aware that other people think differently on the same issue shields us from that god-like certainty which stops all discussion and reduces social relationships to those of an ant heap. A unanimous public opinion tends to eliminate bodily those who differ, for mass unanimity is not the result of agreement, but an expression of fanaticism and hysteria. In contrast to agreement, unanimity does not stop at certain well-defined objects, but spreads like an infection into every related issue.

Thus Jewish unanimity on the Palestine issue has already prompted a somewhat vague and inarticulate shift of Jewish public opinion in the direction of pro-Soviet sympathies, a shift that even affects people who for more than twenty-five years have consistently denounced Bolshevik policies. Even more significant than such changes of mood and general attitude have been the attempts to establish an anti-Western and pro-Soviet orientation inside the Zionist movement. The resignation of Moshe Sneh, the organizer of illegal immigration and formerly prominent in the Haganah, is important in this repsect; and occasional utterances by almost every one of the Palestinian delegates in America point even more strongly in this direction. The program, finally, of the new left-wing Palestinian party formed by the merger of the Hashomer Hatzair and the Ahdut Avodah has put plainly on record as its chief reason for not joining the majority party the desire to have Zionist foreign policy rely on Russia more than on the Western democracies.

The mentality behind this unrealistic understanding of Russian policy and the consequences of subjecting oneself to it has a long tradition in Zionism. As is understandable enough among people without political experience, a childlike hope has always been present that some big brother would come along to befriend the Jewish people, solve their problems, protect them from the Arabs, and present them eventually with a beautiful Jewish state with all the trimmings. This role was filled in Jewish imagination by Great Britain—until the issuance of the White Paper; and because of this naive trust, and an equally naive underestimation of Arab forces, for decades Jewish leaders let slip one opportunity after another to come to an understanding with the Arabs. After the outbreak of the Second World War, and particularly since the Biltmore Program, the imaginary role of the big brother of the Jews fell to the United States. But it has very quickly become clear that America is no more in a position to fill the bill than the British, and so Soviet Russia is now left as the only power upon which foolish hopes can be pinned. It is remarkable, however, that Russia is the first big brother whom even Jews do not quite trust. For the first time a note of cynicism has entered Jewish hopes.

Unfortunately, this healthy distrust is not caused so much by a specific suspicion of Soviet policy as by another traditionally Zionist feeling that has by now seized all sections of the Jewish people: the cynical and deep-rooted conviction that all Gentiles are anti-Semitic, and everybody and everything is against the Jews, that, in the words of Herzl, the world can be divided into *verschämte und unverschämte Antisemiten,* and that the "essential meaning of Zionism is the revolt of the Jews against their pointless and hapless mission—which has been to challenge the Gentiles to be crueler than they dare without forcing them to be as kind as they ought, [with the result that the Zionist revolt has ended in reproducing] in altered perspective the dynamic picture of Israel's mission" (Benjamin Halpern in the *New Leader,* December 1947). In other words, general Gentile hostility, a phenomenon that Herzl thought was directed only at Galut Jewry, and which would therefore disappear wit the normalization of the Jewish people in Palestine, is now assumed by Zionists to be an unalterable, eternal fact of Jewish history that repeats itself under any circumstances, even in Palestine.

Obviously this attitude is plain racist chauvinism and it is equally obvious that this division between Jews and all other peoples—who are to be classed as enemies—does not differ from other master race theories (even though the Jewish "master race" is pledged not to conquest but to suicide by its protagonists). It is also plain that any interpretation of politics oriented according to such "principles" is hopelessly out of touch with the realities of this world. Nevertheless it is a fact that such attitudes tacitly or explicitly permeate the general atmosphere of Jewry; and therefore Jewish leaders can threaten mass suicide to the applause of their audiences, and the terrible and irresponsible "or else we shall go down" creeps into all official Jewish statements, however radical or moderate their sources.

Every believer in a democratic government knows the importance of a loyal opposition. The tragedy of Jewish politics at this moment is that it is wholly determined by the Jewish Agency and that no opposition to it of any significance exists either in Palestine or America.

From the time of the Balfour Declaration the loyal opposition in Zionist politics was constituted by the non-Zionists (certainly this was the case after 1929, when the enlarged Jewish Agency elected half of the Executive from the non-Zionists). But for all practical purposes the non-Zionist opposition no longer exists today. This unfortunate development was encouraged, if not caused, by the fact that the United States and the United Nations finally endorsed an extremist Jewish demand that non-Zionists had always held to be totally unrealistic. With the support of a Jewish state by the great powers, the non-Zionists believed themselves refuted by reality itself. Their sudden loss of significance, and their helplessness in the face of what they felt justified in thinking an accomplished fact, were the result of an attitude that has always identified reality with the sum of those facts created by the powers-that-be—and by them only. They had believed in the Balfour Declaration rather than in the wish of the Jewish people to build its homeland; they had reckoned with the British or American governments rather than with the people living in the Near East. They had refused to go along with the Biltmore program—but they accepted it once it was recognized by the United States and the United Nations.

Now, if the non-Zionists had wanted to act as genuine realists in Jewish politics, they should have insisted and continued to insist that the only permanent reality in the whole constellation was the presence of Arabs in Palestine, a reality no decision could alter—except, perhaps the decision of a totalitarian state, implemented by its particular brand of ruthless force. Instead, they mistook decisions of great powers for the ultimate realities and lacked the courage to warn, not only their fellow-Jews, but also their respective governments of the possible consequences of partition and the declaration of a Jewish state. It was ominous enough that no significant Zionist party was left to oppose the decision of November 29, the minority being committed to the Jewish state, and the others (the majority under Weizmann) to partition; but it was downright tragic that at this most crucial of all moments the loyal opposition of the non-Zionists simply disappeared.

In the face of the "despair and resoluteness" of the Yishuv (as a Palestinian delegate recently put it) and the suicide threats of the Jewish leaders, it might be useful to remind the Jews and the world what it is that will "go down" if the final tragedy should come in Palestine.

Palestine and the building of a Jewish homeland constitute today the great hope and the great pride of Jews all over the world. What would happen to Jews, individually and collectively, if this hope and this pride were to be extinguished in another catastrophe is almost beyond imagining. But it is certain that this would become the central fact of Jewish history and it is possible that it might become the beginning of the self-dissolution of the Jewish people. There is no Jew in the world whose whole outlook on life and the world would not be radically changed by such a tragedy.

If the Yishuv went down, it would drag along in its fall the collective settlements, the kibbutzim—which constitute perhaps the most promising of all social experiments made in the 20th century, as well as the most magnificent part of the Jewish homeland.

Here, in complete freedom and unhampered by any government, a new form of ownership, a new type of farmer, a new way of family life and child education, and new approaches to the troublesome conflicts between city and country, between rural and industrial labor have been created.

The people of the kibbutzim have been too absorbed in

their quiet and effective revolution to make their voices sufficiently heard in Zionist politics. If it is true that the members of the Irgun and the Stern group are not recruited from the kibbutzim, it is also true that the kibbutzim have offered no serious obstacle to terrorism.

It is this very abstention from politics, this enthusiastic concentration on immediate problems, that has enabled the kibbutz pioneers to go ahead with their work, undisturbed by the more noxious ideologies of our times, realizing new laws and new behavior patterns, establishing new customs and new values, and translating and integrating them in new institutions. The loss of the kibbutzim, the ruin of the new type of man they have produced, the destruction of their institutions and the oblivion that would swallow the fruit of their experiences—this would be one of the severest of blows to the hopes of all those, Jewish and non-Jewish, who have not and never will make their peace with present-day society and its standards. For this Jewish experiment in Palestine holds out hope of solutions that will be acceptable and applicable, not only in individual cases, but also for the large mass of men everywhere whose dignity and very humanity are in our time so seriously threatened by the pressures of modern life and its unsolved problems.

Still another precedent, or at least its possibility, would go down with the Yishuv—that of close cooperation between two peoples, one embodying the most advanced ways of European civilization, the other an erstwhile victim of colonial oppression and backwardness. The idea of Arab-Jewish cooperation, though never realized on any scale and today seemingly farther off than ever, is not an idealistic day dream but a sober statement of the fact that without it the whole Jewish venture in Palestine is doomed. Jews and Arabs could be forced by circumstances to show the world that there are no differences between two people that cannot be bridged. Indeed, the working out of such a *modus vivendi* might in the end serve as a model of how to counteract the dangerous tendencies of formerly oppressed peoples to shut themselves off from the rest of the world and develop nationalist superiority complexes of their own.

Many opportunities for Jewish-Arab friendship have already

been lost, but none of these failures can alter the basic fact that the existence of the Jews in Palestine depends on achieving it. Moreover, the Jews have one advantage in the fact that, excluded as they were from official history for centuries, they have no imperialist past to live down. They can still act as a vanguard in international relations on a small but valid scale— as in the kibbutzim they have already acted as a vanguard in social relations despite the relatively insignificant numbers of the people involved.

There is very little doubt about the final outcome of an all-out war between Arabs and Jews. One can win many battles without winning a war. And up to now, no real battle has yet taken place in Palestine.

And even if the Jews were to win the war, its end would find the unique possibilities and the unique achievements of Zionism in Palestine destroyed. The land that would come into being would be something quite other than the dream of world Jewry, Zionist and non-Zionist. The "victorious" Jews would live surrounded by an entirely hostile Arab population, se-cluded inside ever-threatened borders, absorbed with physical self-defense to a degree that would submerge all other interests and activities. The growth of a Jewish culture would cease to be the concern of the whole people; social experiments would have to be discarded as impractical luxuries; political thought would center around military strategy; economic development would be determined exclusively by the needs of war. And all this would be the fate of a nation that—no matter how many immigrants it could still absorb and how far it extended its boundaries (the whole of Palestine and Transjordan is the insane Revisionist demand)—would still remain a very small people greatly outnumbered by hostile neighbors.

Under such circumstances (as Ernst Simon has pointed out) the Palestinian Jews would degenerate into one of those small warrior tribes about whose possibilities and importance history has amply informed us since the days of Sparta. Their relations with world Jewry would become problematical, since their defense interests might clash at any moment with those of other countries where large numbers of Jews lived. Palestine Jewry would eventually separate itself from the larger body of world Jewry and in its isolation develop into an entirely new people. Thus it becomes plain that at this moment and under present circumstances a Jewish state can only be erected at the price of the Jewish homeland.

Fortunately, there are still some Jews left who have shown in these bitter days that they have too much wisdom and too great a sense of responsibility to follow blindly where desperate, fanaticized masses would lead them. There are still, despite all appearances, a few Arabs who are unhappy about the increasingly fascist coloration of their national movements.

Until very recently, moreover, Palestinian Arabs were relatively unconcerned in the conflict with the Jews and the actual fighting against them is even now left to so-called volunteers from neighboring countries. But now even this situation has begun to change. The evacuations of Haifa and Tiberias by their Arab populations are the most ominous occurrences of the whole Arab-Jewish war so far. These evacuations could not have been carried out without careful preparation, and it is hardly likely that they are spontaneous. Nevertheless, it is very doubtful that Arab leadership, which by creating homelessness among Palestinian Arabs aims to arouse the Moslem world, would have succeeded in persuading tens of thousands of city dwellers to desert all their earthly possessions at a moment's notice, had not the massacre of Deir Yassin struck fear of the Jews into the Arab population. And another crime that played into the hands of the Arab leadership had been committed only a few months back in Haifa itself when the Irgun had thrown a bomb into a line of Arab workers outside the Haifa refinery, one of the few places where Jews and Arabs had for years worked side by side.

The political implications of these acts, neither of which had any military objective whatsoever, are all too clear in both instances: they were aimed at those places where neighborly relations between Arabs and Jews had not been completely destroyed; they were intended to arouse the wrath of the Arab people in order to cut off the Jewish leadership from all temptations to negotiate; they created that atmosphere of factual complicity which is always one of the main prerequisites for the rise to power of terrorist groups. And, indeed, no Jewish leadership did come forward to stop the Irgun from taking political matters into its own hands and declaring war on all

Arabs in the name of the Jewish community. The lukewarm protests of the Jewish Agency and the Haganah, forever limping behind, were followed two days later by an announcement from Tel Aviv that Irgun and Haganah were about to conclude an agreement. The Irgun attack on Jaffa, first denounced by Haganah, was followed by an agreement for joint action and the dispatch of Haganah units to Jaffa. This shows to what extent political initiative is already in terrorist hands.

The present Executive of the Jewish Agency and the Vaad Leumi have by now amply demonstrated that they are either unwilling or incapable of preventing the terrorists from making political decision for the whole Yishuv. It is even questionable whether the Jewish Agency is still in a position to negotiate for a temporary truce, since its enforcement would largely depend upon the consent of the extremist groups. It is quite possible that this was one of the reasons why representatives of the Agency, though they must know the desperate needs of their people, allowed the recent negotiations for a truce to break down. They may have been reluctant to reveal to the whole world their lack of effective power and authority.

The United Nations and the United States have up to now simply accepted the elected delegates of the Jewish and the Arab peoples, which was of course the proper thing to do. After the breakdown of truce negotiations, however, it would seem that there are now only two alternatives left for the great powers: either to leave the country (with the possible exception of the holy places) to a war that not only may mean another extermination of Jews but may also develop into a large-scale international conflict; or else to occupy the country with foreign troops and rule it without giving much consideration to either Jews or Arabs. The second alternative is clearly an imperialist one and would very likely end in failure if not carried out by a totalitarian government with all the paraphernalia of police terror.

However, a way out of this predicament may be found if the United Nations could summon up the courage in this unprecedented situation to take an unprecedented step by going to those Jewish and Arab individuals who at present are isolated because of their records as sincere believers in Arab-Jewish cooperation, and asking them to negotiate a truce. On the Jewish side, the so called Ihud group among the Zionists, as well as certain outstanding non-Zionists, are clearly the people most eligible for this purpose at the moment.

Such a truce, or better, such a preliminary understanding— even negotiated between non-accredited parties—would show the Jews and the Arabs that it could be done. We know the proverbial fickleness of masses; there is a serious chance for a rapid and radical change of mood, which is the prerequisite for any real solution.

Such a move, however, could be effective only if concessions are made at once on both sides. The White Paper has been an enormous obstacle, in view of the terrible needs of Jewish DP's. Without the solution of their problem, no improvement in the mood of the Jewish people can be expected. Immediate admission of Jewish DP's to Palestine, though limited in terms of time and number, as well as immediate admission of Jewish and other DP's to the United States outside the quota system, are prerequisites for a sensible solution. On the other hand, the Palestinian Arabs should be guaranteed a well-defined share in the Jewish development of the country, which under any circumstances will still continue to be their common home-land. This would not be impossible if the huge amounts now expended in defense and rebuilding could be used instead for the realization of the Jordan Valley Authority project.

There can be no doubt that a trusteeship as proposed by President Truman and endorsed by Dr. Magnes is the best temporary solution. It would have the advantage of preventing the establishment of sovereignty whose only sovereign right would be to commit suicide. It would provide a cooling-off period. It could initiate the Jordan Valley Authority project as a government enterprise and it could establish for its realiza-tion local Arab-Jewish committees under the supervision and the auspices of an international authority. It could appoint members of the Jewish and the Arab intelligentsia to posts in local and municipal offices. Last but not least, trusteeship over the whole of Palestine would postpone and possibly prevent partition of the country.

It is true that many non-fanatical Jews of sincere good will have believed in partition as a possible means of solving the Arab-Jewish conflict. In the light of political, military, and geographic realities, however, this was always a piece of wishful thinking. The partition of so small a country could at best mean the petrifaction of the conflict, which would result in arrested development for both peoples; at worst it would signify a temporary stage during which both parties would prepare for further war. The alternative proposition of a federated state, also recently endorsed by Dr. Magnes, is much more realistic; despite the fact that it establishes a common government for two different peoples, it avoids the troublesome majority-minority constellation, which is insoluble by definition. A federated structure, moreover, would have to rest on Jewish-Arab community councils, which would mean that the Jewish-Arab conflict would be resolved on the lowest and most promising level of proximity and neighborliness. A federated state, finally, could be the natural stepping-stone for any later, greater federated structure in the Near East and the Mediterranean area.

A federated state, however, such as is proposed by the Morrison Plan, is outside the actual political possibilities of the day. As matters now stand, it would be almost as unwise to proclaim a federated state over the heads and against the opposition of both peoples as it has already been to proclaim partition. This is, certainly, no time for final solutions; every single possible and practicable step is today a tentative effort whose chief aim is pacification and nothing more.

Trusteeship is not an ideal and not an eternal solution. But politics seldom offers ideal or eternal solutions. A United Nations trusteeship could be effectively carried through only if the United States and Great Britain were ready to back it up, no matter what happened. This does not necessarily mean great military commitments. There is still a good chance of recruiting police forces on the spot if the present memberships of the Arab Higher Committee and the Jewish Agency were to be denied authority in the country. Small local units composed of Jews and Arabs under the command of higher officers from countries that are members of the United Nations could become an important school for future cooperative self-government.

Unfortunately, in a hysterical atmosphere such proposals are only too liable to be dismissed as "stabs in the back" or unrealistic.

They are neither; they are, on the contrary, the only way of saving the reality of the Jewish homeland.

No matter what the outcome of the present deadlock, the following objective factors should be axiomatic criteria for the good and the bad, the right and the wrong:

1) The real goal of the Jews in Palestine is the building up of a Jewish homeland. This goal must never be sacrificed to the pseudo-sovereignty of a Jewish state.

2) The independence of Palestine can be achieved only on a solid basis of Jewish-Arab cooperation. As long as Jewish and Arab leaders both claim that there is "no bridge" between Jews and Arabs (as Moshe Shertok has just put it), the territory cannot be left to the political wisdom of its own inhabitants.

3) Elimination of all terrorist groups (and not agreements with them) and swift punishment of all terrorist deeds (and not merely protests against them) will be the only valid proof that the Jewish people in Palestine has recovered its sense of political reality and that Zionist leadership is again responsible enough to be trusted with the destinies of the Yishuv.

4) Immigration to Palestine, limited in numbers and in time, is the only "irreducible minimum" in Jewish politics.

5) Local self-government and mixed Jewish-Arab municipal and rural councils, on a small scale and as numerous as possible, are the only realistic political measures that can eventually lead to the political emancipation of Palestine.

It is still not too late.

Peace or Armistice in the
Near East?

(JANUARY 1950)

Peace in the Near East is essential to the State of Israel, to the Arab people and to the Western world. Peace, as distinguished from an armistice, cannot be imposed from the outside, it can only be the result of negotiations, of mutual compromise and eventual agreement between Jews and Arabs.

The Jewish settlement in Palestine may become a very important factor in the development of the Near East, but it will always remain a comparatively small island in an Arab sea. Even in the event of maximum immigration over a long period of years the reservoir of prospective citizens of Israel is limited to roughly two million, a figure that could be substantially increased only by catastrophic events in the United States or the Soviet Union. Since, however, (apart from the improbability of such a turn of events) the State of Israel owes its very existence to these two world powers, and since failure to achieve a genuine Jewish-Arab understanding will necessarily make its survival even more dependent upon continued sympathy and support of one or the other, a Jewish catastrophe in the two great surviving centers of world Jewry would lead almost immediately to a catastrophe in Israel.

The Arabs have been hostile to the building of a Jewish homeland almost from the beginning. The uprising of 1921, the pogrom of 1929, the disturbances from 1936 to 1939 have been the outstanding landmarks in the history of Arab-Jewish

Note: This paper was written in 1948 upon the suggestion of Judah L. Magnes, the late President of the Hebrew University in Jerusalem, who from the close of World War I to the day of his death in October, 1948, had been the outstanding Jewish spokesman for Arab-Jewish understanding in Palestine. It is dedicated to his memory.

relations under British rule. It was only logical that the evacuation of British troops coincided with the outbreak of a Jewish-Arab war; and it is remarkable how little the accomplished fact of a State of Israel and Jewish victories over Arab armies have influenced Arab politics. All hopes to the contrary notwithstanding, it seems as though the *one* argument the Arabs are incapable of understanding is force.

As far as Arab-Jewish relations are concerned, the war and the Israeli victories have not changed or solved anything. Any settlement short of genuine peace will give the Arabs time to grow stronger, to mend the rivalries between the Arab states, possibly to promote revolutionary changes, social, economic and political. Probably such changes in the Arab world will come about in any event, but the question is whether they will be inspired by the thought of *revanche* and crystallize around a common hostility against Israel, or whether they will be prompted by an understanding of common interests and crystallize around close economic and political cooperation with the Jews, the most advanced and Westernized people of the region. Arab reluctance, on the one hand, to begin direct peace talks and the (implied) admission that they may prefer a peace imposed by an outside power, and Israeli handling of the Arab refugee problem on the other, argue in favor of the first possibility. But all considerations of the self-interest of both peoples speak for the second. To be sure, these reasons are weak in a century when political issues are no longer determined by common sense and when the representatives of great powers frequently behave more like gamblers than statesmen.

To such general considerations must be added the education in irresponsibility which was the concomitant of the mandate system. For twenty-five years, the peoples of Palestine could rely upon the British government to uphold adequate stability for general constructive purposes and feel free to indulge in all kinds of emotional, nationalistic, illusionary behavior. Occasional outbreaks, even if they enlisted almost unanimous popular support (as, for instance, the disturbances of 1936 to 1939 which were preceded by a successful Arab general strike, or the Jewish fight against Arab labor 1934–1935–1936 which was supported by practically the whole Jewish population), led to nothing more serious than another Inquiry Commission or another turn in the complicated game of British imperialist policy.

It is only natural that in an atmosphere where nothing was quite serious both parties grew more and more reckless, were more and more inclined to consider only their own interests and to overlook the vital realities of the country as a whole. Thus the Arabs neglected to take into account the rapid growth of Jewish strength and the far-reaching consequences of economic development, while the Jews ignored the awakening of colonial peoples and the new nationalist solidarity in the Arab world from Iraq to French Morocco. In hope or in hate both peoples have focused their attention so exclusively upon the British that they practically ignored each other: the Jews forgot that the Arabs, not the English, were the permanent reality in Near Eastern policies and the Arabs that Jewish settlers, and not British troops, intended to stay permanently in Palestine.

The British, on the other hand, were quite content with this state of affairs, because it prevented both a working agreement between Jews and Arabs, which might have resulted in a rebellion against British rule, and an open conflict between them, which might have endangered the peace of the country. No doubt, "if the British Government had really applied itself with energy and good will to the establishment of good relations between the Jews and the Arabs, such could have been accomplished" (Chaim Weizmann). Yet, British interest in Arab-Jewish understanding awoke only when the British had decided to evacuate the country—a decision by the way which was caused neither by Jewish terrorism nor by the Arab League, but came as a consequence of the Labor Government's liquidation of the British rule in India. Since then the British have been genuinely interested in an Arab-Jewish settlement and in the prevention of the Balkanization of the region which may again attract a third power. But although the interests of the peoples of the Near East certainly coincide with British interests at this moment, the past record of British imperialism has made it impossible for her to negotiate a reasonable settlement.

But the choice between genuine peace and armistice is by no means only, or even primarily, an issue of foreign policy. The internal structure of the Arab as well the Jewish states will depend upon it. A mere armistice would force the new Israeli state to organize the whole people for permanent potential mobilization; the permanent threat of armed intervention would necessarily influence the direction of all economic and social developments and possibly end in a military dictatorship. The cultural and political sterility of small thoroughly militarized nations has been sufficiently demonstrated in history. The examples of Sparta and similar experiments are not likely to frighten a generation of European Jews who are trying to wipe out the humiliation of Hitler's slaughterhouses with the newly-won dignity of battle and the triumph of victory. Nevertheless, even this generation should be able to realize that an independent Spartan existence will be possible only after the country has been built up and after the Jewish homeland has been definitely established, by no means the case now. Excessive expenditures on armaments and mobilization would mean not only the stifling of the young Jewish economy and the end of the country's social experiments, but lead to an increasing dependence of the whole population upon financial and other support from American Jewry.

A condition of no-peace and no-war will be far easier for the Arabs to bear precisely because of the stagnation of their economic life and the backwardness of their social life. In the long run, however, the poverty-stricken, undeveloped and unorganized Near East needs peace as badly as the Jews; it needs Jewish cooperation in order quickly to achieve the strength to prevent its remaining a power vacuum and to assure its independence. If the Arab states are not just pretending but really are afraid of Russian aggression, their only salvation lies in sincere collaboration with the State of Israel. The Arabs' argument that they can do without Jewish help and prefer to grow slowly and organically rather than be influenced by "foreign" Western methods and ideas may sound very attractive to a few romantics inside and outside the Arab world. The simple truth of the matter is that the world's political pace will not allow them enough time for "organic" development; the Arabs, though potentially stronger than the Jews, are not a great power either and hardly on the way to becoming one. The victories of the Israeli army are dangerous to them not so much because of possible Jewish domination as because of the demonstrated power vacuum. If they continue to be anti-Western, to spend their energies fighting the tiny Jewish state and indulging their sterile pride in keeping the national character intact, they are threatened with something far worse, and much more real, than the bogey of Jewish domination.

In terms of international politics, the danger of this little war between two small peoples is that it inevitably tempts and attracts the great powers to interfere, with the result that existing conflicts explode because they can be fought out by proxy. Until now, neither the Jewish charge of an *Anglo*-Arab invasion nor the Arab countercharge of a *Russian*-Jewish aggression has contained any truth at all. The reason, however, why both legends sound so plausible and are so frequently accepted is that such a situation can indeed develop.

Moreover, the last war showed all too clearly that no better pretext or greater help exists for would-be aggressors than petty national conflicts fought out in chauvinist violence. The peoples of the Near East who show such a disturbing resemblance in psychology and political mentality to the small nations of Central and Eastern Europe, would do well to consider how easily these latter were conquered by Stalin as well as by Hitler, and to compare them with the more fortunate small nations, like the Scandinavian countries and Switzerland, who were not devoured by hate and not torn by chauvinistic passion.

The great good fortune of Jews as well as Arabs at this moment is that America and great Britain not only have no interest in further hostilities, but, on the contrary, are genuinely eager to bring about an authentic pacification of the whole region. Mutual denunciations by Jews and Arabs to the effect that they are either British or Russian agents serve only to cloud the real issues: Jewish determination to keep and possibly extend national sovereignty without consideration for Arab interests, and Arab determination to expel the Jewish "invaders" from Palestine without consideration for Jewish achievements there. If this "independent and sovereign" behavior (Arab unwillingness during the war to take British advice, and the Jewish inclination to interpret as pressure any device which America may offer, for instance, in the question of Arab refugees) goes on unabated, then all independence and sovereignty will be lost. Since a trusteeship under the United Nations has become impossible, continuance of this stubbornness leaves only three kinds of peace which the world may finally be willing to offer the Near East: a Pax Britannica which is very unlikely at the moment, a Pax Americana which is even more unlikely, or a Pax Moscovita which, alas, is the only actual danger.

THE INCOMPATIBILITY OF CLAIMS

A good peace is usually the result of negotiation and compromise, not necessarily of a program. Good relationships between Jews and Arabs will depend upon a changed attitude toward each other, upon a change in the atmosphere in Palestine and the Near East, not necessarily upon a formula. Hardly any conflict in the history of the world has given rise to so many programs and formulae from the outside; yet none of them has ever been acceptable to either side. Each has been denounced as soon as it was published as pro-Jewish by the Arabs and pro-Arab by the Jews.

The reception of the two Bernadotte Peace Proposals is typical. The first report to the United Nations concluded with a series of recommendations, made in the spirit of the United Nations' decision of partition; they provided for political implementation of economic cooperation through a "coordinated foreign policy" and "measures of common defense," for negotiated boundaries and for a limited guarantee of Jewish immigration. The second report, on the contrary, recommended two completely sovereign and independent political entities, separated by neutralized zones, and temporarily supervised by a UN commission. Both reports were denounced equally by both sides. The differences between the two Peace Proposals were hardly recognized because they had one thing in common: the recognition of the existence of a State of Israel on one side, and the existence of an Arab population in Palestine and the Near East on the other.

Since no formula, however good and sensible, seems to be acceptable to either side while the present mood of the two peoples persists, it may well be that any plan, however rudimentary, will be a sufficient basis of negotiations as soon as this mood is changed.

The past two years will stand out in Jewish history for many decades, and perhaps for many centuries to come. Even if the establishment of a Jewish State and the outbreak of an Arab-Jewish war may turn out ultimately to be one of many ephemeral episodes in an unhappy history of a country that has known many changes of rulers and fortune, their place as a turning point in Jewish history has already been decided. The majority of the Jewish people feel that the happenings of the last years have a closer relation to the destruction of the Temple in 70 A.D. and the Messianic yearnings of two thousand years of dispersion, than to the United Nations' decision of 1947, the Balfour Declaration of 1917, or even to fifty years of pioneering in Palestine. Jewish victories are not judged in the light of present realities in the Near East but in the light of a very distant past; the present war fills every Jew with "such satisfaction as we have not had for centuries, perhaps not since the days of the Maccabees" (Ben-Gurion).

This feeling of historical momentum, this determination to regard these recent events as a final verdict of history, is doubtless strengthened by success, but success is not its source. The Jews went into battle against the British occupation troops and the Arab armies with the "spirit of Masadah," inspired by the slogan "or else we shall go down," determined to refuse all compromise even at the price of national suicide. Today the Israeli government speaks of accomplished facts, of Might is Right, of military necessities, of the law of conquest, whereas two years ago, the same people in the Jewish Agency spoke of justice and the desperate needs of the Jewish people. Palestinian Jewry bet on one card—and won.

Against Jewish determination to regard the outcome as final stands the determination of the Arabs to view it as an interlude. Here, too, we are confronted with a decision which is neither deducible from events nor changed in the least by them. Defeats seem to confirm the Arabs' attitude as much as victories do that of the Jews. Arab policy in this respect is very simple and consists mainly in a diplomacy which discounts defeats and states and restates with undisturbed stubbornness the old claim to ownership of the country and refusal to recognize the State of Israel.

This mutual refusal to take each other seriously is perhaps the clearest sign of the seriousness of the situation. During the war, it expressed itself in the dangerous inclination to interpret the whole conflict as the result of a sinister behind-the-scenes conspiracy in which the Arabs were not confronted with 700,000 or 800,000 Palestinian Jews but with the overwhelming strength of American or Russian imperialism or both, while the

Jews insisted that they fought not so much the members of the Arab League as the entire might of the British Empire. That the Arabs should attempt to find a plausible explanation for the fact that six Arab states could not win a single victory against the tiny forces of Palestinian Jewry, and that the Jews should shrink from the idea of being permanently surrounded by hostile neighbors who so hopelessly outnumbered them, is understandable enough. The net result, however, of a propaganda (by itself hardly worthy of consideration) which treats the real opponent as a kind of ghost or tool is an atmosphere where negotiations are impossible: for what is the point of taking statements and claims seriously if you believe that they serve a conspiracy?

This utterly unreal situation is not new. For more than twenty-five years, Jews and Arabs have made perfectly incompatible claims on each other. The Arabs never gave up the idea of a unitary Arab state in Palestine, though they sometimes reluctantly conceded limited minority rights to Jewish inhabitants. The Jews, with the exception of the Revisionists, for many years refused to talk about their ultimate goals, partly because they knew only too well the uncompromising attitude of the Arabs and partly because they had unlimited confidence in British protection. The Biltmore program of 1942 for the first time formulated Jewish political aims officially—a unitary Jewish state in Palestine with the provision of certain minority rights for Palestinian Arabs who then still formed the majority of the Palestinian population. At the same time, the transfer of Palestinian Arabs to neighboring countries was contemplated and openly discussed in the Zionist movement.

Nor is this incompatibility only a matter of politics. The Jews are convinced, and have announced many times, that the world—or history or higher morality—owes them a righting of the wrongs of two thousand years and, more specifically, a compensation for the catastrophe of European Jewry which, in their opinion, was not simply a crime of Nazi Germany but of the whole civilized world. The Arabs, on the other hand, reply that two wrongs do not make a right and that "no code of morals can justify the persecution of one people in an attempt to relieve the persecution of the other." The point of this kind of argumentation is that it is unanswerable. Both claims are nationalistic because they make sense only in the closed framework of one's own people and history, and legalistic because they discount the concrete factors of the situation.

SOCIAL AND ECONOMIC SEPARATION

The complete incompatibility of claims which until now has frustrated every attempt to compromise and every effort to find a common denominator between two peoples whose common interests are patent to all except themselves is only the outward sign of a deeper, more real incompatibility. It is incredible and sad, but it is true, that more than three decades of intimate proximity have changed very little the initial feeling of complete strangeness between Arabs and Jews. The way the Arabs conducted this war has proved better than anything else how little they knew of Jewish strength and the will to fight. To the Jews, similarly, the Arabs they met for so many years in every city, village and rural district, with whom they had constant dealing and conflicts, have remained phantoms, beings whom they have considered only on the irrelevant levels of folklore, nationalist generalizations, or idle idealistic dreams.

The Jewish and Arab failure to visualize a close neighbor as a concrete human being has many explanations. Outstanding among them is the economic structure of the country in which the Arab and Jewish sectors were separated by, so to speak, watertight walls. The few exceptions, such as common export organizations of Jewish and Arab orange growers or a few factories that employed both Jewish and Arab labor, only confirmed the rule. The building of the Jewish homeland, the most important economic factor in the recent history of the entire Near East, never depended on Jewish-Arab cooperation, but exclusively on the enterprise and pioneering spirit of Jewish labor and the financial support of world Jewry. Jewish economy may eventually have to depend heavily if not exclusively on the Arab markets of the Near East. But this stage of mutual dependence is still far off and will be reached only after Palestine has been fully industrialized and the Arab countries have reached a level of civilization that could offer a market for high-quality merchandise, which only Jewish economy will probably be able to produce profitably.

The struggle for political sovereignty, necessarily accompanied by heavy expenditure for armaments and even more decisive losses in work hours, has retarded considerably the development toward economic independence. As long as outside financial support on a large scale is assured, Jewish-Arab cooperation can hardly become an economic necessity for the new Israeli state. The same has been true in the past. The financial support of world Jewry, without which the whole experiment would have failed, signified economically that the Jewish settlement could assert itself without much thought of what was going on in the surrounding world, that it had no vital interest, except on humanitarian grounds, in raising the Arab standard of living and that economic issues could be fought out as though the Jewish National Home were completely isolated from its neighbors.

Naturally economic and social isolation had its good and its bad aspects. Its advantage was that it made possible such experiments as the collective and cooperative settlements, that an advanced and in many respects very promising economic structure could impose itself upon an environment of hopeless misery and sterility. Its economic disadvantage was that the experiment dangerously resembled a hothouse plant and that the social and political problems which arose from the presence of a native population could be handled without consideration of objective factors.

Organized Jewish labor fought and won a relentless battle against cheap Arab labor; the old-time Arab fellahin, even though they were not deprived of their soil by Jewish settlement, quickly became a kind of relic, unfit for and superfluous to the new modernized structure of the country. Under the leadership of Jewish labor, Palestine underwent the same industrial revolution, the same change from a more or less feudal to a more or less capitalist order, as European countries did 150 years ago. The decisive difference was only that the industrial revolution had created and employed its own fourth estate, a native proletariat, whereas in Palestine the same development involved the importation of workers and left the native population a potential proletariat with no prospect of employment as free laborers.

This unhappy potential Arab proletariat cannot be argued away by statistics about land sales nor can it be counted in terms of the destitute. Figures do not show the psychological changes of the native population, their deep resentment against a state of affairs which seemingly left them untouched, and in reality demonstrated to them the possibility of a higher standard of living without ever fulfilling the implied promises. The Jews introduced something new into the country which, through sheer productivity, soon became the decisive factor. Compared to this new life, the primitive Arab economy assumed a ghostlike appearance, and its backwardness and inefficiency seemed to await a catastrophe to sweep it away.

It was, however, no accident that Zionist officials allowed this economic trend to take its course and that none of them ever made, in Judah L. Magnes' words, Jewish-Arab coopera- tion "the chief objective of major policy." Zionist ideology, which after all is at least thirty years older than the Balfour Declaration, started not from a consideration of the realities in Palestine but from the problem of Jewish homelessness. The thought that "the people without a country needed a country without a people" so occupied the minds of the Zionist leaders that they simply overlooked the native population. The Arab problem was always "the veiled issue of Zionist politics" (as Isaac Epstein called it as long ago as 1907), long before economic problems in Palestine forced Zionist leadership into an even more effective neglect.

The temptation to neglect the Arab problem was great indeed. It was no small matter, after all, to settle an urban population in a poor, desertlike country, to educate thousands of young potential tradesmen and intellectuals to the arduous life and ideas of pioneerdom. Arab labor was dangerous because it was cheap; there was the constant temptation for Jewish capital to employ Arabs instead of the more expensive and more rights-conscious Jewish workers. How easily could the whole Zionist venture have degenerated in those crucial years into a white man's colonial enterprise at the expense of, and based upon, the work of natives. Jewish class struggle in Palestine, was for the most part a fight against Arab workers. To be anti-capitalist in Palestine almost always meant to be practically anti-Arab.

The social aspect of Jewish-Arab relationships is decisive because it convinced the only section of the population that had not come to Palestine for nationalistic reasons that it was impossible to come to terms with the Arabs without committing national and social suicide. The crude nationalist demand of "a country without a people," seemed so indisputably right in the light of practical experience that even the most idealistic elements in the Jewish labor movements let themselves be tempted first into forgetfulness and neglect, and then into narrow and inconsiderate nationalistic attitudes.

British administration which, according to the terms of the mandate, was supposed to prepare "the development of self-governing institutions," did nothing to bring the two peoples together and very little to raise the Arab standard of living. In the twenties, this may have been a half-conscious policy of *divide et impera*; in the late thirties, it was open sabotage of the Jewish National Home which the colonial services had always held to be dangerous to imperialist interests and whose ultimate survival, as the British knew perhaps better than Zionist leadership, depended upon cooperation with the Arabs. Much worse, however, though much less tangible, was the romantic attitude of the colonial services; they adored all the charming qualities of Arab life which definitely impeded social and economic progress. The urban Jewish middle class and especially the free professions in Jerusalem, were for a certain time inclined to imitate the British society they met among the administrative personnel. Here they learned, at best, that it was fashionable to be interested in Arab folk life, to admire the noble gestures and customs of the Bedouins, to be charmed by the hospitality of an ancient civilization. What they overlooked was that Arabs were human beings like themselves and that it might be dangerous not to expect them to act and react in much the same way as Jews; in other words, that because of the presence of the Jews in the country, the Bedouins were likely to want even more urgently land to settle down (a revival of the "inherent tendency in nomad society to desert the weariness and hopelessness of pastoral occupations for the superior comforts of agriculture"—H. St. J. B. Philby), the fellahin to feel for the first time the need for machines with which one obtained better products with less toil, and the urban population to strive for a standard of living which they had hardly known before the arrival of the Jews.

The Arab masses awoke only gradually to a spirit of envy and frustrated competition. In their old disease-stricken poverty, they looked upon Jewish achievements and customs as though they were images from a fairy-tale which would soon vanish as miraculously as they had appeared to interrupt their old way of life. This had nothing to do with neighborliness between Jewish and Arab villages which was the rule rather than the exception for a long time, which survived the disturbances of 1936–1939 and came to an end only under the impact of Jewish terrorism in 1947 and 1948. These relations, however, could be so easily destroyed without harming Jewish municipal and economic interests because they had always been without consequence, a simple, frequently touching expression of human neighborliness. With the exception of the Haifa municipality, not a single common institution, not a single common political body had been built up on this basis in all those years. It was as though, by tacit agreement, the neighbors had decided that their ways of life were different to the point of mutual indifference, that no common interests were possible except their human curiosity. No neighborliness could alter the fact that the Jews regarded the Arabs as an interesting example of folk life at best, and as a backward people who did not matter at worst, and that the Arabs considered the whole Jewish venture a strange interlude out of a fairy tale at best, and, at worst, an illegal enterprise which one day would be fair game for looting and robbery.

THE UNIQUENESS OF THE COUNTRY

While the mood of the country was only too typical, quite like other small nations' fierce chauvinism and fanatic provincialism, the realities of Jewish achievement in Palestine were unique in many respects. What happened in Palestine was not easy to judge and evaluate: it was extraordinarily different from anything that had happened in the past.

The building of a Jewish National Home was not a colonial enterprise in which Europeans came to exploit foreign riches with the help and at the expense of native labor. Palestine was and is a poor country and whatever riches it possesses are exclusively the product of Jewish labor which are not likely to survive if ever the Jews are expelled from the country. Exploitation or robbery, so characteristic of the "original accumulation" in all imperialist enterprises, were either completely absent or played an insignificant role. American and

European capital that flooded the country, came not as
dividend-paying capital held by absentee shareholders but as
"charity" money which the recipients were free to expend at
will. It was used for the acquisition and nationalization of the
soil, the establishment of collective settlements, long-term
loans to farmers' and to workers' cooperatives, social and health
services, free and equal education, and generally for the
building of an economy with a pronounced socialist physiog-
nomy. Through these efforts, in thirty years the land was
changed as completely as if it had been transplanted to another
continent, and this without conquest and with no attempt at
extermination of natives.

The Palestinian experiment has frequently been called
artificial, and it is true that everything connected with the
building of a Jewish national home—the Zionist movement as
well as the realities in Palestine—has not been, as it were, in the
nature of things not according to the ways of the world. No
economic necessities prompted the Jews to go to Palestine in
the decisive years when immigration to America was the
natural escape from misery and persecution; the land was no
temptation for capital export, did not in itself offer opportunities for the solution of population problems. The collective
rural settlements, the backbone of Palestinian society and the
expression of pioneerdom, can certainly not be explained by
utilitarian reasons. The development of the soil, the erection of
a Hebrew University, the establishment of great health centers,
were all "artificial" developments, supported from abroad and
initiated by a spirit of enterprise which paid no heed to
calculations of profit and loss.

A generation brought up in the blind faith in necessity—of
history or economy or society or nature—found it difficult to
understand that precisely this artificiality gave the Jewish
achievements in Palestine their human significance. The trouble was that Zionists as well as anti-Zionists thought that the
artificial character of the enterprise was to be reproached rather
than praised. Zionists, therefore, tried to explain the building
of a Jewish National Home as the only possible answer to a
supposedly eternal antisemitism, the establishment of collective settlements as the only solution to the difficulties of Jewish
agricultural labor, the foundation of health centers and the

Hebrew University in terms of national interests. Each of these explanations contains part of the truth and each is somehow beside the point. The challenges were all there, but none of the responses was "natural." The point was that the responses were of much more permanent human and political value than the challenges, and that only ideological distortions made it appear that the challenges by themselves—antisemitism, poverty, national homelessness—had produced something.

Politically, Palestine was under a British mandate, that is a form of government supposedly devised only for backward areas where primitive peoples have not yet learned the elementary rules of self-government. But under the not too sympathetic eye of the British trustee the Jews erected a kind of state within a non-existent state, which in some respects was more modern than the most advanced governments of the Western world. This non-official Jewish government was represented only on the surface by the Jewish Agency, the recognized political body of world Zionism, or by the Vaad Leumi, the official representative of Palestinian Jewry. What actually ruled the Jewish sector of the country much more efficiently than either and became more decisive in everyday life than British administration was the Histadruth, the Palestinian trade unions in which the overwhelming majority of Jewish labor, that is, the majority of the population, were organized. The trade unions stepped into all those areas which are usually regulated by municipal or national government as well as into a great number of activities which in other countries are the domain of free enterprise. All sorts of functions, such as administration, immigration, defense, education, health, social services, public works, communications, etc., were developed upon the initiative and under the leadership of the Histadruth which, at the same time, grew into the largest single employer in the country. This explains the miraculous fact that a mere proclamation of Jewish self-government eventually sufficed to bring a state machine into being. The present government of Israel, though a coalition government in appearance, is actually the government of the Histadruth.

Although the Jewish workers and farmers had an emotional awareness of the uniqueness of their achievements, expressed in a new kind of dignity and pride, neither they nor their leaders realized articulately the chief features of the new experiment. Thus Zionist leadership could go on for decades talking about the natural coincidence between Jewish interests and British imperialism, showing how little they understood themselves. For while they were talking this way, they built up a country that was economically so independent of Great Britain that it fitted into neither the Empire nor the Commonwealth; and they educated the people in such a way that it could not possibly fit into the political scheme of imperialism because it was neither a master nor a subject nation.

This would have been greatly to the credit of the Israeli State and even to its advantage today, if it had only been realized in time. But even now this is not the case. To defend their nationalist aggressiveness Israeli leadership today still insists on old truisms like "no people ever gets anything, least of all freedom, as a gift but has to fight for it," thus proving that they do not understand that the whole Jewish venture in Palestine is an excellent indication that some changes have occurred in the world and one may conquer a country by transforming its deserts into flourishing land.

Ideological explanations are those which do not fit realities but serve some other ulterior interests or motives. This does not mean that ideologies are ineffective in politics; on the contrary, their very momentum and the fanaticism they inspire frequently overwhelm more realistic considerations. In this sense, almost from the beginning, the misfortune of the building of a Jewish National Home has been that it was accompanied by a Central European ideology of nationalism and tribal thinking among the Jews, and by an Oxford-inspired colonial romanticism among the Arabs. For ideological reasons, the Jews overlooked the Arabs, who lived in what would have been an empty country, to fit their preconceived ideas of national emancipation. Because of romanticism or a complete inability to understand what was actually going on, the Arabs considered the Jews to be either old-fashioned invaders or newfangled tools of imperialism.

The British-inspired romanticization of poverty, of "the gospel of bareness" (T. E. Lawrence) blended only too well with the new Arab national consciousness and their old pride, according to which it is better to accept bribes than help. The new nationalist insistence on sovereignty, supported by an older desire to be left alone, served only to bolster exploitation by a few ruling families and prevent the development of the region. In their blind ideological hostility against Western civilization, a hostility which, ironically enough, was largely inspired by Westerners, they could not see that this region would be modernized in any case and that it would be far wiser to form an alliance with the Jews, who naturally shared the general interests of the Near East, than with some big faraway power whose interests were alien and who would necessarily consider them a subject people.

THE NON-NATIONALIST TRADITION

Against this background of ideological thinking the few protagonists of Jewish-Arab cooperation find their true stature. So few in number that they can hardly be called a real opposition force, so isolated from the masses and mass propaganda media that they were frequently ignored or suffocated by that peculiar praise which discredits a man as impractical by calling him an "idealist" or a "prophet," they nevertheless created, on the Jewish as well as the Arab side, an articulate tradition. At least their approach to the Palestinian problem begins in the objective realities of the situation.

Since it is usually asserted that good will toward the Jewish National Home in Palestine was always completely lacking on the Arab side and that Jewish spokesmen for Arab-Jewish understanding never could produce a single Arab of any standing who was willing to cooperate with them, a few instances of Arab initiative in trying to bring about some kind of Jewish-Arab agreement, may be mentioned. There was the meeting of Zionist and Arab leaders in Damascus in 1913 charged with preparing an Arab-Jewish conference in Lebanon. At that time the whole Near East was still under Turkish rule and the Arabs felt that as an oppressed people they had much in common with the Eastern European sections of the Jewish people. There was the famous friendship treaty of 1919 between King Feisal of Syria and Chaim Weizmann which both sides allowed to slip into oblivion. There was the Jewish-Arab conference of 1922 in Cairo when the Arabs showed themselves willing to agree to Jewish immigration within the limitations of the economic capacity of Palestine.

There were negotiations carried on between Judah L. Magnes (with the subsequent knowledge of the Jewish Agency) and the Palestinian Arab Higher Committee at the end of 1936, immediately after the outbreak of the Arab disturbance. A few years later, tentative consulations were carried out between leading Egyptians and the Jews. "The Egyptians," reports Weizmann in his autobiography, "were acquainted and impressed by our progress and suggested that perhaps in the future they might serve to bridge the gulf between us and the Arabs of Palestine. They assumed that the White Paper . . . would be adopted by England, but its effects might be mitigated, perhaps even nullified, if the Jews of Palestine showed themselves ready to cooperate with Egypt."

And last but not least, as late as 1945, Azzam Bey, then Secretary of the Arab League, stated that "the Arabs (were) prepared to make far-reaching concessions toward the gratification of the Jewish desire to see Palestine established as a spiritual and even a material home." To be sure, such Arabs had as little Arab mass support as their Jewish counterparts. But who knows what might have happened if their hesitating and tentative efforts had gotten a more sympathetic reception on the other side of the table? As it was, these Arabs were discredited among their own people when they discovered that the Jews either ignored them (as happened to Azzam Bey's statement), or broke off negotiations as soon as they hoped to find support from an outside ruling power (the Turkish government in 1913 and the British in 1922), and generally made the solution of the problem dependent upon the British who naturally "found its difficulties insuperable" (Ch. Weizmann). In the same way Jewish spokesmen for Arab-Jewish understanding were discredited when their very fair and moderate demands were distorted and taken advantage of, as happened with the efforts of the Magnes group in 1936.

The necessity of Jewish-Arab understanding can be proved by objective factors; its possibility is almost entirely a matter of subjective political wisdom and personalities. Necessity, based on economic, military and geographic considerations, will make itself felt in the long run only, or possibly, at a time when it is too late. Possibility is a matter of the immediate present, a question of whether there is enough statesmanship on both sides to anticipate the direction of long-range necessary trends and channel them into constructive political institutions.

It is one of the most hopeful signs for the actual possibility of a common Arab-Jewish policy that its essentials have only recently been formulated in very cogent terms by at least one outstanding Arab, Charles Malik, the representative of Lebanon to the United Nations, and one outstanding Palestinian Jew, Judah L. Magnes, the late President of the Hebrew University and Chairman of the Palestinian group of Ihud (Unity).

The speech Dr. Malik made on May 28, 1948, before the Security Council of the United Nations on the priority of Jewish-Arab agreement over all other solutions of the Palestinian problem is noteworthy for its calm and open insistence on peace and the realities of the Near East, and also because it found a "responsive echo" in the Jewish Agency's delegate, Major Aubrey Eban.

Dr. Malik, addressing the Security Council, warned the great powers against a policy of *fait accompli*. "The real task of world statesmanship," he said, was "to help the Jews and the Arabs not to be permanently alienated from one another." It would be a grave disservice to Jews to give a Jewish state a false sense of security as the result of successful manipulation of international machinery, for this would distract them from the fundamental task of establishing a "reasonable, workable, just, abiding understanding with the Arabs."

Dr. Malik's words sound like a late echo to Martin Buber's (the philosopher of the Hebrew University) earlier denunciation of the Zionist Biltmore program as "admitting the aim of the minority to 'conquer' the country by means of international maneuvers." But Dr. Magnes' statement of the case and the conditions for Jewish-Arab cooperation before the Anglo American Committee of Inquiry in 1946, when the White Paper's ban on Jewish immigration was still in force, read like an anticipated response from the Jewish side to the Arab challenge: "Our view is based on two assumptions, first that Jewish-Arab cooperation is not only essential, it is also possible. The alternative is war. . . ."

Dr. Magnes recognized that Palestine is a Holy Land for three monotheistic religions. To it the Arabs have a natural right and the Jews historical rights, both of equal validity. Thus, Palestine was already a bi-national state. This means political equality for the Arabs and justifies numerical equality for the Jews, that is, the right of immigration to Palestine. Dr.

Magnes did not believe that all Jews would be satisfied with his proposal but he thought that many would accept it since they wanted the Jewish State mainly because they wanted a place to which to migrate. He urged the necessity of revising the whole concept of the state. To the Arabs he argued that sovereign independence in tiny Palestine was impossible. Indeed, he called for Palestinian participation in a middle east regional federation as both a practical necessity and as a further assurance to the Arabs. "What a boon to mankind it would be if the Jews and Arabs of Palestine were to strive together in friendship and partnership to make this Holy Land into a thriving peaceful Switzerland in the heart of this ancient highway between East and West. This would have incalculable political and spiritual influence in all the Middle East and far beyond. A bi-national Palestine could become a beacon of peace in the world."

THE HEBREW UNIVERSITY
AND THE COLLECTIVE SETTLEMENTS

If nationalism were nothing worse than a people's pride in outstanding or unique achievement, Jewish nationalism would have been nourished by two institutions in the Jewish National Home: the Hebrew University and the collective settlements. Both are rooted in permanent non-nationalist trends in Jewish tradition—the universality and predominance of learning and the passion for justice. Here was a beginning of something true liberals of all countries and nationalities had hoped for when the Jewish people, with its peculiar tradition and historical experience, were given freedom and cultural autonomy, a hope no one expressed better than Woodrow Wilson who called for "not merely the rebirth of the Jewish people, but the birth also of new ideals, of new ethical values, of new conceptions of social justice which shall spring as a blessing for all mankind from that land and that people whose lawgivers and prophets . . . spoke those truths which have come thundering down the ages." (Quoted from Selig Adler, "The Palestine Question in the Wilson Era" in *Jewish Social Studies*, October 1948).

These two institutions, the *Kibbutzim* (collective settlements) on one hand, the Hebrew University on the other, supported and inspired the non-nationalist, anti-chauvinist trend and opposition in Zionism. The University was supposed to represent the universalism of Judaism in the particular Jewish land. It was not conceived just as the University of Palestine, but as the University of the Jewish people.

It is highly significant that the most consistent and articulate spokesmen for Jewish-Arab understanding came from the Hebrew University. The two groups that made cooperation with the Arabs the cornerstone of their political philosophy, the Brith Shalom (Covenant of Peace) in the twenties and the Ihud (Unity) Association in the forties—both founded and inspired by Judah L. Magnes, the co-founder and President of the Hebrew University since 1925—are not simply the expression of Western-educated intellectuals who find it difficult to swallow the crude slogans of a Balkanized nationalism. From the beginning Zionism contained two separate tendencies that met only in their agreement about the necessity of a Jewish homeland.

The victorious trend, the Herzlian tradition, took its chief impulse from the view of antisemitism as an "eternal" phenomenon in all countries of Jewish dispersion. It was strongly influenced by other nineteenth century small national liberation movements and denied the possibility of Jewish survival in any country except Palestine, under any conditions except those of a full-fledged sovereign Jewish state. The other trend, dating back to Ahad Haam, saw in Palestine the Jewish cultural center which would inspire the spiritual development of all Jews in other countries, but would not need ethnic homogeneity and national sovereignty. As far back as the nineties of the last century, Ahad Haam insisted on the presence in Palestine of an Arab native population and the necessity for peace. Those who followed him never aimed to make "Palestine as Jewish as England is English" (in the words of Weizmann), but thought that the establishment of a center of higher learning was more important for the new revival movement than the foundation of a State. The main achievement of the Herzlian tradition is the Jewish State; it came about (as Ahad Haam feared at the turn of the century and as Judah L. Magnes warned for more than twenty-five years) at the price of an Arab-Jewish war. The main achievement of the Ahad Haam tradition is the Hebrew University.

Another part of the movement, influenced by though not

connected with Ahad-Haam Zionism, grew out of Eastern-European socialism, and ultimately led to the foundation of collective settlements. As a new form of agricultural economy, social living and workers' cooperatives, it became the mainstay of the economic life of the Jewish homeland. The desire to build a new type of society in which there would be no exploitation of man by man did more to attract the best elements of Eastern European Jewry—that is, the powerful revolutionary ferment in Zionism without which not a single piece of land would have been tilled or a single road built—than the Herzlian analyses of Jewish assimilation, or Jabotinsky's propaganda for a Jewish State, or the cultural Zionists' appeal for a revival of the religious values of Judaism.

In the rural collective settlements, an age-old Jewish dream of a society based on justice, formed in complete equality, indifferent to all profit motives, was realized, even if on a small scale. Their greatest achievement was the creation of a new type of man and a new social elite, the birth of a new aristocracy which differed greatly from the Jewish masses in and outside of Palestine in habits, manners, values and way of life, and whose claim to leadership in moral and social questions was clearly recognized by the population. Completely free and unhampered by any government, a new form of ownership, a new type of farmer, a new way of family life and child education, and new approaches to the troublesome conflicts between city and country, between rural and industrial labor were created. Just as the very universalism of teaching and learning at the Hebrew University could be trusted to secure firm links between the Jewish National Home, world Jewry and the international world of scholarship, so could the collective settlements be trusted to keep Zionism within the highest tradition of Judaism whose "principles call for the creation of a visible tangible society founded upon justice and mercy" (M. Buber). At the same time these experiments hold out hope for solutions that may one day become acceptable and applicable for the large mass of men everywhere whose dignity and humanity are today so seriously threatened by the standard of a competitive and acquisitive society.

The only larger groups who ever actively promoted and preached Jewish-Arab friendship came from this collective settlement movement. It was one of the greatest tragedies for the new State of Israel that these labor elements, notably the Hashomer Hatsair, sacrificed their bi-national program to the *fait accompli* of the United Nations' partition decision.

THE RESULTS OF THE WAR

Uninfluenced by the voices raised in a spirit of understanding, compromise and reason, events have been allowed to take their course. For more than twenty-five years, Dr. Magnes and the small group of his followers in Palestine and in Zionism had predicted that there would be either Jewish-Arab cooperation or war, and there has been war; that there could be either a bi-national Palestine or domination of one people by the other, and there has been the flight of more than 500,000 Arabs from Israeli-dominated territory; that the British White-Paper policy and its ban on immigration in the years of the Jewish European catastrophe had to be immediately annulled or the Jews would risk everything to obtain a State if only for the sake of immigration, and, with no one on the British side willing to make any concessions, there is the fact that the Jews obtained a sovereign state.

Similarly, and despite the great impression which Dr. Malik's speech made on his colleagues in the Security Council of the United Nations, the whole policy not only of Israel but of the United Nations and the United States itself is a policy of *fait accompli*. True, on the surface it looks as though the armed forces of Israel had created the *fait accompli* of which Dr. Malik warned so eloquently. Yet, who would doubt that no number of victories in themselves would have been sufficient to secure Israel's existence without the support of the United States and American Jewry?

The most realistic way to measure the cost of the peoples of the Near East of the events of the past year is not by casualties, economic losses, war destruction or military victories, but by the political changes, the most outstanding of which has been the creation of a new category of homeless people, the Arab refugees. These not only form a dangerous potential irredenta dispersed in all Arab countries where they could easily become the visible uniting link; much worse, no matter how their exodus came about (as a consequence of Arab atrocity propaganda or real atrocities or a mixture of both), their flight from

Palestine, prepared by Zionist plans of large-scale population transfers during the war and followed by the Israeli refusal to readmit the refugees to their old home, made the old Arab claim against Zionism finally come true: the Jews simply aimed at expelling the Arabs from their homes. What had been the pride of the Jewish homeland, that it had not been based upon exploitation, turned into a curse when the final test came: the flight of the Arabs would not have been possible and not have been welcomed by the Jews if they had lived in a common economy. The reactionary Arabs of the Near East and their British protectors were finally proved right: they had always considered "the Jews dangerous not because they exploit the fellaheen, but because they do not exploit them" (Ch. Weizmann).

Liberals in all countries were horrified at the callousness, the haughty dismissal of humanitarian considerations by a government whose representatives, only one year ago, had pleaded their own cause on purely humanitarian grounds, and were educated by a movement that, for more than fifty years, had based its claims exclusively on justice. Only one voice eventually was raised in protest to Israel's handling of the Arab refugee question, the voice of Judah L. Magnes, who wrote a letter to the editor of *Commentary* (October 1948):

> It seems to me that any attempt to meet so vast a human situation except from the humane, the moral point of view will lead us into a morass. ... If the Palestine Arabs left their homesteads "voluntarily" under the impact of Arab propaganda and in a veritable panic, one may not forget that the most potent argument in this propaganda was the fear of a repetition of the Irgun-Stern atrocities at Deir Yassin, where the Jewish authorities were unable or unwilling to prevent the act or punish the guilty. It is unfortunate that the very men who could point to the tragedy of Jewish DP's as the chief argument for mass immigration into Palestine should now be ready, as far as the world knows, to help create an additional category of DP's in the Holy Land.

Dr. Magnes, feeling the full significance of actions which forfeited the old proud claim of Zionist pioneerdom that theirs was the only colonizing venture in history not carried out with bloody hands, based his protest on purely humanitarian grounds—and laid himself wide open to the old accusations of quixotic morality in politics where supposedly only advantage and success count. The old Jewish legend about the thirty-six unknown righteous men who always exist and without whom the world would go to pieces says the last word about the necessity of such "quixotic" behavior in the ordinary course of events. In a world like ours, however, in which politics in some countries has long since outgrown sporadic sinfulness and entered a new stage of criminality, uncompromising morality has suddenly changed its old function of merely keeping the world together and has become the only medium through which true reality, as opposed to the distorted and essentially ephemeral factual situations created by crimes, can be perceived and planned. Only those who are still able to disregard the mountains of dust which emerge out of and disappear into the nothingness of sterile violence can be trusted with anything so serious as the permanent interests and political survival of a nation.

FEDERATION OR BALKANIZATION?

The true objectives of a non-nationalist policy in the Near East and particularly in Palestine are few in number and simple in nature. Nationalist insistence on absolute sovereignty in such small countries as Palestine, Syria, Lebanon, Iraq, Transjordan, Saudi Arabia and Egypt can lead only to the Balkanization of the whole region and its transformation into a battlefield for the conflicting interests of the great powers to the detriment of all authentic national interests.

In the long run, the only alternative to Balkanization is a regional federation, which Magnes (in an article in *Foreign Affairs*) proposed as long ago as 1943, and which more recently was proclaimed as a distant but desired goal by Major Aubrey Eban, Israeli representative at the United Nations. While Dr. Magnes' original proposal comprised only those countries which the Peace Treaties of 1919 had dismembered but which had formed an integrated whole under Turkish government, that is, Palestine, Transjordan, Lebanon and Syria, the concept of Aubrey Eban (as published in an article in *Commentary* in

1948) aimed at a "Near Eastern League, comprising all the diverse nationalities of the area, each free within its own area of independence and cooperating with others for the welfare of the region as a whole." A federation which according to Eban might possibly include "Turkey, Christian Lebanon, Israel and Iran as partners of the Arab world in a league of non-aggression, mutual defense and economic cooperation" has the great advantage that it would comprise more than the two peoples, Jews and Arabs, and thus eliminate Jewish fears of being outnumbered by the Arabs.

The best hope for bringing this federation nearer would still be a Confederation of Palestine, as Dr. Magnes and Ihud proposed after partition and a sovereign Jewish State had become an accomplished fact. The very term Confederation indicates the existence of two independent political entities as contrasted with a federal system which is usually regarded "as a multiple government in a single state," (Encyclopedia of Social Sciences) and could well serve also as a model for the difficult relationships between Moslem Syria and Christian Lebanon. Once such small federated structures are established, Major Eban's League of Near Eastern countries will have a much better chance of realization. Just as the Benelux agreement was the first hopeful sign for an eventual federation of Europe, so the establishment of lasting agreement between two of the Near Eastern peoples on questions of defense, foreign policy and economic development could serve as a model for the whole region.

One of the chief advantages of federal (or confederate) solutions of the Palestinian problem has been that the more moderate Arab statesmen (particularly from Lebanon) agreed to them. While the plan for a federal state was proposed only by a minority of the United Nations' Special Committee on Palestine in 1947, namely by the delegates of India, Iran and Yugoslavia, there is no doubt that it could very well have served as a basis for a compromise between Jewish and Arab claims. The Ihud group at that time practically endorsed the minority report; it was in basic accordance with the principles set down and best expressed in the following sentence: "The federal state is the most constructive and dynamic solution in that it eschews an attitude of resignation towards the question of the ability of Arabs and Jews to cooperate in their common interest, in favor of a realistic and dynamic attitude, namely, that under changed conditions the will to cooperate can be cultivated." Mr. Camille Chamoun, representative of Lebanon, speaking before the United Nations' General Assembly on November 29, 1947, in a desperate effort to reach a compromise formula on the very day partition was decided, called once more for an independent state of Palestine to be "constituted on a federal basis and ... [comprise] a federal government and cantonal governments of Jewish and Arab cantons." Like Dr. Magnes in his explanation of the plan for a Confederation of Palestine, he invoked the Constitution of the United States of America to serve as a model for the future constitution of the new state.

The plan for a Confederate Palestine with Jerusalem as a common capital, was nothing more or less than the only possible implementation of the UN partition decision, which made economic union a prerequisite. The purely economic approach of the United Nations would have met with difficulty under any circumstances because, as Major Eban rightly stressed, "the economic interdependence of all Palestine was much overrated by the General Assembly." It would, moreover, have run into the same difficulties as the European Recovery Program, which also pre-supposed the possibility of economic cooperation without political implementation. These inherent difficulties in an economic approach became plain impossibility with the outbreak of the war, which first of all can be concluded only by political measures. Moreover the war has destroyed all sectors of a combined Jewish-Arab economy and eliminated, with the explusion of almost all Arabs from Israeli-held territories, the very small common economic basis upon which hopes for a future development of common economic interests had rested.

Indeed, an obvious shortcoming of our arguments for peace as against a precarious armistice and for confederation as against further Balkanization, is that they can hardly be based upon anything like economic necessity. In order to arrive at a correct estimate of the impact of war on the Israeli economy, one cannot simply add up the staggering losses in working hours and destruction of property which Israel has suffered. Against them stands a very substantial increase in income from "charity" which never would have been given without the establishment of a state and the present tremendous immigration, both of which were the direct causes of the Jewish-Arab war. Since Jewish economy in Palestine in any case depended largely upon investment through donation, it may even be possible that the gains obtained through emergency outweigh the losses suffered through war.

Pacification of the region might well attract more dividend paying investment capital from American Jewry and even international loans. Yet it would also automatically diminish the Israeli income in nondividend paying money. At first glance, such a development may seem to lead to a sounder economy and greater political independence. Actually it may well mean greatly reduced resources and even increased interference from the outside for the simple reason that the investing public is likely to be more businesslike and less idealistic than mere donors.

But even if we assume that American Jewry, after the European catastrophe, would not have needed the emergency of war and the stimulation of victories to mobilize support to the extent of a hundred and fifty million dollars a year, the economic advantages of the war probably outweigh its losses. There are first the clear gains resulting from the flight of the Arabs from Israeli-occupied territory. This evacuation of almost fifty per cent of the country's population in no way disrupted Jewish economy because it had been built in almost complete isolation from its surroundings. But more important than these gains, with their heavy moral and political mortgage, is the factor of immigration itself. The new immigrants, who are partly settled in the deserted homesteads of Arab refugees, were urgently needed for reconstruction purposes and to offset the great loss in manpower brought about by mobilization; they are not only an economic burden to the country, they constitute also its surest asset. The influx of American money, chiefly raised and used for the resettlement of DP's, combined with the influx of manpower, may stimulate Israeli economy in much the same way, only on a much larger scale, as, ten years ago, the influx of American money together with the immigration of youngsters (Youth Aliya) helped the enlargement and modernization of the collective settlements.

The same absence of economic necessity marks the argument for confederation. As things stand today, the Israeli State is not only a Jewish island in an Arab sea and not only a Westernized and industrialized outpost in the desert of a stagnant economy: it is also a producer of commodities for which no demand exists in its immediate neighborhood. Doubtless this situation will change some time in the future, but nobody knows how close or how distant this future may be. At the moment, at any rate, federation could hardly base itself on existing economic realities, on a functioning interdependence. It could become a working device only if—in the words of Dr. Magnes in 1947—"Jewish scientific ability, Jewish organizing power, perhaps finance, perhaps the experience of the West, which many of the countries of this part of the world have need of, [would] be placed at their disposal for the good of the whole region."

Such an enterprise would call for great vision and even sacrifices, though the sacrifices might be less difficult to bear if the channeling of Jewish pioneering skill and capital into Arab countries were connected with some agreement about the resettlement of Arab DP's. Without such a modernization of the Near East, Israel will be left in economic isolation, without the prerequisites for a normal exchange of its products, even more dependent on outside help than now. It is not and never has been an argument against the great achievements of the Jewish National Home that they were "artificial," that they did not follow economic laws and necessities but sprang from the political will of the Jewish people. But it would be a tragedy if, once this home or this state has been established, its people continued to depend upon "miracles" and were unable to accommodate themselves to objective necessities, even if these are of a long-range nature. Charity money can be mobilized in great quantities only in emergencies, such as in the recent catastrophe in Europe or in the Arab-Jewish war; if the Israeli government cannot win its economic independence from such money it will soon find itself in the unenviable position of being forced to create emergencies, that is, forced into a policy of aggressiveness and expansion. The extremists understand this situation very well when they propagate an artificial prolongation of the war which, according to them, never should have ended before the whole of Palestine and Transjordan are conquered.

In other words, the alternative between federation and

Balkanization is a political one. The trouble is not that rampant nationalism has disrupted a common economic structure, but that justified national aspirations could develop into rampant nationalism because they were not checked by economic interests. The task of a Near East Federation would be to create a common economic structure, to bring about economic and political cooperation and to integrate Jewish economic and social achievements. Balkanization would isolate even further the new Jewish pioneer and worker who have found a way to combine manual labor with a high standard of culture and to introduce a new human element into modern life. They, together with the heirs of the Hebrew University, would be the first victims of a long period of military insecurity and nationalistic aggressiveness.

But only the first victims. For without the cultural and social *hinterland* of Jerusalem and the collective settlements, Tel Aviv could become a Levantine city overnight. Chauvinism of the Balkan type could use the religious concept of the chosen people and allow its meaning to degenerate into hopeless vulgarity. The birth of a nation in the midst of our century may be a great event; it certainly is a dangerous event. National sovereignty which so long had been the very symbol of free national development has become the greatest danger to national survival for small nations. In view of the international situation and the geographical location of Palestine, it is not likely that the Jewish and Arab peoples will be exempt from this rule.

PART III:

The Eichmann
Controversy

Organized Guilt
and Universal Responsibility

(JANUARY 1945)

The greater the military defeats of the Wehrmacht in the field, the greater becomes that victory of Nazi political warfare which is so often incorrectly described as mere propaganda. It is the central thesis of this Nazi political strategy that there is no difference between Nazis and Germans, that the people stand united behind the government, that all Allied hopes of finding part of the people uninfected ideologically and all appeals to a democratic Germany of the future are pure illusion. The implication of this thesis is, of course, that there is no distinction as to responsibility, that German anti-Fascists will suffer from defeat equally with German Fascists, and that the Allies had made such distinctions at the beginning of the war only for propaganda purposes. A further implication is that Allied provisions for punishment of war criminals will turn out to be empty threats because they will find no one to whom the title of war criminal could not be applied.

That such claims are not mere propaganda but are supported by very real and fearful facts, we have all learned in the past seven years. The terror organizations which were at first strictly separated from the mass of the people, admitting only persons who could show a criminal past or prove their preparedness to become criminals, have since been continually expanded. The ban on party membership for members of the army has been dissolved by the general order which subordinates all soldiers to the party. Whereas those crimes which have always been a part of the daily routine of concentration camps since the beginning of the Nazi regime were at first a jealously guarded monopoly of the SS and Gestapo, today members of the Wehrmacht are assigned at will to duties of mass murder. These crimes were at first kept secret by every possible means and any publication of such reports was made punishable as atrocity propaganda. Later, however, such reports were spread by Nazi-organized whispering campaigns and today these crimes are openly proclaimed under the title of "measures of liquidation" in order to force "Volksgenossen" whom difficulties of organization made it impossible to induct into the "Volksgemeinschaft" of crime at least to bear the onus of complicity and awareness of what was going on. These tactics resulted in a victory for the Nazis, as the Allies abandoned the distinction between Germans and Nazis. In order to appreciate the decisive change of political conditions in Germany since the lost battle of Britain, one must note that until the war and even until the first military defeats only relatively small groups of active Nazis, among whom not even the Nazi sympathizers were included, and equally small numbers of active anti-Fascists really knew what was going on. All others, whether German or non-German, had the natural inclination to believe the statements of an official, universally recognized government rather than the charges of refugees, which, coming from Jews or Socialists, were suspect in any case. Even of those refugees, only a relatively small proportion knew the full truth and even a smaller fraction was prepared to bear the odium of unpopularity involved in telling the truth.

As long as the Nazis expected victory, their terror organizations were strictly isolated from the people and, in time of war, from the army. The army was not used to commit atrocities and SS troops were increasingly recruited from "qualified" circles of whatever nationality. If the planned New Order of Europe should have succeeded, we would have been witnesses of an inter-European organization of terror under German leadership. The terror would have been exercised by members of all European nationalities with the exception of Jews in an organization graded according to the racial classification of the various countries. The German people, of course, would not have been spared by it. Himmler was always of the opinion that authority in Europe should be in the hands of a racial élite, organized in SS troops without national ties.

It was only their defeats which forced the Nazis to abandon this concept and pretend to return to old nationalist slogans.

The active identification of the whole German people with the Nazis was part of this trend. National Socialism's chances of organizing an underground movement in the future depend on no one's being able to know any longer who is a Nazi and who is not, on there being no visible signs of distinction any longer, and above all on the victorious powers' being convinced that there really are no differences between Germans. To bring this about, an intensified terror in Germany, which proposed to leave no person alive whose past or reputation proclaimed him an anti-Fascist, was necessary. In the first years of the war the regime was remarkably "magnanimous" to its opponents, provided they remained peaceful. Of late, however, countless persons have been executed even though, by reason of years without freedom of movement, they could not constitute any immediate danger to the regime. On the other hand, prudently foreseeing that in spite of all precautionary measures the Allies might still find a few hundred persons in each city with an irreproachable anti-Fascist record—testified to by former war prisoners or foreign laborers, and supported by records of imprisonment or concentration camp internment—the Nazis have already provided their own trusted cohorts with similar documentation and testimony, making these criteria worthless. Thus in the case of inmates of concentration camps (whose number nobody knows precisely, but which is estimated at several million), the Nazis can safely either liquidate them or let them escape: in the improbable event of their survival (a massacre of the type which already occurred in Buchenwald is not even punishable under the war-crimes provisions)—it will not be possible to identify them unmistakably.

Whether any person in Germany is a Nazi or an anti-Nazi can be determined only by the One who knows the secrets of the human heart, which no human eye can penetrate. Those, at any rate, who actively organize an anti-Nazi underground movement in Germany today—and there are such persons in Germany, of course—would meet a speedy death if they failed to act and talk precisely like Nazis. In a country where a person attracts immediate attention by failing either to murder upon command or to be a ready accomplice of murderers, this is no light task. The most extreme slogan which this war has evoked among the Allies, that the only "good German" is a "dead German," has this much basis in fact: the only way in which we

can identify an anti-Nazi is when the Nazis have hanged him.
There is no other reliable token.

II

These are the real political conditions which underlie the
charge of the collective guilt of the German people. They are
the consequences of a policy which, in the deepest sense, is a-
and anti-national; which is entirely determined that there shall
be a German people only if it is in the power of its present
rulers; and which will rejoice as at its greatest victory if the
defeat of the Nazis involves with it the physical destruction of
the German people. The totalitarian policy, which has completely destroyed the neutral zone in which the daily life of
human beings is ordinarily lived, has achieved the result of
making the existence of each individual in Germany depend
either upon committing crimes or on complicity in crimes. The
success of Nazi propaganda in Allied countries, as expressed in
the attitude commonly called Vansittartism, is a secondary
matter in comparison. It is a product of general war propaganda, and something quite apart from the specific modern
political phenomenon described above. All the documents and
pseudo-historical demonstrations of this tendency sound like
relatively innocent plagiarism of the French literature of the
last war—and it makes no essential difference that a few of
those writers who twenty-five years ago kept the presses rolling
with their attacks on "perfidious Albion" have now placed their
experience at the Allies' disposal.

But even the best-intended discussions between the defen-
ders of the "good Germans" and the accusers of the "bad" not
only miss the essence of the question but plainly do not even
apprehend the magnitude of the catastrophe. Either they are
betrayed into trivial general comments on good and bad
people, and into a fantastic over-estimation of the power of
education, or they simply adopt an inverted version of Nazi
racial theory. There is a certain danger in all this only because
since Churchill's famous statement on the subject, the Allies
have refrained from fighting an ideological war and have thus
unconsciously given an advantage to the Nazis (who, without
regard to Churchill, are organizing their defeat ideologically)
and a chance of survival to all racial theories.

The true problem however is not to prove what is self-evident, namely that Germans have not been potential Nazis ever since Tacitus' times, nor what is impossible, that all Germans harbor Nazi views. It is rather to consider how to conduct ourselves and how to bear the trial of confronting a people among whom the boundaries dividing criminals from normal persons, the guilty from the innocent, have been so completely effaced that nobody will be able to tell in Germany whether in any case he is dealing with a secret hero or with a former mass murderer. In this situation we will not be aided either by a definition of those responsible, nor by the punishment of "war criminals." Such definitions by their very nature can apply only to those who not only took responsibility upon themselves, but produced this whole inferno—and yet strangely enough are still not to be found on the lists of war criminals. The number of those who are responsible *and* guilty will be relatively small. There are many who share responsibility without any visible proof of guilt. There are many more who have become guilty without being in the least responsible. Among the responsible in a broader sense must be included all those who continued sympathetic to Hitler as long as it was possible, who aided his rise to power, and who applauded him in Germany and in other European countries. Who would dare to brand all these ladies and gentlemen of high society as war criminals? And as a matter of fact they really do not deserve such a title. Unquestionably they have proved their inability to judge modern political groupings, some of them because they regarded all principles as moralistic nonsense in politics, others because they were affected by a romantic predilection for gangsters whom they confused with "pirates" of an older time. Yet these people, who were co-responsible for Hitler's crimes in a broader sense, did not incur any guilt in a stricter sense. They, who were the Nazis' first accomplices and their best aides, truly did not know what they were doing nor with whom they were dealing.

The extreme horror with which particularly persons of good will react whenever the case of Germany is discussed is not evoked by those irresponsible co-responsibles, nor even by the particular crimes of the Nazis themselves. It is rather the product of that vast machine of administrative mass murder, in whose service not only thousands of persons, nor even scores of thousands of selected murderers, but a whole people could be and was employed: In that organization which Himmler has prepared against the defeat, everyone is either an executioner, a victim, or an automaton, marching onward over the corpses of his comrades—chosen at first out of the various storm-troop formations and later from any army unit or other mass organization. That everyone, whether or not he is directly active in a murder camp, is forced to take part in one way or another in the workings of this machine of mass murder—that is the horrible thing. For systematic mass murder—the true consequence of all race theories and other modern ideologies which preach that might is right—strains not only the imagination of human beings, but also the framework and categories of our political thought and action. Whatever the future of Germany, it will not be determined by anything more than the inevitable consequences of a lost war—conquences which in the nature of the case are temporary. There is no political method for dealing with German mass crimes, and the destruction of seventy or eighty million Germans, or even their gradual death through starvation (of which, of course, nobody except a few psychotic fanatics dream), would simply mean that the ideology of the Nazis had won, even if power and the rights of might had fallen to other peoples.

Just as there is no political solution within human capacity for the crime of administrative mass murder, so the human need for justice can find no satisfactory reply to the total mobilization of a people for that purpose. Where all are guilty, nobody in the last analysis can be judged.[1] For that guilt is not accompanied by even the mere appearance, the mere pretense of responsibility. So long as punishment is the right of the criminal—and this paradigm has for more than two thousand years been the basis of the sense of justice and right of Occidental man—guilt implies the consciousness of guilt, and punishment evidence that the criminal is a responsible person. How it is in this matter has been well described by an American

1. That German refugees, who had the good fortune either to be Jews or to have been persecuted by the Gestapo early enough, have been saved from this guilt is of course not their merit. Because they know this and because their horror at which might have been still haunts them, they often introduce into discussions of this kind that insufferable tone of self-righteousness which frequently and particularly among Jews, can turn into the vulgar obverse of Nazi doctrines; and in fact already has.

correspondent, in a story whose dialogue material is worthy of the imagination and creative power of a great poet.

Q. Did you kill people in the camp? A. Yes.

Q. Did you poison them with gas? A. Yes.

Q. Did you bury them alive? A. It sometimes happened.

Q. Were the victims picked from all over Europe? A. I suppose so.

Q. Did you personally help kill people? A. Absolutely not. I was only paymaster in the camp.

Q. What did you think of what was going on? A. It was bad at first but we got used to it.

Q. Do you know the Russians will hang you? A. (Bursting into tears) Why should they? *What have I done?* (Italics mine. PM, Sunday, Nov. 12, 1944.)

Really he had done nothing. He had only carried out orders and since when has it been a crime to carry out orders? Since when has it been a virtue to rebel? Since when could one only be decent by welcoming death? What then had he done?

In his play, *Last Days of Mankind,* about the last war, Karl Kraus rang down the curtain after Wilhelm II had cried, "I did not want this." And the horribly comic part of it was that this was the fact. When the curtain falls this time, we will have to listen to a whole chorus calling out, "We did not do this." And even though we shall no longer be able to appreciate the comic element, the horrible part of it will still be that this is the fact.

III

In trying to understand what were the real motives which caused people to act as cogs in the mass-murder machine, we shall not be aided by speculations about German history and the so-called German national character, of whose potentialities those who knew Germany most intimately had not the slightest idea fifteen years ago. There is more to be learned from the characteristic personality of the man who can boast that he was the organizing spirit of the murder. Heinrich Himmler is not one of those intellectuals stemming from the dim No-Man's Land between the Bohemian and the Pimp, whose significance in the composition of the Nazi élite has been repeatedly stressed of late. He is neither a Bohemian like Goebbels, nor a sex criminal like Streicher, nor a perverted fanatic like Hitler, nor an adventurer like Goering. He is a "bourgeois" with all the outer aspect of respectability, all the habits of a good *paterfamilias* who does not betray his wife and anxiously seeks to secure a decent future for his children; and he has consciously built up his newest terror organization, covering the whole country, on the assumption that most people are not Bohemians nor fanatics, nor adventurers, nor sex maniacs, nor sadists, but, first and foremost job-holders, and good family-men.

It was Péguy, I believe, who called the family man the "grand aventurier du 20e siècle." He died too soon to learn that he was also the great criminal of the century. We had been so accustomed to admire or gently ridicule the family man's kind concern and earnest concentration on the welfare of his family, his solemn determination to make life easy for his wife and children, that we hardly noticed how the devoted *paterfamilias*, worried about nothing so much as his security, was transformed under the pressure of the chaotic economic conditions of our time into an involuntary adventurer, who for all his industry and care could never be certain what the next day would bring. The docility of this type was already manifest in the very early period of Nazi "gleichschaltung" [equal rule]. It became clear that for the sake of his pension, his life insurance, the security of his wife and children, such a man was ready to sacrifice his beliefs, his honor, and his human dignity. It needed only the satanic genius of Himmler to discover that after such degradation he was entirely prepared to do literally anything when the ante was raised and the bare existence of his family was threatened. The only condition he put was that he should be fully exempted from responsibility for his acts. Thus that very person, the average German, whom the Nazis notwithstanding years of the most furious propaganda could not induce to kill a Jew on his own account (not even when they made it quite clear that such a murder would go unpunished) now serves the machine of destruction without opposition. In contrast to the earlier units of the SS men and Gestapo, Himmler's over-all organization, relies not on fanatics, nor on congenital murderers, nor on sadists; it relies entirely upon the normality of jobholders and family-men.

We need not specially mention the sorry reports about Latvians, Lithuanians, or even Jews who have participated in Himmler's murder organization in order to show that it requires no particular national character in order to supply this new type of functionary. They are not even all natural murderers or traitors out of perversity. It is not even certain that they would do the work if it were only their own lives and future that were at stake. They felt (after they no longer needed to fear God, their conscience cleared through the bureaucratic organization of their acts) only the responsibility toward their own families. The transformation of the family man from a responsible member of society, interested in all public affairs, to a "bourgeois" concerned only with his private existence and knowing no civic virtue, is an international modern phenomenon. The exigencies of our time—"bedenkt den Hunger und die gross Kaelte in diesem Tale, das von Jammer schallt" (Brecht)—can at any moment transform him into the mob-man and make him the instrument of whatsoever madness and horror. Each time society, through unemployment, frustrates the small man in his normal functioning and normal self-respect, it trains him for that last stage in which he will willingly undertake any function, even that of hangman. A Jew released from Buchenwald once discovered among the SS men who gave him the certificates of release a former schoolmate, whom he did not address but yet stared at. Spontaneously the man stared at remarked: "You must understand, I have five years of unemployment behind me. They can do anything they want with me."

It is true that the development of this modern type of man who is the exact opposite of the "citoyen" and whom for lack of a better name we have called the "bourgeois," enjoyed particularly favorable conditions in Germany. Hardly another country of Occidental culture was so little imbued with the classic virtues of civic behavior. In no other country did private life and private calculations play so great a role. This is a fact which the Germans in time of national emergency disguised with great success, but never altered. Behind the facade of proclaimed and propagandized national virtues, such as "love of the fatherland," "German courage," "German loyalty," etc., there lurked corresponding real national vices. There is hardly another country where on the average there is so little patriotism as Germany; and behind the chauvinistic claims of loyalty and courage, a fatal tendency to disloyalty and betrayal for opportunistic reasons is hidden.

The mob man, however, the end-result of the "bourgeois," is an international phenomenon; and we would do well not to submit him to too many temptations in the blind faith that only the German mob-man is capable of such frightful deeds. What we have called the "bourgeois" is the modern man of the masses, not in his exalted moments of collective excitement, but in the security (today one should rather say the insecurity) of his own private domain. He has driven the dichotomy of private and public functions, of family and occupation, so far that he can no longer find in his own person any connection between the two. When his occupation forces him to murder people he does not regard himself as a murderer because he has not done it out of inclination but in his professional capacity. Out of sheer passion he would never do harm to a fly.

If we tell a member of this new occupational class which our time has produced that he is being held to account for what he did, he will feel nothing except that he has been betrayed. But if in the shock of the catastrophe he really becomes conscious that in fact he was not only a functionary but a murderer, then his way out will not be that of rebellion, but suicide—just as so many have already chosen the way of suicide in Germany, where it is plain that there has been one wave of self-destruction after another. And that too would be of little use to us.

IV

It is many years now that we meet Germans who declare that they are ashamed of being Germans. I have often felt tempted to answer that I am ashamed of being human. This elemental shame, which many people of the most various nationalities share with one another today, is what finally is left of our sense of international solidarity, and it has not yet found an adequate political expression. Our fathers' enchantment with humanity was of a sort which not only light-mindedly ignored the national question; what is far worse, it did not even conceive of the terror of the idea of humanity and of the

Judeo-Christian faith in the unitary origin of the human race. It was not very pleasant even when we had to bury our false illusions about "the noble savage," having discovered that men were capable of being cannibals. Since then peoples have learned to know one another better and learned more and more about the evil potentialities in men. The result has been that they have recoiled more and more from the idea of humanity and become more susceptible to the doctrine of race which denies the very possibility of a common humanity. They instinctively felt that the idea of humanity, whether it appears in a religious or humanistic form, implies the obligation of a general responsibility which they do not wish to assume. For the idea of humanity, when purged of all sentimentality, has the very serious consequence that in one form or another men must assume responsibility for all crimes committed by men and that all nations share the onus of evil committed by all others. Shame at being a human being is the purely individual and still nonpolitical expression of this insight.

In political terms, the idea of humanity, excluding no people and assigning a monopoly of guilt to no one, is the only guarantee that one "superior race" after another may not feel obligated to follow the "natural law" of the right of the powerful, and exterminate "inferior races unworthy of survival"; so that at the end of an "imperialistic age" we should find ourselves in a stage which would make the Nazis look like crude precursors of future political methods. To follow a non-imperialistic policy and maintain a non-racist faith becomes daily more difficult because it becomes daily clearer how great a burden mankind is for man.

Perhaps those Jews, to whose forefathers we owe the first conception of the idea of humanity, knew something about that burden when each year they used to say "Our Father and King, we have sinned before you," taking not only the sins of their own community but all human offenses upon themselves. Those who today are ready to follow this road in a modern version do not content themselves with the hypocritical confession, "God be thanked, I am not like that," in horror at the undreamed of potentialities of the German national character. Rather, in fear and trembling, have they finally realized of what man is capable—and this is indeed the precondition of any modern political thinking. Such persons will not serve very well as functionaries of vengeance. This, however, is certain: upon them and only upon them, who are filled with a genuine fear of the inescapable guilt of the human race, can there be any reliance when it comes to fighting fearlessly, uncompromisingly, everywhere against the incalculable evil that men are capable of bringing about.

About "Collaboration"

(OCTOBER 1948)

Dear Sir:

The August issue of *Jewish Frontier* carried an article by Ben Halpern, "The Partisan in Israel," in which, together with Robert Weltsch and Ernst Simon, I was singled out for an attack on my political views and my personal motives. Since Mr. Halpern's attack on the latter was based on an unexplained and certainly unexpected insight into my "subconsciousness," I don't think it necessary to reply to it. However, some of the political points which his article raised seem to be pertinent enough to merit closer attention.

Mr. Halpern is correct in stating that there exists an opposition to present Zionist politics which is based on a long-term analysis of the Jewish position in the Near East on one hand, and on a moral and political distrust of all racial chauvinist attitudes on the other, and that this opposition will not be silenced or disproved through the changing constellations of the moment. He also is correct in stating that apprehensions voiced by some members of this opposition and, especially by myself, have most fortunately been unfounded for the time being.

I do not think that the time has come to discuss the very complicated and very dangerous political background of the military victories of the State of Israel. Even without such an analysis, no "metaphysical" interpretation should be needed in order to understand the difference in emphasis and importance between a few military successes in a small country against ill-armed, ill-trained soldiers and the solid threatening opposition of many millions of people from Morocco down to the Indian

237

Ocean. This and similar constellations constitute the long-range reality, which certainly is not less "real" than what happens in Jerusalem or in the Galilee. The trouble with reality is that, without transcending into another world, it sometimes does not lie before our noses.

What Mr. Halpern, like many of our politically interested intellectuals, does not understand is that we deal in politics only with warnings and not with prophecies. If I were foolish and resigned enough to play the role of the prophet, I certainly should also be content to share his eternal fate, which is to be proved wrong time and again, except at the decisive moment, when it is too late.

Much more to the point than this controversy about "realism" are those paragraphs in Halpern's article which deal with the difference between the "type of the partisan" and the "type of the collaborationist." (Here Mr. Halpern uses Max Weber's method of constructing *Idealtypen* and thus proves how difficult it seems to be to avoid "a type of reasoning which [is] . . . in essence metaphysical.") The term "collaborationist" is, of course, a defamation: actually, however, Halpern restores it to its non-committal and literal meaning. For it is perfectly true that all the people attacked by him have been concerned, in different ways, with the relationship between the Yishuv and the outside world, and have been constantly on the look-out for countries, persons, and institutions with which one might collaborate. This has been notably the case with Dr. Magnes' outstanding effort to bring about a Jewish-Arab agreement as the basis for any solution to the Palestinian problem. Halpern dismisses the Ikhud group, of course, as unpractical. Yet, Dr. Magnes' recent proposal of a Confederation of Palestine is in agreement with some of the basic ideas contained in Count Bernadotte's Peace Proposals of July 4th. Does Mr. Halpern think that the Mediator was a very unpractical man?

The central question in this controversy is really the question whether one wants or does not want to collaborate. And this question, again, is tied up with an older troublesome question of Zionist politics, that is, the problem of the distinction between friend and foe. When, in the 30's, the Jewish Agency concluded a "Transfer Agreement" with Nazi Germany, the problem of this distinction was involved. Official Zionism thought the agreement a wise step because it made possible the transfer of part of Jewish property from Germany to Palestine in the form of German merchandise. The agreement was severely criticized by a large part of Jewry because, from a long-range political point-of-view, it seemed unwise for a Jewish political agency to do business with an anti-Semitic government. A similar error in judgment, though in an opposite sense, is one of the basic conflicts between official Zionism and its current "collaborationist" opposition, and it has misled Mr. Halpern into a complete misunderstanding of my analysis of the all-or-nothing attitude. Indeed, if Great Britain were an enemy of the Jews, like Nazi Germany, the all-or-nothing attitude would be justified. The point is precisely that today a certain general hysteria imposes all-or-nothing policies upon a moderately friendly world. This is chauvinism; it tends to divide the world into two halves, one of which is one's own nation, which fate, or ill-will, or history has pitted against a whole world of enemies.

Neither the Arabs nor the British are enemies against whom an all-or-nothing attitude could be justified. With both, we shall have to live in peace. The struggle in Palestine takes place within a broad international framework, and the right distinction between friend and foe will be a life-or-death matter for the State of Israel. Changing opportunities of the moment are now dangerously blurring such fundamental distinctions. The program of left-wing Labor in Israel with respect to Russia on the one hand, and to England on the other, is a case in point.

This is also one of the reasons why the "partisan" attitude cannot be generalized—no matter how tempting Halpern's enthusiastic description may sound. A closer analysis would easily show that the moment the "partisan" is backed by the machinery of state power, he changes into that type of "political soldier" whom we know only too well in totalitarian governments. What the new State of of Israel will need most are responsible citizens (the "type of the *citoyen*," to speak of Mr. Halpern's language), who don't lose their pioneer qualities and who, after having lost their faith in internationalist ideologies, may acquire a new, more sober and juster international outlook upon the world that still surrounds them.

HANNAH ARENDT

"Eichmann in Jerusalem"

An Exchange of Letters between Gershom Scholem and Hannah Arendt*

Jerusalem, June 23, 1963

DEAR HANNAH,

Six weeks have passed since I received your book on the Eichmann trial; and, if I write belatedly, it is because only now do I have the leisure to devote myself to a proper study of it. I have not, let me say, gone into the question of the factual and historical authenticity of the various statements you make. To judge by your treatment of those aspects of the problem with which I happen to be familiar, however, I fear that your book is not free of error and distortion. Still, I have no doubt that the question of the book's factual authenticity will be taken up by other critics—of whom there will be many—and it is not in any case central to the critique I wish to offer here.

Your book moves between two poles: the Jews and their bearing in the days of catastrophe, and the responsibility of Adolf Eichmann. I have devoted, as you know, a good part of my time to a consideration of the case of the Jews, and I have studied a not insignificant volume of material on the subject. I am well aware, in common with every other spectator of the events, how complex and serious, how little reducible or transparent, the whole problem is. I am aware that there are aspects of Jewish history (and for more than forty years I have concerned myself with little else) which are beyond our comprehension; on the one hand, a devotion to the things of this world that is near-demonic; on the other, a fundamental uncertainty of orientation in this world—an uncertainty which must be contrasted with that certainty of the believer concern-

* Permission to reprint this letter was given by Gershom Scholem although he registers his strong objections to the title of this book, which he finds most offensive.—Ed.

ing which, alas, your book has so little to report. There has been weakness, too, though weakness so entwined with heroism that it is not easily unraveled; wretchedness and power-lust are also to be found there. But these things have always existed, and it would be remarkable indeed if, in the days of catastrophe, they were not to make their appearance once again. Thus it was in the year 1931, at the beginning of that generation of catastrophe; and so it has been in our own time. The discussion of these matters is, I believe, both legitimate and unavoidable— although I do not believe that our generation is in a position to pass any kind of historical judgment. We lack the necessary perspective, which alone makes some sort of objectivity possible—and we cannot but lack it.

Nevertheless, we cannot put these questions aside. There is the question thrown at us by the new youth of Israel: why did they allow themselves to be slaughtered? As a question, it seems to me to have a profound justification; and I see no readily formulated answer to it. At each decisive juncture, however, your book speaks only of the *weakness* of the Jewish stance in the world. I am ready enough to admit that weakness; but you put such emphasis upon it that, in my view, your account ceases to be objective and acquires overtones of malice. The problem, I have admitted, is real enough. Why, then, should your book leave one with so strong a sensation of bitterness and shame—not for the compilation, but for the compiler? How is it that your version of the events so often seems to come between us and the events—events which you rightly urge upon our attention? Insofar as I have an answer, it is one which, precisely out of my deep respect for you, I dare not suppress; and it is an answer that goes to the root of our disagreement. It is that heartless, frequently almost sneering and malicious tone with which these matters, touching the very quick of our life, are treated in your book to which I take exception.

In the Jewish tradition there is a concept, hard to define and yet concrete enough, which we know as *Ahabath Israel*: "Love of the Jewish people. . . ." In you, dear Hannah, as in so many intellectuals who came from the German Left, I find little trace of this. A discussion such as is attempted in your book would seem to me to require—you will forgive my mode of expression—the most old-fashioned, the most circumspect, the most exacting treatment possible—precisely because of the feelings aroused by this matter, this matter of the destruction of one-third of our people—and I regard you wholly as a daughter of our people, and in no other way. Thus I have little sympathy with that tone—well expressed by the English word "flippancy"—which you employ so often in the course of your book. To the matter of which you speak it is unimaginably inappropriate. In circumstances such as these, would there not have been a place for what I can only describe with that modest German word—"*Herzenstakt*"? You may laugh at the word; although I hope you do not, for I mean it seriously. Of the many examples I came upon in your book—and came upon not without pain—none expresses better what I mean than your quotation (taken over without comment from a Nazi source!) about the traffic with the armbands with the Star of David in the Warsaw Ghetto, or the sentence about Leo Baeck "who in the eyes of both Jews and Gentiles was the 'Jewish *Führer*'. . . ." The use of the Nazi term in this context is sufficiently revealing. You do not speak, say, of the "Jewish leader," which would have been both apt and free of the German word's horrific connotation—you say precisely the thing that is most false and most insulting. For nobody of whom I have heard or read was Leo Baeck—whom we both knew—ever a "*Führer*" in the sense which you here insinuate to the reader. I too have read Adler's book about Theresienstadt. It is a book about which a great many things could be said. But it was not my impression that the author—who speaks of some people, of whom I have heard quite different accounts, with considerable harshness—it was not my impression that Adler ever spoke of Baeck in this fashion, either directly or indirectly. Certainly, the record of our people's suffering is burdened with a number of questionable figures who deserve, or have received, their just punishment: how could it have been otherwise in a tragedy on so terrible a scale? To speak of all this, however, in so wholly inappropriate a tone—to the benefit of those Germans in condemning whom your book rises to greater eloquence than in mourning the fate of your own people—this is not the way to approach the scene of that tragedy.

In your treatment of the problem of how the Jews reacted to these extreme circumstances—to which neither of us was exposed—I detect, often enough, in place of balanced judgment, a kind of demagogic will-to-overstatement. Which of us can say today what decisions the elders of the Jews—or whatever we choose to call them—ought to have arrived at in the circumstances? I have not read less than you have about these matters, and I am still not certain; but your analysis does not give me confidence that your certainty is better founded than my uncertainty. There were the *Judenräte*, for example; some among them were swine, others were saints. I have read a great deal about both varieties. There were among them also many people in no way different from ourselves, who were compelled to make terrible decisions in circumstances that we cannot even begin to reproduce or reconstruct. I do not know whether they were right or wrong. Nor do I presume to judge. I was not there.

Certainly, there were people in Theresienstadt—as every former inmate can confirm—whose conduct is deserving of the severest judgment. But in case after case we find that the individual verdict varies. Why was Paul Eppstein, one of these "questionable figures," shot by the Nazis, for example? You give no reason. Yet the reason is clear enough: he had done precisely that which according to you he could afford to do without serious danger—he told people in Theresienstadt what awaited them at Auschwitz. Yet he was shot twenty-four hours later.

Nevertheless, your thesis that these machinations of the Nazis served in some way to blur the distinction between torturer and victim—a thesis which you employ to belabor the prosecution in the Eichmann trial—seems to me wholly false and tendentious. In the camps, human beings were systematically degraded; they were, as you say, compelled to participate in their own extermination, and to assist in the execution of fellow-prisoners. Is the distinction between torturer and victim thereby blurred? What perversity! We are asked, it appears, to confess that the Jews, too, had their "share" in these acts of genocide. That is a typical *quaternio terminorum*.

Recently, I have been reading about a book, written during the days of catastrophe in full consciousness of what lay ahead, by Rabbi Moses Chaim Lau of Piotrkov. This rabbi attempted to define as precisely as possible what was the duty of the Jew in such extremities. Much that I read on this moving and

terrible book—and it does not stand alone—is congruent with
your general thesis (though not with your tone). But nowhere
in your book do you make plain how many Jews there were who
acted as they did in full consciousness of what awaited them.
The Rabbi in question went with his flock to Treblinka—
although he had previously called on them to run away, and his
flock had called on him to do likewise. The heroism of the Jews
was not always the heroism of the warrior; nor have we always
been ashamed of that fact. I cannot refute those who say that
the Jews deserved their fate, because they did not take earlier
steps to defend themselves, because they were cowardly, etc. I
came across this argument only recently in a book by that
honest Jewish anti-semite, Kurt Tucholsky. I cannot express
myself, of course, with Kurt Tucholsky's eloquence, but I
cannot deny that he was right: if all the Jews had run away—in
particular, to Palestine—more Jews would have remained alive.
Whether, in view of the special circumstances of Jewish history
and Jewish life, that would have been possible, and whether it
implies a historical share of guilt in Hitler's crime, is another
question.

I shall say nothing concerning that other central question of
your book: the guilt, or the degree of guilt, of Adolf Eichmann.
I have read both the text of the judgment delivered by the
Court, and the version you substituted for it in your book. I
find that of the Court rather more convincing. Your judgment
appears to me to be based on a prodigious *non sequitur*. Your
argument would apply equally to those hundreds of thousands,
perhaps millions of human beings, to whom your final sentence
is relevant. It is the final sentence that contains the reason why
Eichmann ought to be hanged, for in the remainder of your
text you argue in detail your view—which I do not share—that
the prosecution did not succeed in proving what it had set out
to prove. As far as that goes, I may mention that, in addition to
putting my name to a letter to the President of Israel pleading
for the execution not to be carried out, I set out in a Hebrew
essay why I held the execution of the sentence—which
Eichmann had in every sense, including that of the prosecution, deserved—to be historically wrong, precisely because of
our historical relationship with the German people. I shall not
argue the case again here. I wish to say only that your

description of Eichmann as a "convert to Zionism" could only come from somebody who had a profound dislike of everything to do with Zionism. These passages in your book I find quite impossible to take seriously. They amount to a mockery of Zionism; and I am forced to the conclusion that this was, indeed, your intention. Let us not pursue the point.

After reading your book I remain unconvinced by your thesis concerning the "banality of evil"—a thesis which, if your sub-title is to be believed, underlies your entire argument. This new thesis strikes me as a catchword: it does not impress me, certainly, as the product of profound analysis—an analysis such as you gave us so convincingly, in the service of a quite different, indeed contradictory thesis, in your book on total-itarianism. At that time you had not yet made your discovery, apparently, that evil is banal. Of that "radical evil," to which your then analysis bore such eloquent and erudite witness, nothing remains but this slogan—to be more than that it would have to be investigated, at a serious level, as a relevant concept in moral philosophy or political ethics. I am sorry—and I say this, I think, in candor and in no spirit of enmity—that I am unable to take the thesis of your book more seriously. I had expected, with your earlier book in mind, something different.

GERSHOM SCHOLEM

New York City, July 24, 1963

DEAR GERHARD,

I found your letter when I got back home a week ago. You know what it's like when one has been away for five months. I'm writing now in the first quiet moment I have; hence my reply may not be as elaborate as perhaps it should be.

There are certain statements in your letter which are not open to controversy, because they are simply false. Let me deal with them first so that we can proceed to matters which merit discussion.

I am not one of the "intellectuals who come from the German Left." You could not have known this, since we did not know each other when we were young. It is a fact of which I am in no way particularly proud and which I am somewhat reluctant to emphasize—especially since the McCarthy era in this country. I came late to an understanding of Marx's importance because I was interested neither in history nor in politics when I was young. If I can be said to "have come from anywhere," it is from the tradition of German philosophy.

As to another statement of yours, I am unfortunately not able to say that you could not have known the facts. I found it puzzling that you should write "I regard you wholly as a daughter of our people, and in no other way." The truth is I have never pretended to be anything else or to be in any way other than I am, and I have never even felt tempted in that direction. It would have been like saying that I was a man and not a woman—that is to say, kind of insane. I know, of course, that there is a "Jewish problem" even on this level, but it has never been my problem—not even in my childhood. I have always regarded my Jewishness as one of the indisputable factual data of my life, and I have never had the wish to change or disclaim facts of this kind. There is such a thing as a basic gratitude for everything that is as it is; for what has been *given* and was not, could not be, *made*; for things that are *physei* and not *nomǭ*. To be sure, such an attitude is pre-political, but in exceptional circumstances—such as the circumstances of Jewish politics—it is bound to have also political consequences though, as it were, in a negative way. This attitude makes certain types of behavior impossible—indeed precisely those which you chose to read into my considerations. (To give another example: In his obituary of Kurt Blumenfeld, Ben-Gurion expressed his regret that Blumenfeld had not seen fit to change his name when he came to live in Israel. Isn't it obvious that Blumenfeld did not do so for exactly the same reasons that had led him in his youth to become a Zionist?) My stand in these matters must surely have been known to you, and it is incomprehensible to me why you should wish to stick a label on me which never fitted in the past and does not fit now.

To come to the point: let me begin, going on from what I have just stated, with what you call "love of the Jewish people" or *Ahabath Israel*. (Incidentally, I would be very grateful if you could tell me since when this concept has played a role in Judaism, when it was first used in Hebrew language and literature, etc.) You are quite right—I am not moved by any "love" of this sort, and for two reasons: I have never in my life "loved" any people or collective—neither the German people, nor the French, nor the American, nor the working class or anything of that sort. I indeed love "only" my friends and the only kind of love I know of and believe in is the love of persons.

Secondly, this "love of the Jews" would appear to me, since I am myself Jewish, as something rather suspect. I cannot love myself or anything which I know is part and parcel of my own person. To clarify this, let me tell you of a conversation I had in Israel with a prominent political personality who was defending the in my opinion disastrous—non-separation of religion and state in Israel. What he said—I am not sure of the exact words any more—ran something like this: "You will understand that, as a Socialist, I, of course, do not believe in God; I believe in the Jewish people." I found this a shocking statement and, being too shocked, I did not reply at the time. But I could have answered: the greatness of this people was once that it believed in God, and believed in Him in such a way that its trust and love towards Him was greater than its fear. And now this people believes only in itself? What good can come out of that?—Well, in this sense I do not "love" the Jews, nor do I "believe" in them; I merely belong to them as a matter of course, beyond dispute or argument.

We could discuss the same issue in political terms; and we should then be driven to a consideration of patriotism. That there can be no patriotism without permanent opposition and criticism is no doubt common ground between us. But I can admit to you something beyond that, namely, that wrong done by my own people naturally grieves me more than wrong done by other peoples. This grief, however, in my opinion is not for display, even if it should be the innermost motive for certain actions or attitudes. Generally speaking, the role of the "heart" in politics seems to me altogether questionable. You know as well as I how often those who merely report certain unpleasant facts are accused of lack of soul, lack of heart, or lack of what you call *Herzenstakt*. We both know, in other words, how often these emotions are used in order to conceal factual truth. I cannot discuss here what happens when emotions are displayed in public and become a factor in political affairs; but it is an important subject, and I have attempted to describe the disastrous results in my book *On Revolution* in discussing the role of compassion in the formation of the revolutionary character.

It is a pity that you did not read the book before the present campaign of misrepresentation against it got under way from the side of the Jewish "establishment" in Israel and

America. There are, unfortunately, very few people who are able to withstand the influence of such campaigns. It seems to me highly unlikely that without being influenced you could possibly have misunderstood certain statements. Public opinion, especially when it has been carefully manipulated, as in this case, is a very powerful thing. Thus, I never made Eichmann out to be a "Zionist." If you missed the irony of the sentence—which was plainly in *oratio obliqua*, reporting Eichmann's own words—I really can't help it. I can only assure you that none of dozens of readers who read the book before publication had ever any doubt about the matter. Further, I never asked why the Jews "let themselves be killed." On the contrary, I accused Hausner of having posed this question to witness after witness. There was no people and no group in Europe which reacted differently under the immediate pressure of terror. The question I raised was that of the cooperation of Jewish functionaries during the "Final Solution," and this question is so very uncomfortable because one cannot claim that they were traitors. (There were traitors too, but that is irrelevant.) In other words, until 1939 and even until 1941, whatever Jewish functionaries did or did not do is understandable and excusable. Only later does it become highly problematical. This issue came up during the trial and it was of course my duty to report it. This constitutes our part of the so-called "unmastered past," and although you may be right that it is too early for a "balanced judgment" (though I doubt this), I do believe that we shall only come to terms with this past if we begin to judge and to be frank about it.

I have made my own position plain, and yet it is obvious that you did not understand it. I said that there was no possibility of resistance, but there existed the possibility of *doing nothing*. And in order to do nothing, one did not need to be a saint, one needed only to say: "I am just a simple Jew, and I have no desire to play any other role." Whether these people or some of them, as you indicate, deserved to be hanged is an altogether different question. What needs to be discussed are not the people so much as the arguments with which they justified themselves in their own eyes and in those of others. Concerning these arguments we are entitled to pass judgment. Moreover, we should not forget that we are dealing here with conditions which were terrible and desperate enough, but which were not the conditions of concentration camps. These decisions were made in an atmosphere of terror but not under the immediate pressure and impact of terror. These are important differences in degree, which every student of totalitarianism must know and take into account. These people had still a certain, limited freedom of decision and of action. Just as the SS murderers also possessed, as we now know, a limited choice of alternatives. They could say: "I wish to be relieved of my murderous duties," and nothing happened to them. Since we are dealing in politics with men, and not with heroes or saints, it is this possibility of *"nonparticipation"* (Kirchheimer) that is decisive if we begin to judge, not the system, but the individual, his choices and his arguments.

And the Eichmann trial was concerned with an individual. In my report I have only spoken of things which came up during the trial itself. It is for this reason that I could not mention the "saints" about whom you speak. Instead I had to limit myself to the resistance fighters whose behavior, as I said, was the more admirable because it occurred under circumstances in which resistance had really ceased to be possible. There were no saints among the witnesses for the prosecution, but there was one utterly pure human being, old Grynszpan, whose testimony I therefore reported at some length. On the German side, after all, one could also have mentioned more than the single case of Sergeant Schmidt. But since his was the only case mentioned in the trial, I had to restrict myself to it.

That the distinction between victims and persecutors was blurred in the concentration camps, deliberately and with calculation, is well known, and I as well as others have insisted on this aspect of totalitarian methods. But to repeat: this is not what I mean by a Jewish share in the guilt, or by the totality of the collapse of all standards. This was part of the system and had indeed nothing to do with Jews.

How you could believe that my book was "a mockery of Zionism" would be a complete mystery to me, if I did not know that many people in Zionist circles have become incapable of listening to opinions or arguments which are off the beaten track and not consonant with their ideology. There are exceptions, and a Zionist friend of mine remarked in all innocence that the book, the last chapter in particular (recognition of the competence of the court, the justification of the kidnapping), was very pro-Israel—as indeed it is. What confuses you is that my arguments and my approach are different from what you are used to; in other words, the trouble is that I am independent. By this I mean, on the one hand, that I do not belong to any organization and always speak only for myself, and on the other hand, that I have great confidence in Lessing's *selbstdenken* for which, I think, no ideology, no public opinion, and no "convictions" can ever be a substitute. Whatever objections you may have to the results, you won't understand them unless you realize that they are really my own and nobody else's.

I regret that you did not argue your case against the carrying out of the death sentence. For I believe that in discussing this question we might have made some progress in finding out where our most fundamental differences are located. You say that it was "historically false," and I feel very uncomfortable seeing the spectre of History raised in this context. In my opinion, it was *politically* and *juridically* (and the last is actually all that mattered) not only correct—it would have been utterly impossible not to have carried out the sentence. The only way of avoiding it would have been to accept Karl Jaspers' suggestion and to hand Eichmann over to the United Nations. Nobody wanted that, and it was probably not feasible; hence there was no alternative left but to hang him. Mercy was out of the question, not on juridical grounds— pardon is anyhow not a prerogative of the juridical system—but because mercy is applicable to the person rather than to the deed; the act of mercy does not forgive murder but pardons the murderer insofar as he, as a person, may be more than anything he ever did. This was not true of Eichmann. And to spare his life without pardoning him was impossible on juridical grounds.

In conclusion, let me come to the only matter where you have not misunderstood me, and where indeed I am glad that you have raised the point. You are quite right: I changed my mind and do no longer speak of "radical evil." It is a long time since we last met, or we would perhaps have spoken about the subject before. (Incidentally, I don't see why you call my term "banality of evil" a catchword or slogan. As far as I know no one has used the term before me; but that is unimportant.) It is indeed my opinion now that evil is never "radical," that it is only extreme, and that it possesses neither depth nor any demonic dimension. It can overgrow and lay waste the whole world precisely because it spreads like a fungus on the surface. It is "thought-defying," as I said, because thought tries to reach some depth, to go to the roots, and the moment it concerns itself with evil, it is frustrated because there is nothing. That is its "banality." Only the good has depth and can be radical. But this is not the place to go into these matters seriously; I intend to elaborate them further in a different context. Eichmann may very well remain the concrete model of what I have to say.

You propose to publish your letter and you ask if I have any objection. My advice would be not to recast the letter in the third person. The value of this controversy consists in its epistolary character, namely in the fact that it is informed by personal friendship. Hence, if you are prepared to publish my answer simultaneously with your letter, I have, of course, no objection.

Hannah Arendt

Footnotes to the Holocaust

by Walter Z. Laqueur

(NOVEMBER 1965)

A Review of *And the Crooked Shall Be Made Straight: The Eichmann Trial, The Jewish Catastrophe and Hannah Arendt's Narrative* by Jacob Robinson. Macmillan, 406 pp., $6.95.

The storm that followed the publication of Hannah Arendt's *Eichmann in Jerusalem* raged for a long time; it provoked violent denunciation or emphatic assent; it even, I am told, poisoned personal relations among intellectuals in New York and to a lesser degree elsewhere. Above all, it drew attention to the many controversial issues in the as yet unwritten history of the Jewish catastrophe during the Second World War. The Arendt debate generated more heat than light; precisely because passions ran so strongly, historical truth at times suffered. It also seems, in retrospect, that a great many people felt impelled to take a position without sufficient knowledge to support their arguments. This does not mean that discussion of the Jewish fate in Europe should be restricted to the professional students of that period; this would be about as absurd as the attempt to confine the discussion of the outstanding political issues of our time to political scientists. But a minimum of factual knowledge is needed to make a genuine contribution to the debate if it is not to turn, as it has done on occasion, into a controversy about moral (or political) dilemmas in general, without reference to time, place, and circumstance.

The author of the present book clearly thinks that Miss Arendt did not have that essential minimum of factual knowledge. Dr. Robinson's own credentials are formidable; an eminent authority on international law, he brings great erudition, a knowledge of many languages, and an unrivaled mastery of the sources to this full-scale attempt to refute Miss Arendt. Miss Arendt's name is no doubt one to conjure with in literary circles and among students of political science and the philosophy of history. Dr. Robinson is less well known, but he belongs to a generation that still produced polymaths. His standing among students of contemporary Jewish history is high. Although he does not say so directly, Dr. Robinson was clearly outraged by Miss Arendt's book. He dissents strongly from her views. He no doubt felt, as many did, that the entire tenor of her work was deplorable, that the murder of six million people was not a fitting occasion for a display of cleverness, occasionally even flippancy. But his rejection of Miss Arendt's work was also clearly motivated by the resentment felt by the professional against the amateur.

It has been Dr. Robinson's task to coordinate research between the various institutes devoted to the study of the Jewish catastrophe. He knows probably better than anyone else the complexity of the issues involved, having had to deal for many years with the problems of tracing, sifting, analyzing, and publishing the immense amount of all chapters in Jewish history. More than anyone else he has encouraged the laborious and painful work of collecting such documents as the protocols of local Jewish Councils in Poland, of innumerable eyewitness accounts in Polish, Russian, Hebrew, and many other languages. Most of this immense documentation cannot have been known to Miss Arendt, whose research was based largely upon secondary materials, such as the books of Reitlinger and Hilberg. These are valuable studies as far as they go, but they are based only on Nazi sources. As Mr. Hilberg says in his Preface to *The Destruction of the European Jews:* "This is not a book about Jews, it is a book about the people who destroyed the Jews." Can one write about Jewish behavior in the face of the disaster without constant reference to the enormous amount of documentation which Dr. Robinson and others have collected?

Dr. Robinson clearly does not think so; he went over Miss Arendt's book with a fine-toothed comb and a powerful magnifying glass. His scholarly apparatus is awe-inspiring—

about one hundred pages of notes and bibliographical references to both published and unpublished material in many languages. Dr. Robinson proves beyond any shadow of doubt that Miss Arendt has made literally hundreds of mistakes, has used incorrect statistics, and has quoted out of context. The relevance of all these corrections is not, however, always immediately obvious. For example, Dr. Robinson notes that Italy joined the Hague Convention in 1907, whereas Miss Arendt didn't think so; he devotes four pages—exactly as much space as he devotes to the fate of French Jewry—to the question of whether, from a constitutional point of view, the crown of Hungary went with that of the Holy Roman Empire. There is thus a sense of imbalance, and the impression is created that the lawyer in Dr. Robinson too often gets the better of the historian. From a lawyer's point of view it is no doubt of decisive importance to discredit a hostile expert by showing that he is not really master of his subject. Now Miss Arendt's trip to Jerusalem did not make her an expert on contemporary Jewish history, and for a specialist like Dr. Robinson, this is not difficult to prove. But there is a tendency to overdo it; even if Miss Arendt gives the name of an SS *Obergruppenfuehrer* as Hans, and Dr. Robinson points out that it really should be Hanns, this does not necessarily disqualify her from commenting on SS policy.

Dr. Robinson's intention was to put the record straight and he had therefore to go into considerable detail. But such immersion in detail can be dangerous; he is a most painstaking scholar, but not an infallible one. Had Miss Arendt a team of researchers at her disposal they could, no doubt, find mistakes in Dr. Robinson's book. They would show for instance that Freisler, president of the Nazi People's Court, was killed in February 1945 and not in 1944 (as Dr. Robinson says), that Martin Luther (not the Protestant theologian, but a high Nazi official) did not die a natural death, that it ought to be *Sudetendeutscher* rather than *Sudetedeutscher*, and so forth. What would it prove? Very little, if anything. It is, I admit, unfair to equate Miss Arendt's attitude towards facts with Dr. Robinson's almost obsessive scholarly accuracy. But attacking Miss Arendt's book mainly in its details is not wholly effective. As a result there is all too often no real confrontation between Miss Arendt, half philosopher and half journalist, with a somewhat cavalier attitude towards facts, and her antagonist, who hardly ever pauses for general reflection between his footnotes. Dr. Robinson is devastating on matters of detail, but less persuasive when it comes to summing up the discussion of the broader issues and their political and moral implications. In his section on "Jewish behavior in the face of disaster," half of Dr. Robinson's space is given to quoting an eyewitness account by a Christian Pole who lived in the Cracow ghetto. The same witness had just before been quoted for twelve consecutive pages. However valuable his information may be, at this stage the reader expects the author's own conclusions.

How important was Adolf Eichmann? Most Jews came to regard him as both the brains and the chief engineer of the final solution; in fact, he was only one part of the vast machine of destruction (albeit a very large one). Miss Arendt tried to show that he didn't really matter very much, that he was a man full of contradictions, and that evil as personified by him was a very banal figure indeed. Dr. Robinson argues that Eichmann was neither without intelligence nor without convictions, and that Miss Arendt by making him more complex than he really was, introduced much unnecessary confusion. Eichmann cut a sorry figure at the trial, which induced Miss Arendt to develop her theory of the banality of evil. But Hitler himself would not have emerged as a hero in similar conditions. Once they cease to inspire fear, dictators and their servants are bound to become pathetic creatures and it is difficult to understand in retrospect how anyone could ever have been overawed by them. Miss Arendt's appraisal of Eichmann, in brief, is too much influenced, I feel, by his performance in Jerusalem. Men tend to be banal in prison.

The next two sections in Robinson's book deal with the legal problems of war crime trials in general and the Eichmann trial in particular. Here for once there is limited agreement between Miss Arendt and Dr. Robinson, for both devote what seems to me excessive space to the whole issue. Miss Arendt with great fervor and pathos argues that justice was not done in Jerusalem, that there were countless irregularities and abnor- malities, that Eichmann should have been hanged not as *hostis Judaeorum*, but as *hostis generis humani*. Dr. Robinson on the other hand, with countless legal references and precedents to war crime trials, reaches the conclusion that the Jerusalem trial was entirely correct and in full accordance with the practices and rules of national and international law. There is a growing, largely technical, literature on this subject and the discussion will go on, I suspect, for a long time, for in legal philosophy there are not the same certainties as in, say, physics. It is difficult to believe that irreparable harm was done to the rule of law among nations because Eichmann was hanged, as Miss Arendt thinks, by the wrong court and for the wrong reasons. These disputations seem of considerably less importance than the discussion of Jewish resistance and collaboration in Nazi-occupied Europe. Miss Arendt, it will be recalled, argues that the *Judenräte* collaborated with the Nazis in organizing the final solution; her indictment of the Jewish leadership is based on the assumption that without this help it would have been far more difficult, perhaps impossible, for the Nazis to kill so many Jews. Her thesis, Dr. Robinson shows, is untenable in this form; by not taking into account the specific conditions in which most Jewish communities were then living, she seems not to be aware of their particular vulnerability. The *Judenräte* were not essential to the "final solution"; the Nazis managed only too well in those parts of Europe where these organizations did not exist or where they had no part in preparing the infamous lists—USSR, France, Yugoslavia, Greece etc. But why was there not more active resistance? Those who have tried to find out more about the psychological attitudes prevailing among Jews in Europe during the war have all stressed their enormous will to live in the midst of the basest degradation; mere survival was thought to be a victory over an enemy who wanted the extinction of the Jewish people. The time factor was of the greatest importance, as was the naive belief that something would turn up. In the desperate race against time, "convinced that the scales of war would soon turn, the Jews invoked through bribery and procrastination the traditional ways which had enabled their fathers and forefathers to survive the hostility of surrounding populations."

In the heat of his polemic Dr. Robinson tends to be inconsistent on the subject of "collaboration." He says at one point that much further study is needed, but on another occasion he implies that there was no collaboration and no treason at all. This is difficult to accept: there were traitors and criminals among Jews as there were among all other peoples; a few of them took advantage of the situation created during the war. As for the Jewish leaders, Miss Arendt's sweeping accusation is untenable. It could be argued with equal justice that every person of working age in Nazi-occupied Europe "collaborated"—unless he took to the woods, acted as a spy for the Allies, or found some other way to sabotage the German war effort. The borderline between passive resistance and the legitimate defense of Jewish interests, on the one hand, and activities that helped the Nazis to carry out their policy of mass murder on the other, does not appear always very distinct even now—how much less clear was it at the time. To pass judgment on these men is an immensely complicated task requiring, as Dr. Robinson rightly says, the most careful analysis of each individual case and community. It is obvious that there were enormous differences between the situation of Jews in Denmark and in Poland. But even within Poland, Nazi policy varied between one ghetto and another, and so did the behavior of the Jews.

The issue is by no means closed even if Miss Arendt emerges from this as something less than an authority on Jewish contemporary history. She had stumbled on what seemed a hornet's nest but is in fact a very intricate and painful problem. But a real problem it is; if it were not, the publication of her book would have scarcely caused the outcry it did. I am almost sure that Miss Arendt would have written a different book had she devoted more time to the study of the subject. But it is also true that in the course of such further research she could have come, in all probability, across material bearing witness to betrayal and collaboration—along with other documents giving evidence of heroism and resistance. Not only knowledge, but imagination are needed to decide *post factum* whether in given circumstances a certain leader or *Judenrat* did the only thing they could do or whether they should have acted differently. This debate will not be settled by Dr. Robinson's book; that it continues is shown, for example, by the current heated controversy in Holland following Dr. Presser's recently published work on the destruction of Dutch Jewry (*Ondergang—de vervolging en verdelging van hets Nederlandse Jodendom 1940–45*). This huge work, brought out by the Dutch government publishing house, has provoked exchanges very much like the Arendt debate, although at a higher level of factual knowledge and understanding.

The point that cannot be made too strongly is that the

whole issue of Jewish survival, of resistance and "collaboration," must at last be tackled. It ought not to be the happy hunting ground for amateurs or those eager to write a *roman à thèse*. But neither should a veil be drawn over this most tragic chapter in Jewish history. Twenty years after the end of the war there is still no comprehensive attempt to undertake this task. It is precisely the absence of such works that provoked Miss Arendt's book and the great debate around it. In this respect Dr. Robinson's complaints about Miss Arendt resemble the criticism leveled by professional historians at Mr. Shirer as an authority on Nazi Germany and, perhaps to a lesser extent, at Mr. Werth as an authority on the Soviet-German war. It was precisely the reluctance of the professional historians to tackle these large subjects, that induced Messrs. Shirer and Werth to write their books, and assisted in their success. Historians in America and Israel from whom we expected authoritative studies on the holocaust and who have not so far provided them cannot entirely escape responsibility for the emergence of a literature they strongly dislike. They deserve praise for collecting masses of source material, but documentation is not an end in itself. It is not good enough to say that there is now a very good dissertation on the fate of Danish Jewry in Hebrew, and that an excellent study has been published in Italy on the fate of Italian Jewry, that a great many monographs in Hebrew and Yiddish, published and unpublished, are available in Jerusalem. So long as the more important studies are not made accessible to a wider circle of students in at least one major language they might as well not exist for the purposes of modern historiography. Those who think it too early to write definite histories have several arguments: the holocaust belongs to the very recent past; the wounds are still open; is it not asking too much of flesh and blood to approach this subject with scholarly detachment? There are technical difficulties as well: certain important materials are not yet available. We do not know enough, for instance, about Allied policies and attitudes in 1942–45; the British archives will not be opened for many years to come. These are real obstacles and I do not wish to belittle them, but the historian's life is never an easy one. If definitive histories can be written only by historians of a future generation, this should not prevent those now alive from doing their duty beyond the collection of documents. If this does not happen, others less qualified will step in, and will shape the image of that entire period—and handwringing and protests will not help.

I do not know whether this book was necessary, nor how great an effect it will have. On balance it is regrettable that Dr. Robinson's great knowledge of the period has been employed in a book of comments on another book, rather than in preparation of the major work which is so badly needed. Dr. Robinson has found in Isaiah an apt quotation for his title. I wish he had been guided by the saying from *Pirkei Avot*: "The day is short and the work is great."

"The Formidable Dr. Robinson": A Reply by Hannah Arendt

(JANUARY 1966)

Miss Arendt, said Mr. Laqueur in his review of Jacob Robinson's book *And the Crooked Shall Be Made Straight* (NYR, Nov. 11) "had stumbled on what seemed a hornets' nest but is in fact a very intricate and painful problem." This sentence would be true if it read: "She stumbled on what in fact was a hornets' nest because she had touched upon what seemed an intricate problem and is indeed a painful one."

Reviewing Robinson's "full-scale attempt to refute" my report of the Eichmann trial, Mr. Laqueur was so overwhelmed by his author's "eminent authority" that he thought it superfluous to acquaint himself with the subject under attack. He accepts Mr. Robinson's basic distortion, contained in the subtitle of his book, "The Jewish Catastrophe and Hannah Arendt's Narrative," which implies that I recounted part of "Jewish contemporary history," while in fact I have criticized the prosecution for taking the Eichmann Trial as a pretext for doing just that. (Needless to say, I would never have gone to Jerusalem if I had wanted to write a book on "contemporary Jewish history.") Mr. Laqueur believes that *I* asked "why was there not more active resistance" among the Jews, while it was the prosecution that had brought up this question; I had reported this incident and dismissed the question twice as "silly and cruel, since it testified to a fatal ignorance of the conditions of the time" (pp. 11 and 283 of the second edition). He claims that I have been unaware of the "particular vulnerability" of the Jewish communities in the face of organized persecution, whereas I actually have enumerated these vulnerabilities—no territory, no government, no army, no government in exile, no weapons, no youth with military training (p. 125). He insists that I "argue that justice was not done in Jerusalem," while I actually argue that *despite* a number of carefully enumerated irregularities, the very opposite of "countless" ones, justice was done insofar as the trial's "main purpose—to prosecute and to defend, to judge and to punish Adolf Eichmann—was achieved," a passage even quoted in Robinson's book.

Nowhere did I say, as Mr. Laqueur claims, that "Eichmann was hanged . . . by the wrong court and for the wrong reasons," or that "irreparable harm was done to the rule of law." On the contrary, I justified the competence of the court and the kidnapping of the accused (pp. 259–265) and stated that the trial in Jerusalem was "no more, but also no less, than the last of the numerous Successor Trials which followed the Nuremberg Trials." Finally, Mr. Laqueur—knowing neither my book nor the trial in Jerusalem—believes that I attacked the court proceedings as a whole, whereas what I attacked was the prosecution. (The conflict between bench and prosecution ran like a red thread through the proceedings; I reported it, and sided in nearly all cases with the bench—which was rather common among the members of the press.) Had Mr. Laqueur been at all familiar with the subject matter, he would not have been so naive as to identify "betrayal and collaboration," for the whole point of the matter is that the members of the Jewish Councils as a rule were *not* traitors or Gestapo agents, and *still* they became the tools of the Nazis. (The distinction was made by the witnesses for the prosecution; if the members of the Jewish Councils had been scoundrels, there would be no "problem," let alone a "painful and intricate" one.)

After misinforming the reader about the subject matter of my book, Mr. Laqueur proceeds to enumerate my opponent's "formidable credentials." He deplores that Mr. Robinson's name is not well known among "students of political science," which is true, and not "one to conjure with in literary circles," which is untrue: Since the appearance of my book, Mr. Robinson's name has become famous, particularly in New York's literary circles, and especially among writers for *Partisan Review* and *Dissent*. Paralleling the publisher's blurb, Mr. Laqueur draws attention to this "eminent authority on international law" and assures us that "his standing is high among students of contemporary Jewish history" (something of a let-down, for the publisher has claimed eminence for this field as well). He rounds out the picture with praise of "unrivaled mastery of the sources," "great erudition," and "awe-inspiring," "almost obsessive" scholarship. Finally, he tells us what Mr. Robinson's present position is: He "coordinates research be-tween the various institutes devoted to the study of the Jewish catastrophe" ("throughout the world," as the publisher has it), but he does not tell us what these institutes are. Are they too numerous to be enumerated? Hardly. They are the YIVO (the Yiddish Scientific Institute) in New York, the Wiener Library in London, the Centre de Documentation Juive in Paris, and Yad Washem in Jerusalem. There are reasons not to be too specific in these matters. Mr. Laqueur himself, the reviewer of Mr. Robinson's book, is Director of Research in one of the co-ordinated research centers, the Wiener Library.

In view of the recent vintage of Mr. Robinson's "eminent authority" Mr. Laqueur's information is deplorably vague. Let us see whether we can help the reader. Since Mr. Laqueur so closely follows publishers' blurbs, we may note that in 1960 when Mr. Robinson's last book was published, the jacket did not yet know that he was either "eminent" or an "authority." Then, in the summer of 1963, a couple of months after the publication of *Eichmann in Jerusalem,* he wrote a propaganda pamphlet for the (B'nai B'rith's) Anti-Defamation League, called *Facts,* directed against my book. The change in his worldly fortunes was sudden and radical. While on earlier publishers' jackets he was mentioned as "special consultant on *Jewish Affairs*" at the Nuremberg Trial, he was now described as "special consultant" *tout court*—obviously a much greater distinction for an "authority" on international law, especially if one is aware of the minor role the crime against the Jewish people had played at Nuremberg. These still rather modest beginnings—compared to his present status—show already that, while Mr. Robinson recently acquired a number of startlingly new qualities, he also lost a few which up to then had been his very own. Nowhere are we any longer told that Mr. Robinson's specialty is "Minorities Problems," that he founded the Institute of Jewish Affairs, sponsored by the American and

World Jewish Congress, where, with the exception of an article on the United Nations, all of Mr. Robinson's contributions since 1940 appeared, and, most surprisingly, nowhere in Mr. Laqueur's review is there any mention at all of Mr. Robinson's very important role in Jerusalem. In the A.D.L. pamphlet, the reader is still told of his having been "a special consultant to the prosecution of the Eichmann trial," on the jacket of the present book he merely "advised the Israelis on questions of documentation and law"—no special connection with the prosecution any longer!—whereas in fact, and according to the Israeli press handouts, giving "brief biographies" of the team of prosecutors, "Dr. Jacob Robinson" ranked directly after Gideon Hausner, the Attorney General, and was then followed by two Deputy State Attorneys; hence, Mr. Robinson was second in importance for the prosecution only to the Attorney General himself. From which one may conclude that Mr. Robinson had a personal interest in "prosecuting" me for a change, and in defending the case for the prosecution. *It was, in fact, his own case.*

Since Mr. Laqueur believes that the core of the conflict between Mr. Robinson and myself consists of the antagonism of "professional historians" and "amateurs . . . eager to write a *roman à thèse*," he may be surprised to learn that prior to 1963 Mr. Robinson was not a historian—the Israeli trial authorities correctly mention his training as a lawyer—and that the present book, published in cooperation with the Jewish Publication Society, is in fact his first venture into the field of Jewish history. The best way to settle this difficult question of who is the amateur and who the professional is perhaps to consult the *Guide to Jewish History Under Nazi Impact*, a bibliography covering all languages, including Hebrew and Yiddish, published under the coauthorship of the late Philip Friedman and Jacob Robinson by the YIVO and Yad Washem in 1960. There, Mr. Robinson appears with two entries: a short preface to a book by Boris Shub (1943) and a five-page study on "Palestine and the United Nations" (1947), a subject totally unrelated to the question that came up during the Eichmann trial. But most surprising of all, at that time Mr. Robinson must have thought that I was much more a "professional" than he himself, for I appear there with four items, one of them a book more substantial and relevant to modern Jewish history and to the period in question than anything by the two authors.

II

Shortly after the appearance of my book, Mr. Robinson said he had found "hundreds of factual errors"—four hundred, to be exact, a figure which he later upped to six hundred. However, upon closer inspection it turned out that these were miscalculations; the number of mistakes can be counted only by the number of words I used. This would make it rather difficult to reply under all circumstances but is actually the least of the difficulties. Mr. Laqueur is vaguely aware of certain shortcomings in Mr. Robinson's book; he ascribes them to a refusal to think, to "pause for reflection between footnotes," and it is indeed true that the greatest difficulty in dealing meaningfully with this book is its complete lack of consistent argument or point of view. To be sure, Mr. Robinson has one overriding interest, namely, to contradict me line by line, and one overriding ambition, namely, to display his "erudition." But while the former led him more often than not into a kind of super-quibbling the like of which I never saw in black and white (when I say: "According to international law, it was the privilege of the sovereign German nation to declare to be a national minority whatever part of its population it saw fit," he replies: no, not at all, except that "there is no prohibition . . . in international law to declare part of a population a national minority," p. 73), the latter tempted him into filling countless pages with complete irrelevancies—as for instance a four-page excursion into Hungarian history, complete with "basic sources," though all his facts could be found in a one-volume *Encyclopedia of World History*. This is no proof of scholarship but of its very opposite.

In addition to these difficulties, the book displays in all innocence a total unawareness of the most common distinctions in the historical sciences. Such questions as : How many Jews lived in Rome in 1943? (Mr. Robinson's figure taken from the year 1925, is certainly too high.) When did the Hitler regime become fully totalitarian? (Mr. Robinson actually believes that this can be found out by consulting a *Zeittafel*, a chronological enumeration of events.) Are there connections between the Final Solution and the earlier euthanasia program? (Gerald Reitlinger, as I stated, has proved these connections "with documentary evidence that leaves no doubt"; Mr. Robinson prefers to ignore my statement as well as Reitlinger's evidence, simply ascribing the discovery of these connections to me and claiming that they did not exist.) All these and many more questions are treated on exactly the same level, or rather they are reduced to the level of the first question, an isolated fact which, to be established, needs neither the context of a story nor the support of interpretation nor the judgment of the reporter.

Clearly, the number of "mistakes" one can discover in any book with the help of Mr. Robinson's extraordinary methods is staggering. And we have by no means exhausted them yet. Mr. Robinson belongs among the happy few who are psychologically color blind; they see only black and white. Hence, when I described Eichmann as not at all stupid and yet entirely thoughtless, or point out that on the basis of the evidence he was not an inveterate liar and yet lied occasionally, and then proceed to give some instances where he actually lied, Mr. Robinson is firmly convinced that these are "contradictions," "hopping back and forth," in his inimitable jargon. Needless to say, my "contradictions" are almost as countless as my "mistakes." All these methodological difficulties, however, which perhaps can be excused in a book written by a lawyer and meant to restate a prosecutor's case, are overshadowed by a truly dazzling display of sheer inability to read.

In his Preface, Robinson charges me with "misreading" documents and books, and on page 2 of his book he starts to pile up examples of what he understands by reading and what by misreading, until at the end one finds oneself overwhelmed by a unique *embarras de richesse*. There are first the endlessly repeated instances in which Eichmann's words, often given by me in indirect discourse and sometimes even in quotation marks, are misread for direct discourse of the author. Thus quoting from a passage, which is introduced in the original by "*According to the version* [*Eichmann*] *gave* at the police examination" and is liberally sprinkled with clear indications of indirect discourse ("as he saw it," etc.), Mr. Robinson writes:

"*According to Miss Arendt,* the story of Adolf Eichmann is a 'bad luck story if there ever was one.' " But even when I quote verbatim from the police examination, in which Eichmann had described his visit to Auschwitz to meet Mr. Storfer and said: "We had a normal human encounter,' " and conclude the episode by saying, "Six weeks after this normal human encounter, Storfer was dead," Mr. Robinson thinks that *I* "considered it a 'normal human encounter.' " And since he apparently wrote his book without consulting the "primary sources," namely the trial proceedings, he can write, "*In the face of what she says* [Eichmann] referred to 'a cross-examination that lasted longer than any known before,' " completely unaware of the fact that Eichmann (in the 106th session) had said literally: "Above all I wish that . . . my sons can say . . . 'Please, he was in the longest cross-examination that ever was known . . .' "

Another difficulty with Mr. Robinson's strange reading habits comes to light whenever he accuses me of not offering "explanation" or "support" for my statements. In all these instances he would have had to turn the page, and in some instances a couple of pages, to find lengthy explanations, and while he may find this too complicated because he seems incapable of remembering what he read only a few short sentences before, it is, unfortunately, indispensable for reading books or documents. Thus he can for instance quote me correctly on one page: "*To a Jew* this role of the Jewish leaders in the destruction of their own people is undoubtedly the darkest chapter of the whole dark story," and then on the very next page reply: "The destruction of six million Jews—not 'the role of the Jewish leaders'—is the 'darkest chapter' of Jewish history," as though he never read the qualifying clause. The difference between what I say and what Mr. Robinson makes me say is the difference between "patriotism"—"that wrong done by my own people naturally grieves me more than wrong done by other peoples," as I put it in my reply to Gershom Scholem (*Encounter,* January 1964)—and a monstrous lie. And the alternative to assuming Mr. Robinson's inability to read would be to charge him with character assassination. However, the alternative of bad faith is difficult to entertain in view of the fact that Mr. Robinson's difficulties with sentence structure occasionally work against his own interest. Thus he begins his treatment of "Behavior of the Victims" (p. 187 ff.) by ascribing to me a description which was taken, word for word, from the Attorney General's examination of witnesses during the 22nd session and was quoted by me for the deliberate purpose of denouncing Mr. Hausner's attack on these survivors. Since Mr. Robinson honestly believes he denounces me and not his colleague, he finds now what he failed to discover when he advised him, i.e., that this "picture contrasts radically with reality," which, of course, was my whole point to begin with.

Mr. Laqueur found in Mr. Robinson's book a few inconsequential mistakes and believes that more could be found by "a team of researchers." Actually, the book abounds in monumental errors, of which I can give here only two representative examples. The first concerns the Nazi legal system, a clear understanding of which was of course of the greatest importance for the Jerusalem trial. The second deals with the widespread anti-Semitism in Europe prior to Nazi occupation, because this was an important contributing factor to the success of the Final Solution.

(1) The discussion of the Nazi legal system occurs on pp. 274–276 of Robinson's book, and only after having read these pages did it dawn upon me that the case for the prosecution had been presented in honest ignorance of it. That this legal system was actually criminal did not make it any less "legal" for those who lived in the country. Robinson obviously never heard of the famous Nazi slogan, *Führerworte haben Gesetzes Kraft*, "the Führer's *words* have the force of law," because he does not recognize it in the English paraphrase. Hence, he does not know that the Führer's orders, whether given orally or in writing, "canceled all *written* law" (Hans Buchheim). He therefore believes that the sections in the German Criminal Code dealing with murder made Hitler's order "illegal," and is in doubt "whether [the order for the Final Solution] emanated from Hitler or Himmler (p. 371). Only a "specialist," as Mr. Laqueur would put it, can judge how fantastic this doubt is. That many of these orders were secret is a matter of course, but this by no means prevented them from being legally binding, because, contrary to what Mr. Robinson thinks, promulgation was not "the very essence of the binding force of law" in Nazi

Germany; he simply does not know that there exist five fat volumes of *Verfügungen, Anordnungen, Bekanntgaben* (Decrees, Ordinance, Notices) which regulated very important areas in the life of the German people and still were classified as "top secret." (Four of these volumes, published by the *Parteikanzlei,* are available in the archives of the Hoover Library.) In short, the order for the Final Solution was binding law in Nazi Germany because Germany had become a criminal state, and nothing could be more preposterous than to assert that it "constituted nothing but an illegal secret promise of the Führer of immunity from prosecution."

(2) In my discussion of the situation in the Netherlands, I stated that "the prewar Dutch government had officially declared [Jewish refugees] to be 'undesirable'." Mr. Robinson declares categorically as usual: "This never happened," because he never heard of the circular letter, issued by the Dutch government on May 7, 1938, in which refugees are declared to be "undesirable aliens." I would not have mentioned this if it were merely a factual error, but the point of the matter is that the attitude of the Dutch government was only more outspoken than that of other European countries. Refugees, and especially Jewish refugees, were "undesirable" all over Europe, and Mr. Robinson tries in all instances to present the situation of Jews in Europe prior to the Nazi occupation in rosy colors. (His only exception to the rule is Italy, where anti-Semitic legislation actually was enacted, in 1938, only under pressure from Berlin—the evidence is too well known to be quoted. For reasons best known to Mr. Robinson, I suddenly stand accused of "whitewashing Mussolini.") The rampant Jew-hatred in Eastern Europe and the rapidly growing anti-Semitism in Western Europe can be interpreted and explained in many different ways, but there is no doubt about the extent to which it facilitated later Hitler's Final Solution. This attempt to deny the historical truth is especially noticeable in Mr. Robinson's discussion of Rumania. The drift of his argument is to accuse me of "minimizing German influence in Rumania's *Judenpolitik,*" and to deny, in the face of all evidence, that Rumania, in the words of Reitlinger, was the "nation which began its deportations to Russia before Hitler had even given the signal, but which was constrained ... through jealousy of the Ger-

mans." Mr. Robinson, because of his mistaken notions about scholarship, despises standard works (which explains, incidentally, why he is at a loss to find out how I "know" that Hitler thought Antonescu to be more "radical" than the Nazis (p. 362); I cited a famous remark of Hitler to Goebbels, well known to all "professionals"); he prefers to base his presentation on an admittedly highly "selective" *(lückenhafte)* collection of documents, prepared for the trial by the United Restitution Organization, a group established to press Jewish claims against Germany; it includes a research department whose *raison d'être* is of course to "prove" that all initiative during this period came from Berlin, and therefore to "minimize" indigenous anti-Semitism.

III

A major part of Mr. Robinson's book is devoted to "Jewish Behavior in the Face of Disaster," which in my book played a minor role. Even the admiring Mr. Laqueur thinks that this chapter is the most disappointing of Robinson's book. And it is true that much of its space is wasted on proving what nobody ever doubted—namely, that the Jewish Councils were established by the Nazis—as well as on a thesis that no one at all familiar with concentration and extermination camps will ever believe—namely, that there was no deliberate and infernal blurring of the line between victims and executioners. In the center of these sections are the Jewish Councils, and Robinson's main thesis is expressed in two sentences: First, "Legally and morally, the members of the Jewish Councils can no more be judged accomplices of their Nazi rulers than can a store owner be judged an accomplice of an armed robber to whom he surrenders *his store* at gunpoint" (p. 159, italics added). The worst reproach one could level at the Jewish Councils would indeed be to accuse them of disposing of Jewish lives and properties as though they *owned* them, and no one to my knowledge has ever dared to go that far before Mr. Robinson, with his inability "to pause for reflection," appeared on the scene. And since he cannot remember what he wrote on p. 159 when he comes to p. 223, we hear, second, that whoever "accepted appointment to a Council . . . did so as a rule out of feeling of responsibility," hence was by no means forced at gunpoint. Mr. Robinson's second thesis has become common property among writers for the Jewish Establishment. The first thesis had a certain success in New York's literary circles, partly, to be sure, because they knew absolutely nothing of the whole issue, but partly also, I am afraid, because of a moral obtuseness which Mary McCarthy very pointedly exposed in *Partisan Review*. (No one, of course, ever combined the two before for obvious reasons.)

This moral obtuseness (like tone deafness) is actually the most alarming aspect of the whole book. Mr. Robinson quotes endlessly from announcements and deliberations of the *Judenräte*, one more terrible than the next, and then mentions—as though this was no more than one among many legitimate opinions—an instance in which the rabbinate intervened and told the *Judenrat* in Vilna "that he had no right to select Jews and deliver them to the Germans" in accordance with the old prescription: If the Gentiles should tell you " 'give us one of yours and we shall kill him, otherwise we shall kill all of you,' they should all be killed and not a single Jewish soul should be delivered." At this point, not knowing what he is doing, Mr. Robinson raises one of the most disturbing "problems" of the whole issue, a problem I had been careful not to raise because it was not raised at the trial and therefore was not my business: the conduct of the European rabbinate during the catastrophe. It seems there was not one Rabbi who did what Dompropst Bernhard Lichtenberg, a Catholic priest, or Propst Heinrich Grüber, a Protestant minister, had tried to do—to volunteer for deportation.

These are serious and even terrible questions, and neither the present unanimity of Jewish official opinion nor any "coordination" of research will be able to prevent independent scholars from asking them and trying to find an answer. The greatest weakness of this unanimity is that it is of so very recent origin. History textbooks used in Israeli schools abound in the most extreme opinions on Jewish behavior; generally they are as unable to distinguish between the behavior of the victims and the conduct of the Jewish leadership as Mr. Hausner was when he questioned his witnesses. He complained about the lack of Jewish resistance in general terms because this was "a popular view among many Israeli writers," who held that "Hitler was helped in exterminating all European Jews by appeasement tactics of Jewish leaders," and because "Jews went to their death like sheep to slaughter." (See Mark M. Krug's "Young Israelis and Jews Abroad—A Study of Selected History Textbooks," in *Comparative Education Review,* October 1963.)

Naturally, I know much more about this issue today than when I wrote my book and could only be marginally concerned with it. My insufficient knowledge of the intricacies of the problem came out in many letters from survivors, and the most knowledgeable and interesting one came from a colleague of mine who was in Hungary under the Nazi occupation and in Israel during the Kastner trial. (Rudolf Kastner had been the most prominent member of the Hungarian *Judenrat*.) He said that I was in error when I wrote "that Kastner was murdered by Hungarian survivors," that "during the trial it came out that out of the four or five accused . . . there was only one who was not at one time or another in the service of the Israeli Security Service," though "none of them was actually in the Service at the time of the murder." And he told me, what I had not known, that "the Government did everything in its power to support Kastner. The reason for this, apart from the dirty-linen argument, was that there was and is a strong link between the Establishment in Israel and the leadership which was in charge in Europe during the war." (Kastner was of course a case in point; at the time of his trial he was a high public officer in Israel although his role in Hungary was known to everybody.) This, and nothing else, makes the problem "intricate" in addition to "painful," for it won't be possible to elucidate it until the archives of the respective Jewish organizations have been opened.

IV

To anyone willing and able to read, the result of Mr. Robinson's long labors will look like a prime example of a non-book. But this is not to deny that its author is "formidable" and "awe-inspiring." It *is* formidable that the book found two respectable publishers and was reviewed in respected magazines; and it *is* awe-inspiring that for years now, simply on his having said so, the news has echoed around the globe that my book contained "hundreds of factual errors" and that I had not written a trial report but "scrutinized the data concerned with the Nazi extermination of European Jewry"—as a student paper recently put it, without, of course, meaning any harm. Even apart from these spectacular successes, how could anybody deny the formidableness of a man who represented the government of Israel, and thus can count upon its unflinching support, together with its consulates, embassies, missions, etc. throughout the world, is backed by both the American and the World Jewish Congress, by B'nai B'rith, with its powerful Anti-Defamation League and student organizations on all campuses, and who has four coordinated research institutes at his beck and call?

And these are merely the organizations in whose name Mr. Robinson has the right to speak. To them we must add his allies, also international in scope, though perhaps a shade less powerful. They are best represented by Dr. Siegfried Moses— State Comptroller of Israel now in retirement, President of the Leo Baeck Institute, with headquarters in Jerusalem, New York, and London, and on the board of the Council of Jews from Germany, with branches in the United States, Israel, Europe, and South America—who wrote me (in a letter in German, dated March 3, 1963) that he had come to New York with a draft statement against Raul Hilberg's book, to be published by the Council of Jews from Germany, but that now he had to send *me* "a declaration of war" instead. (The Council did indeed publish a protest on March 12 against Hilberg and me, and it was considerably less than an act of war: it defended the activities of the Nazi-established *Reichsvereinigung* by citing the work done by its predecessor, the independent *Reichsvertretung*, which was not under attack; admitted that Jewish "leaders and officials" had given "technical assistance in the execution" of Nazi orders; claimed "secret resistance" for which "no documentary evidence existed"; and finally mentioned a single known case where "Nazi orders had not been *fully* carried out" [italics added]—all of which, of course tended to prove my point.)

I do not know to what extent Moses, a high Israeli government official, was instrumental in measures taken by the Israeli government; the first reaction of the Israeli press to my book had been sympathetic: the *Jerusalem Post* printed a friendly report from its correspondent; *Haaretz* published long excerpts; and the Schocken Publication House asked for, and then canceled, an option on the Hebrew edition. I was informed by reliable Israeli sources that Ben-Gurion himself had intervened to change this atmosphere. However, I am reasonably sure that Dr. Moses's "war" consisted not in the harmless declaration of the Council but in organizing attacks by former functionaries of German-Jewish organizations who are now dispersed all over the world.

The "war" in America, at any rate, preceded by no friendly declaration, began on March 11, 1963, when the Anti-Defamation League sent out its first memorandum—from Arnold Forster to all Regional Offices, National Commissions, and National Committees—informing them of the article series in *The New Yorker*, and stating its fear that my "concept about Jewish participation in the Nazi holocaust . . . *may plague Jews for years to come*" (italics added). This was followed two weeks later by another Memorandum, which summed up the articles in five sentences and recommended this summary to "book reviewers and others when the volume appears." The points to be attacked were as follows:

(1) "That Eichmann was, as he himself claimed, only a small cog in the extermination machine." (Not even Eichmann, let alone I, had ever claimed this. It was the thesis of the defense.)

(2) "That the trial did not fulfill an original Israeli Government hope—enlarging international law to include the crime of racial and religious [?] genocide." (Just plain nonsense; no one had accused the Israeli Government of not fulfilling a non-existent promise.)

(3) "That the Eichmann trial was little more than a legal circus." (I never thought or said so, but this was indeed a widespread opinion, shared incidentally by quite a number of old and trusted Zionists: Martin Buber told me in Jerusalem that the trial was part of "Ben-Gurion's policies of *panis et*

circenses," and a well-known Jewish journalist wrote me (in August, 1963): "No one can seriously question that the trial was a political and not a juridical act"—firmly believing, incidentally, that this was my opinion too!)

(4) "That the Jewish victims of the Holocaust in Nazi Europe failed, by and large, to resist the *final solution,"* which was, as I said before, the point insisted upon by the prosecutor.

(5) "That Europe's Jewish organizations, in the main, played a 'disastrous role' by cooperating with the Nazi exter- mination machine. As a result, the Jews, themselves, bear a large share of the blame for the murder of millions of their kinsmen killed by the Nazis." (In other words, as everybody soon knew and repeated, my "thesis" was that the Jews had murdered themselves.)

This summary was then once more summed up for the press by Gideon Hausner himself: According to the New York *Daily News* (May 20, 1963), he "flew here to answer Hannah Arendt's bizarre defense of Eichmann in her book *Eichmann in Jerusalem.* The author would have you believe that Eichmann really wasn't a Nazi, that the Gestapo aided Jews, that Eichmann was actually unaware of Hitler's evil plans. The record, to the contrary, that Eichmann shipped 434,351 Jews to the Auschwitz gas chamber." (One really would like to know how Mr. Hausner arrived at this figure.)

Those who are familiar with the ensuing "controversy" will know that four of the A.D.L.'s five sentences were used from then on by almost every reviewer, just as Mr. Forster had suggested it, as though, in Mary McCarthy's telling phrase, they came out of a "mimeographing machine," which in fact they did, although it must be admitted that, apart from colleague Robinson, only Michael Musmanno, in *The New York Times,* reflected fully Hausner's line. (With the result that the Jewish Center Lecture Bureau of the National Jewish Welfare Board recommended him to Jewish communities all over the country.)

Mr. Robinson's present book is only the last, the most elaborate, and the least competent variation of this "image" of a posthumous defense of Eichmann, a book that no one ever wrote but of whose reality even people who had read my book became convinced and under this stupendous barrage, quickly changed their minds. It is in the nature of such campaigns that they gain in momentum and viciousness as they proceed. (A.D.L.'s first communication still stressed that mine was an "otherwise masterful report," that "Dr. Arendt is a recognized scholar," "a person of eminent respectability"—characterizations which must make them shudder today if ever they consult their old files.) This is due to the fact that the more successful the image-makers are the more likely they are to fall victim not only to their own fabrication but to its inherent logic. The image they had created was that of an "evil book"; now they had to prove that it was written by an "evil person." When this happened there were still quite a few Jewish functionaries who thought that things had gone too far. Thus, I received a letter from an officer of the United Restitution Organization—on whose help Mr. Robinson so heavily relied—telling me that he could only "shake his head in uneasiness" when he read the "very vicious [*gehässige*] discussion, especially in the whole Jewish press" (mentioning, incidentally, the "*New York Times* and the London *Observer*"), and he singled out the articles "of Syrkin, Steiner, Nehemiah Robinson, Jacob Robinson, etc." This was in July 1963; a few months later, this communication would have been impossible.

No one will doubt the effectiveness of modern image-making, and no one acquainted with Jewish organizations and their countless channels of communication outside their immediate range will underestimate their possibilities in influencing public opinion. For greater than their direct power of control is the voluntary outside help upon which they can draw from Jews who, though they may not be at all interested in Jewish affairs, will flock home, as it were, out of age-old fears (no longer justified, let us hope, but still very much alive) when their people or its leaders are criticized. What I had done according to their lights was the crime of crimes: I had told "the truth in a hostile environment," as an Israeli official told me, and what the A.D.L. and all the other organizations did was to hoist the danger signal. At this moment, all those among us who still think "their honor precarious, their liberty provisional . . . their position unstable" feared that "the days of funeral disaster when the majority rally round the victim as the

Jews rallied round Dreyfus" (in Proust's great description of
Jewish and homosexual society) were drawing close. It was of
course a farce, but it was effective.

Or was it? After all, the denunciation of book and author,
with which they achieved great, though by no means total,
success, was not their goal. It was only the *means* with which to
prevent the discussion of an issue "which may plague Jews for
years to come." And as far as this goal was concerned, they
achieved the precise opposite. If they had left well enough
alone, this issue, which I had touched upon only marginally,
would not have been trumpeted all over the world. In their
efforts to prevent people from reading what I had written, or,
in case such misfortune had already happened, to provide the
necessary reading glasses, they blew it up out of all proportion,
not only with reference to my book but with reference to what
had actually happened. They forgot that they were mass
organizations, using all the means of mass communication, so
that every issue they touched at all, *pro* or *contra*, was liable to
attract the attention of masses whom they then no longer
could control. So what happened after a while in these
meaningless and mindless debates was that people began to
think that all the nonsense the image-makers had made me say
was the actual historical truth.

Thus, with the unerring precision with which a bicyclist on
his first ride will collide with the obstacle he is most afraid of,
Mr. Robinson's formidable supporters have put their whole
power at the service of propagating what they were most
anxious to avoid. So that now, as a result of their folly, literally
everybody feels the need for a "major work" on Jewish conduct
in the face of catastrophe. I doubt that such a book is as "badly
needed" as Mr. Laqueur thinks, but Mr. Robinson, in any case,
is most unlikely to produce it. The methods used in the pursuit
of historical truth are not the methods of the prosecutor, and
the men who stand guard over facts are not the officers of
interest groups—*no matter how legitimate their claims*—but
the reporters, the historians, and finally the poets.

A Reply to Hannah Arendt

by *Walter Z. Laqueur*

(FEBRUARY 1966)

At the very opening of my review of Mr. Robinson's book, I wrote that the Arendt debate provoked both violent denunciation and emphatic assent, that it generated more heat than light; precisely because passions run so strongly, historical truth has suffered. I am sorry to see from Miss Arendt's reply that my attempt to reduce the temperature has not been very successful. I do not think detailed comment on Miss Arendt's very long letter is called for: some of the issues she raises cannot possibly be of public interest. Surely Miss Arendt is the only reader of my review who gained the impression that I am the "admiring Mr. Laqueur." Much of the letter concerns Mr. Robinson's book, not what I wrote about it, and I am glad my review provided an opportunity for Miss Arendt to make her comments. But I see little point in perpetuating an increasingly acrimonious polemic, based on unedifying personal denunciations, semantic hair-splitting, and the wish to score points and to denigrate rather than to understand the opposing point of view. This is not a level on which truths can be established and insight gained. The basic points I tried to make in my review (and which apparently need restating) are very briefly these: Miss Arendt touched on some disturbing aspects of the holocaust which ought not to be glossed over but should be studied in detail. But her book is deficient in both factual knowledge and judgment.

As for Mr. Robinson, I made it fairly clear that with all his knowledge of matters of detail he did not come to grips with

the basic issues, and that for this reason his book is disappointing. The suggestion that I am in some way an employee of Dr.
Robinson, implied in Miss Arendt's letter, is ridiculous; I fear,
however, that whatever I say will not convince her because she
knows that all this is part of a conspiracy.

Miss Arendt is convinced that it was her cardinal sin in the
eyes of the Jewish establishment to "tell the truth in an hostile
environment," but that the attacks against her, by some
Hegelian cunning of reason, achieved exactly the opposite
effect from that intended. They provoked a discussion of
Jewish conduct in the face of the catastrophe, an issue "which
may plague Jews for generations to come." I see the effect of
Miss Arendt's book in a different light. It was not meant to
display the fruits of original research; as far as recent Jewish
history is concerned it said nothing that had not been said
before. Miss Arendt was attacked not so much for what she
said, but for how she said it. Her attackers, on the other hand,
were all too often inclined to throw out the baby with the
bathwater. Incensed by offensive remarks or misconstructions
in Miss Arendt's book, they brushed aside the discussion of the
real issue she had raised, and this became so highly charged that
a rational discussion of this complex of questions has been
much more difficult during the last few years. In Miss Arendt's
eyes, all this of course, is the fault of her critics.

There is no deliberate conspiracy, I believe, on the part of
the "Jewish establishment" to hide the truth. There has been
and is great reluctance to pass judgment on certain Jewish
leaders. They may have failed, they may have to be condemned; and yet, who does not feel that there but for the grace
of God, go I? The real sins of omission committed by what
Miss Arendt calls "the officers of interest groups" she does not
mention; perhaps she is not aware of them. Some of them tried
to monopolize the historiography of the catastrophe in their
own hands; they did valuable work in collecting source material
but discouraged all "outsiders" and all the more ambitious
projects to write the history of the period in one of the world's
main languages; they failed to enlist younger historians and
make them partners in their work. (Mr. Robinson's book was
apparently meant to be the final word on the subject—at least
for the time being.) This was a mistaken policy and it has

resulted in a serious crisis; the whole future of this official historiography is now in the balance. Common human failings underlie this crisis; its causes are less dramatic and sinister than Miss Arendt believes. I think I can assure her that the Elders of Zion are not yet out to get her.

Other Books by Hannah Arendt

The Origins of Totalitarianism in three parts: *Antisemitism, Imperialism, Totalitarianism*. New York: Harcourt, Brace & World, Inc., 1968. Originally published in 1951.

Rahel Varnhagen: The Life of a Jewish Woman. New York: Harcourt Brace Jovanovich, Inc., 1974. Originally published in 1957.

The Human Condition. Chicago: The University of Chicago Press, 1958.

Between Past and Future. New York: The Viking Press, 1968. Originally published in 1961.

On Revolution. New York: The Viking Press, 1965. Originally published in 1963.

Eichmann in Jerusalem: A Report on the Banality of Evil. New York: The Viking Press. Revised and enlarged edition 1965, originally published in 1963.

Men in Dark Times. New York: Harcourt, Brace & World, Inc., 1968.

Crises of the Republic. New York: Harcourt Brace Jovanovich, Inc., 1972.

The Life of the Mind in two volumes: *One/Thinking, Two/Willing*. New York: Harcourt Brace Jovanovich, Inc., 1978.

Index

284 / *Index*